D1226726

The Spirit of Catholicism

THE SPIRIT OF CATHOLICISM

VIVIAN BOLAND OP

BLOOMSBURY CONTINUUM
LONDON · OXFORD · NEW YORK · NEW DELHI · SYDNEY

BLOOMSBURY CONTINUUM
Bloomsbury Publishing Plc
50 Bedford Square, London, WC1B 3DP, UK
29 Earlsfort Terrace, Dublin 2, Ireland

BLOOMSBURY, BLOOMSBURY CONTINUUM and the Diana logo are
trademarks of Bloomsbury Publishing Plc

First published in Great Britain 2021
Copyright © Vivian Boland, 2021

Vivian Boland has asserted his right under the Copyright, Designs and Patents Act,
1988, to be identified as Author of this work

All rights reserved. No part of this publication may be reproduced or transmitted
in any form or by any means, electronic or mechanical, including
photocopying, recording, or any information storage or retrieval system,
without prior permission in writing from the publishers

A catalogue record for this book is available from the British Library

Library of Congress Cataloguing-in-Publication data has been applied for

ISBN: HB: 978-1-4411-7802-2; eBook: 978-1-4411-1138-8;
ePDF: 978-1-4411-7781-0

2 4 6 8 10 9 7 5 3 1

Typeset by Deanta Global Publishing Services, Chennai, India
Printed and bound in Great Britain by CPI Group (UK) Ltd, Croydon CR0 4YY

To find out more about our authors and books visit www.bloomsbury.com
and sign up for our newsletters

CONTENTS

Introduction   7

PART ONE

1   A People of God?   21

PART TWO

2   Christ, Image and Sacrament of God   41

3   The Church, Sacrament of Christ   57

4   Embodiment Means Life and Structure   73

5   Forms of Corruption in this Body   91

PART THREE

6   Christ's Threefold Mission and the Church's
    Threefold Nature   113

7   Authority, Service and Leadership   129

8   Take All Thought Captive   151

9   The Life of a Community   171

PART FOUR

10 With the Son: Christ, the Head of Humanity   197

11 In the Spirit: The Love of Christ Urges Us On   223

12 To the Father: From Glory to Glory   243

    Notes   259
    Index   265

INTRODUCTION

In 1924 Karl Adam (1876–1966) published a book with the title *The Spirit of Catholicism* in which he considered the distinctive characteristics and teachings of Roman Catholicism. Henri de Lubac (1896–1991) followed suit in 1938 with his classic work *Catholicism: Christ and the Common Destiny of Man*. Already the privatization or spiritualization of religion was an issue: de Lubac's concern was to stress the social and embodied character of Catholicism, a fact that he regarded as crucial not just for giving a true account of the Catholic faith but for responding to the social and political situation in which the world was then finding itself. Adam's book is also all about the Church, and for him, too, the distinctive characteristic and teaching of Catholicism is that this religious faith is embodied, transmitted and experienced only ever in social and institutional forms, as the life of a visibly organized and historical community. Each of them looked back to important works on the Church composed in the previous century, the most important of which were J. A. Möhler's *Unity in the Church* (1825) and John Henry Newman's *An Essay on the Development of Christian Doctrine* (1845).

Many commentators draw parallels between what is happening today and what was happening, particularly in Europe, in the years between the two world wars. Adam and de Lubac were professional theologians, but of such a kind that their political and cultural antennae, far from being numbed or distorted by that activity, were highly sensitized by it. In response to the fascism already established, and to the communism then growing in strength, they proposed the Catholic Church as at least a sign pointing to an alternative understanding of a shared human life and a common human destiny.

Romano Guardini (1885–1968), another important Catholic thinker of the first half of the twentieth century, living in Berlin in the darkest days of the Second World War, composed a series of essays in which he sought to restate, in terms of contemporary life and experience, the 'eternal spiritual and humane verities', and so to help people confused and troubled by all that was happening.[1] Although in those essays he does not focus on the Church as Adam and de Lubac do, his essays, surreptitiously circulated for as long as possible, are still of strongly Catholic inspiration and teaching. It is striking that the first of them is on 'Adoration', the bowing down of creation before God who alone is worthy of adoration. It is the safeguard of our mental health, Guardini says, and of our inmost intellectual soundness, pointing our loyalty and our devotion in the right direction. Olivier Clément (1921–2009) explains the same point: 'Whenever Caesar, as an individual or an institution, pretends to explain humankind entirely by history, he is demanding to be worshipped … [but] the secret masters of history, although they do not know it, are people of adoration.'[2] The fundamental purpose of the Church is to bear witness to this fact: only God is worthy of our adoration.

If we think about what Catholic theology might have to offer today, and in particular of what the existence and life of the Church holds out, voices will immediately be raised about the failures of that particular community to live up to its own moral and spiritual teachings. These are voices that must be heard and the experience informing them acknowledged. In fact, such voices not only echo from outside but come also from within – within the Church, within oneself: how could they not? – where they are likewise informed by experience that must be acknowledged. More than that, these voices must be allowed to inform all that follows here as we seek to appreciate anew the treasure carried in this undeniably earthly vessel. Although this book does not have an explicitly apologetic purpose, 'to defend the Catholic Church before the world' – who would want to take on such a task today? – such an orientation cannot be avoided completely, at least implicitly, at a time when public perceptions of the Catholic

Church in some parts of the world are often simply negative, a situation brought about to a significant extent by the actions and inactions of members of the Church themselves.

THE SPIRIT IS IN THE BODY

It seems like a contradiction to say that the spirit of something is embodiment. A number of things point us in this direction, however, when we are asked to think about the spirit of Catholicism. G. K. Chesterton (1874–1936), in his biography of Saint Thomas Aquinas, says that Thomas, together with that even more famous friar of the thirteenth century, Francis of Assisi, 'saved us from Spirituality'.[3] It is a startling statement, a typical Chestertonian paradox and provocation. All the more so at a time when many people believe there is more integrity in declaring themselves 'spiritual but not religious'.

What Chesterton means is that the charism of Francis of Assisi, with his celebration of creation, and the philosophical and theological work of Thomas Aquinas, in defending the inherent goodness of the material creation, served to illuminate and to protect the doctrine that is the heart of Christianity: in Chesterton's words, 'the wedding of God with Man and therefore with Matter'.[4]

If we recall summarily the doctrines of Catholic Christianity that became most controversial in modern times, even among other Christians, they are all connected with embodiment: the Eucharist (the real presence of the body of Christ under the form of bread?), the role of the Blessed Virgin Mary (immaculate conception? virgin birth? bodily assumption?) and the position of the Pope (a monarchical and hierarchical form of government in this body?).

The Eucharist, with the transformation of bread and wine into the body and blood of Christ, is understood by the Catholic Church to mean the real presence of Christ's body and blood, given in sacrifice once and for all on Calvary but renewed in this way every day as food for those who attach themselves to him and seek to live from his life. The Eucharist is obviously symbolic, to anybody who might wander in and look and listen – a piece of what looks like bread is held up and described as a lamb: obviously something strange is going on and that is not the half of it! But it is symbolic in the very particular sense that Catholic Christianity sees in those symbols it calls 'sacraments'. More about this as we go along, but enough for the moment to recall words reputedly first uttered by the American Catholic author Flannery O'Connor (1925–64) concerning the Eucharist: 'If it's a symbol, to hell with it' (more about that later also).[5]

The Virgin Mary, the mother of Jesus, is the woman about whom the undivided Christian Church has proclaimed two doctrines – that she is rightly honoured as the Mother of God and that she is ever-virgin – and about whom Roman Catholicism has proclaimed two further doctrines: that she was immaculately conceived (proclaimed in 1854) and that after her death she was assumed body and soul into heaven (proclaimed in 1950). Each of these raises many questions: the point for the moment is simply to note that they are all intimately and unavoidably connected with the physical body of Mary – her own conception, her motherhood of Jesus, her virginity and the fate of her body after her death.

The Bishop of Rome, recognized even beyond the denominational boundaries of Roman Catholicism as having some kind of primacy in the government of the Church, stands at the head of a hierarchy that structures the Catholic community as an institution. Like any other association of human beings that is formally established and that endures for any length of time, the Church constitutes a 'body politic' and is, therefore, institutional: necessarily so and we might be tempted even to say irredeemably so. It can therefore seem like the opposite of what a religion ought to be. Should it not be spiritual rather than institutional? Some have proposed that the 'real' Church must be a spiritual reality, for the moment invisible to us, and only to be revealed in the age to come. The social and political reality we encounter as 'the Church' is a more or less remote sign pointing to a kingdom that is to come – usually more rather than less remote, sometimes remote to the point of seeming to contradict the very mission it claims to serve.

Everybody knows that these teachings and beliefs about the Eucharist, Mary and the papacy are characteristic of Catholicism. We might be tempted to say that they were stressed – perhaps even exaggerated? – in response to the criticisms of other Christians, particularly following the schism between East and West and exacerbated in reaction to the Protestant Reformation. Could we say that 'Roman Catholicism' came into existence in the sixteenth century, taking its characteristic shape in response to the controversies of the day, and is therefore as much a post-Reformation denomination as any of the Protestant Churches themselves? But we could just as easily say that those controversies, like earlier moments of doctrinal conflict, actually helped the Church to realize, and where necessary to reappropriate, things that are essential to the teaching of Christ and to what the Church itself is meant to be, to teach and to live.

If Francis of Assisi and Thomas Aquinas saved us from spirituality, as Chesterton claimed, for what did they save it? For materiality? For embodiment? For the truth of the declaration that 'the Word became flesh and dwelt among us' (Jn 1.14)?[6] Is it just a nice idea or does that conviction – with the scandal of particularity that it involves: that the Eternal came to dwell in a unique way in a particular human being, in a particular place, at a particular time – take us to the heart of God's dealings with humanity, dealings that did not end with the death of Jesus but that continue in the life now shared within the body of believers? The Word became flesh through the body of his mother. The Word becomes flesh in the sacrament we are to eat (Jesus does not spare our sensitivities in John 6 when talking about masticating his flesh and drinking his blood!). The Word becomes flesh in the human beings who are incorporated in him through baptism – the very word 'incorporation' refers to embodiment, since it means to make to be of one body with oneself. The Word becomes flesh in the all too human beings whom he chose, and continues to choose, to guide the body of believers.

11

So there are many reasons why it seems appropriate to say that the spirit of Catholicism is embodiment, the continuation in human history of the Incarnation of the Son of God. The term 'incarnation' itself also refers to embodiment since it means the 'enfleshment' of the Word.

A consequence is that the spirit of Catholicism is only ever found 'in the midst of the occasions of falling', as Teresa of Avila (1515–82) puts it in encouraging her nuns not to withdraw into sealed contemplative bubbles but to engage with each other, with the Lord in prayer and with the people with whom they have to deal in their daily activities.[7] It is therefore a body that, in spite of its establishment by Christ and the Holy Spirit, remains susceptible to the weaknesses and corruptions to which flesh is heir. And, as we know all too well, even more so. The demons that come to tease and mock the one who would write about the spirit of Catholicism have an easy task, considering the very physical and so undeniable character of this body's corruptions.

SACRAMENT AND SACRAMENTALITY

The embodied life so shared within the Catholic Church is understood in terms of 'sacramentality'. Christ may be described as the sacrament of God – pointing to God while making God present – and the Church, analogously, may be described as the sacrament of Christ – pointing to Christ while making Christ present. Following Saint Paul, we say that the Church is the body of Christ. The significant life of this community is the sacramental life shared among its members – those rituals, signs and actions in which that life is celebrated and made present. They also call those who participate in them to make this life present in the world not just in sign but in reality, not just as promise but as realization, not just as a personal lifestyle choice but as a shared quest for the communion of which Jesus speaks and which – so he has revealed to the world – is what God is. We must, as Saint Paul says, 'discern the body' (1 Cor. 11.29). He is referring not just to the presence of Christ's body in the Eucharist under the form of bread but also to Christ's body as the community of those who have come to believe in Christ. This is the 'earthen vessel' in which a treasure is carried (2 Cor. 4.7) and Catholicism acknowledges, and even celebrates, this embodiment.

As we move towards the centenary of Adam's book, the bicentenary of Möhler's book, we can say that these themes of embodiment and sacramentality remain the distinctive themes that give definition to the *res catholica*, the 'Catholic thing'. Catholicism indicates a community of human beings united in a communion of faith. In order to understand it we need to talk about history and tradition, since it is a community of human beings spread across time and sharing a common life across that time. As a community of human beings, it is a community of creatures made 'in the image and likeness of God', creatures who clearly have special gifts among the animals of the world but who also therefore carry special responsibilities. Catholicism places high value on the goodness of the created order, wounded by sin but not rendered absolutely corrupt, seeing a surviving integrity and intelligibility both in nature and in human reason.

As a body, a community sharing a common life, the Church must have some structure, since the life of any living thing we know is always a structured life. So, we must say something about hierarchy, a distinctive characteristic of this body that refers in the first place to its articulation as an organism, the ways in which its different parts are related to each other in mutual dependence and receptivity. For too long the term 'hierarchy' has been understood vertically and one-sidedly; the time is long overdue for a recovery of the richer implications the term had when it was first introduced.

In what follows we will speak not only about the Church's own life (communion, *koinonia*, faith, hope, love) and structure (hierarchy, collegiality, synodality, ministry, subsidiarity, infallibility), but also about its relations with all who are 'outside', and also about its mission, the kind of fruitfulness it is called to make possible for human beings.

As a body with a long life, the Catholic Church has learned to incorporate many things from the cultures and peoples who came to share its life and whose life it came to share. Its predominant tendency is to incorporate and integrate, within its own life, the practices and traditions, all that is good, true and beautiful, in the cultures of the earth. The contrast is often made between communities of the Reformation, who gain a certain kind of strength from their emphasis on the *sola* – *sola fides*, *sola scriptura*, *solus Christus* – and Catholicism, which manifests another kind of strength with its concern to integrate both faith and reason, both scripture and tradition, both Christ and the Church.

THE ELEMENTS OF HEALTHY RELIGION

If we are to speak about the body that is the Church, then it is clear from the beginning that, because it is a body belonging to the human world, it will not always be healthy: it will grow and decline, it will wax and wane. And yet the faith that inspired the works of the great theologians of the last two centuries – only some of whom have been mentioned at this point – is 'the faith of the Church', a treasure that is mysteriously carried in the earthen vessel that the Church is. At the heart of Catholic faith is the conviction that in Jesus of Nazareth the Word became flesh (Jn 1.14), that as the Father sent him so he sent his disciples, and that the word of God's grace and the life it establishes continue to be transmitted in these conditions of time and space through the teaching, life and worship of the Church.

John Henry Newman (1801–90) spoke about a threefold aspect to Catholicism, in which it mirrors the threefold ministry of Christ as priest, prophet and king. Catholicism is, he says, a philosophy, a political power and a religious rite. These three aspects are based on different principles (truth, government and worship), involve different means (intellectual work and teaching, authority and obedience, devotion and spirituality) and are liable to different corruptions (rationalism, ambition and tyranny, superstition and enthusiasm). Newman's idea was taken up and developed by Friedrich von Hügel (1852–1925), whose discussion of the elements of religion shows how what he terms the institutional, the intellectual and the mystical-active need to balance and correct each other. Any one of these can succeed in dominating the others to the detriment of all; likewise, any two can conspire against the third, once again to the detriment of all.

Along with the notion of sacramentality, the presentation of Catholicism given here will also depend significantly on this threefold distinction coming from Newman and von Hügel. It is a distinction that has its roots in the Bible itself, with its promise of a Messiah who would be priest, prophet and king.

IMAGES, METAPHORS, ANALOGIES, MODELS OF THE CHURCH

Besides the notion of sacrament and the threefold articulation of the elements of healthy religion, a third tool or key for getting at the spirit of Catholicism is that provided by the dozens of images, metaphors, analogies and models for the Church that we find throughout the scriptures and that are drawn on here in order to help keep our consideration of the Church concrete and practical. Some presentations of Catholicism have offered a smaller number of such 'models' and, more or less explicitly, encouraged the reader to consider which model he or she might prefer. The approach here is to include as many of them as possible, to accept that each one catches something of the concrete and particular character of this human community, and that therefore each one needs to be acknowledged. Some of these metaphors and models have more power than others, either from the use made of them in the scriptures themselves or from the importance they took on in the course of the Church's history. Think of the Church being named 'the body of Christ', for example, or 'the temple', as examples of images that have gained greater theological weight. Think of 'you are the aroma of Christ' or you are 'lambs who rule' as images that have not gained as much attention but that add something to the overall picture.

What will be regarded here as the best definition of the Church comes from Saint Cyprian of Carthage (c.205–58), who described it as 'a people brought into unity from the unity of the Father, the Son and the Holy Spirit'.[8] It is best because it points directly to the source of the Church's communion, what it is that holds these people together in one body, namely their participation in the unified life of the Blessed Trinity, Father, Son and Holy Spirit. It is with meditations on that unique understanding of God, and what it means for the life of the Church, that this book will end.

THE VIEW FROM OUTSIDE

It will be clear very quickly that the main sources of inspiration and influence on these meditations on the Church have been the New Testament, particularly Saint Paul, and the works of Saint Thomas Aquinas (1225–74). What about sources outside the tradition of Catholicism itself: what do they say we are? There is certainly help from outside the visible boundaries of Catholicism towards a fuller understanding of it, not least of the difficulties and challenges it presents for people. Perhaps we can find also some help from outside the Church towards a renewed appreciation of its strengths, and certainly of its distinctive character, even while the same help enables us to see its weaknesses more clearly.

From the broader Christian world two writers in particular have helped to shape what follows and have sustained the author in his work. One is Olivier Clément, from the perspective of Eastern Orthodox Christianity, already mentioned. His rich presentation of the teaching of the undivided Church is a powerful stimulus to Catholicism to remember its full integrity, the importance of keeping together the mystical and the intellectual, and the importance of that collaboration in sustaining the institutional. Another such influence is Walter Brueggemann, from the perspective of Protestant Christianity. His study of the Old Testament has proved to be not just enlightening but also stimulating and fruitful, applying to contemporary church life the various experiences of the people of Israel as interpreted by the prophets, in particular the experience of exile interpreted by the great prophets of that period. For understanding where Catholicism stands today, and what it needs, the help of non-Catholic Christian thinkers such as these proves to be invaluable.

It will be necessary to consider Catholicism's relations with other religions – not only with Judaism and Islam, the other members of the so-called Abrahamic faiths, but with Buddhism, Hinduism and other religious traditions. Nicholas Healy wrote about the importance of 'an other' if a Church community is to grow in knowledge of itself.[9] Particularly remarkable individuals such as Simone Weil (1909–43) and Etty Hillesum (1914–43), 'outsiders' to Catholicism in its sacramental visibility, nevertheless have many essential things to bring back to its collective memory. There are many other men and women of goodwill, seeking truth and goodness with sincere hearts, whose presence, questions and loving interest all serve to confirm the quest of each one to live in the light, whether visibly within or without Catholicism.

This book does not aspire to emulate either Karl Adam or Henri de Lubac, John Henry Newman or Friedrich von Hügel. I believe, however, that the social and cultural situation of our time, as well as the challenges the Church is facing, require that the same distinctive characteristics and teachings of Catholicism should be highlighted.

I am indebted in particular to three friends who generously agreed to read the text as it developed. Paul Murray, O.P. and Thomas McCarthy, O.P. are friends, colleagues and brothers in the Order of Preachers for more years than any of us care to remember. Rebecca K. Morrison, a cherished friend for many years, gave this book the benefit of her keen mind, her publishing experience and her rich cultural formation. Between them they have served my readership well, saving me from many theological and literary stumbles. Robin Baird-Smith conceived the idea of this book many years ago and he has shown remarkable patience in waiting for its delivery. Finally, I would like to dedicate this work to the memory of another Dominican brother and friend, Eddie Conway, O.P. (1952–2018). He made profession in the Order and was ordained to the priesthood along with Tom McCarthy and myself. May he rest in peace and be raised in the glory of the resurrection.

Vivian Boland, O.P.

PART ONE

I

A People of God?

EXPERIENCES OF THE CHURCH

It can be difficult to get behind initial perceptions of the Church in order to reflect on what its nature and purpose is. There is a lot of history informing those perceptions. The same goes for people's actual experiences of the Church: for some these will have been positive but for others there are negative experiences they can quickly call to mind.

Most people will probably identify some positive aspects of the Church. It means belonging to a people or a community, perhaps even to another kind of family. The Church brings people together and unites them. The Latin term for church, *ecclesia*, derives from the Greek *kaleo*, which means 'I call'. An *ecclesia* is a gathered assembly, a group of people called together. The Latin and Greek terms are derived in turn from, or at least are easily related to, the Hebrew term *qahal*, used in the Old Testament to refer to the assembly of the people.

We can offer a first unpacking of the term *ecclesia* in the phrase 'the community of the disciples', the community of people who have come to believe in Jesus Christ. The assembly is not random or accidental but is on the basis of a shared enterprise, a 'society' therefore in the technical sense, a group of people who recognize themselves as belonging together because there is something in which they share that makes them to be a community. The Latin term *communio*, which translates the Greek *koinonia*, is another term with a solid basis in the New Testament and is used to describe this aspect of the Church: it is a communion, human beings sharing life with each other and, as they believe, with God.

For some people the positive aspect of the Church that stands out is more personal and individual. It offers a purpose and a meaning in life. The Church acknowledges and celebrates the dignity of each person, in particular of those whose dignity might be less appreciated elsewhere: the poor, the disabled, the waifs and strays of society, who (when all is going well) will find a sense of self-worth and dignity in belonging to this community. Some people, already rich in terms of career, family life and social position, still feel the need for a deeper meaning and purpose to their life and some of these find it in the Church. The human being is there appreciated in a more holistic way than is normally the case in society generally. It is not just material prosperity or professional success that are valued, but each person in and for themselves, their spiritual as well as their physical well-being. The Church, keeping alive the teaching of Jesus, offers guidance for living human life well.

Staying for the moment with positive experiences of the Church, still others will focus immediately on the theological meaning of the Church, what it offers in relation to God. The primary thing then is that the Church is a community whose fundamental concern is people's relationship with God. It is the place in which people gather to worship God, the normal setting for the celebration of the sacraments, and the place in which, or from which, members of the community (or indeed anybody who asks for help) can expect pastoral care. Pastoral care means kindness, compassion, material help, spiritual support, a listening heart, moral guidance, a place in which one hopes to be received kindly and treated lovingly. In many parts of the developed world, where religious practice has become weak, people still value the ways in which the Church celebrates rites of passage, in particular the moments of birth, marriage and death.

For each positive experience of the Church, however, one can find a corresponding negative experience. The pathologies of religion (religion become sick, or even gone mad) have been found and presumably will continue to be found also in Catholicism. Ritual celebrations, appreciated by some as positive, will be experienced by others as ritualistic, formal and empty. The awe and wonder that characterize the mystery of God, appreciated as such by some through the life and teaching of the Church, for others is experienced as something fearful in a negative sense, encouraging shame and guilt, pulling people down and subverting their self-esteem rather than building them up with a sense of their dignity. Some will find the Church intrusive, coming between God and individual persons, complicating and distorting their relationship with God rather than strengthening and supporting it. Some may find 'happy-clappy' versions of Christianity attractive, but as many, if not more, will be turned off by manifestations of 'joy' that seem unreal, superficial and forced.

People often dismiss religious people as hypocrites, seeing contradictions between the teachings they profess and how they live their social and political lives. A number of initial thoughts ought to accompany this accusation. A hypocrite does not practise what he preaches, but if Christian teachers were to preach only what they practise, the higher and finer aspects of Christ's way would rarely if ever be preached. Those who see themselves as publicans over against hypocritical Pharisees need to be careful (Lk. 18.9-14). The whole point of that parable of Jesus is to trap not just self-righteous Pharisees but self-righteous publicans, who on hearing the parable might be tempted to say, 'Thank God I am not like those Pharisees' (for Pharisees read clerics, bishops, Catholics, or whatever).

At the same time, it cannot be denied that the failures of Catholics, in particular in recent years in relation to the protection of children and vulnerable adults, have done untold damage to the credibility of the Church in many parts of the world. This is an enormous problem that the Church still struggles to negotiate and it will take a long time to recover the trust of many, probably never in the case of some.

Combined with these failures in relation to the protection of children is the significant gulf between the Catholic Church's teaching about sexuality and the generally accepted *mores* of modern societies. The Catholic Church is the last remaining institutional voice opposing, with traditional teachings that were once universally accepted, many of the liberalizations in sexual morality that characterize modern culture. The Church's teaching on contraception, sexual relations between unmarried people, remarriage after divorce, and homosexuality are all now out of step not only with how many people live but also with the ways in which many people think it is good to live. John Paul II made a supreme effort in his 'theology of the body' to think through on a new basis the Church's theology of sexuality and marriage in defence of traditional moral teaching in these areas. Pope Francis, in an interview he gave near the beginning of his pontificate, spoke of how the Church needs to think out again, *ab initio* as it were, how to present its moral teachings effectively and convincingly to the modern world.[1]

A kind of 'bottom line' in all this is that, alongside these positive and negative experiences, many people come to believe, or continue to believe, that there is a truth to be found in the Church, a contact with God and with God's grace, that obliges one to acknowledge it even if difficulties and questions remain. Thomas Aquinas says that there is a thinking (cogitation) that precedes the act of faith and there is a thinking (cogitation) that accompanies the act of faith. In what way the Church itself is an object of faith will be considered below.

The part of theology that considers the origin, nature, structure and life of the Church is called 'ecclesiology'. It has become fashionable in some places to use the term 'church' without the definite article, in such expressions as 'wanting to be church together', 'how to be church today'. It may seem unimportant, but these meditations seek to show that it is essential to refer to 'the Church', definite article and capital 'C', in order to indicate something that Catholic Christianity wants to say about itself. This is not in the first place something triumphalist. It is in order to show that 'church' is not some kind of Platonic form that can be instantiated in different times and places as a kind of perfection or quality or characteristic of some group. Rather, 'the Church' is a subject in history, to be related to in the first place as we relate to a subject and not to a thing, a quality or even an institution. In other words, relating to the Church is more akin to a personal relationship than it is to any other kind of relationship. Once again, more about that as we go along.

IMAGES FOR THE CHURCH

The opening chapter of Vatican II's Dogmatic Constitution on the Church, *Lumen gentium*, gathers a range of imagery the Bible uses to refer to the Church.[2] It is tempting to describe the biblical images spoken of in *LG* 6 as 'models' of the Church, a term that became popular as a result of an influential book by an American Jesuit, later a cardinal, Avery Dulles. He called his book simply *Models of the Church* and it was very influential in its day.[3] But there are reasons for resisting the use of the term 'models', at least for the moment.

Some of the biblical images are *pastoral* and *agricultural*, to do with the tending of flocks and the husbanding of crops. Jesus describes himself as the good shepherd and as the gate of the sheepfold (Jn 10.7-16), developing earlier references to the people as a flock of which God is the shepherd (Isa. 40.11; Ezek. 34.11-16). Saint Paul speaks of the early Christian community as a field and of himself as a worker in God's tillage (1 Cor. 3.5-9; 2 Cor. 10.13-18). Paul speaks also of the Church as a holy olive tree whose roots are in the prophets and onto which a new branch, the Gentiles, is being grafted so that all human beings might belong to God's people (Rom. 11.13-24). Jesus's use of the image of the vineyard (Jn. 15) also has roots in earlier biblical poetry where Israel is described as a choice vineyard planted by the heavenly cultivator (Isa. 5.1-10; Ezek. 19.10 and Ps. 80(79).8-19. Cf. also Mt. 21.33-41; Mk 12.1-12; Lk. 20.9-19).

Other images are taken from the world of construction, from *buildings* and *cities*. Thus, the Church is described as God's building (1 Cor. 3.9-17) established on the foundation of the apostles (Eph. 2.20; Rev. 21.14), an image of solidity and unity in spite of the notorious unreliability of the apostles! The Church is the house of God in which his family dwells, the household of God in the Spirit (Eph. 2.19-22). God revealed himself to Moses long ago as a God who would be with his people and the covenant he established and renewed with them confirmed this relationship: 'I will be their God and they will be my people.' That statement echoes through the centuries of the relationship and comes to a climax in a vision of a new heaven and a new earth in which the holy city, new Jerusalem, is now the dwelling place of God among people (Rev. 21.1-3). This vision of a new city, Mount Zion, the heavenly Jerusalem, the city of the living God, is found also in the Letter to the Hebrews, which makes it explicit that in this new reality God dwells with the assembly (*ekklesia*, the Church: Heb. 12.22-24). The Book of Revelation closes with this striking image of the holy city, God's dwelling place, coming down when the world is made anew, mixing its metaphors by saying then that this city will be like a bride adorned for her husband (Rev. 21.1f.). One final reference to building ought to be noted. This is the frequent reference, in the preaching of Jesus as well as in the post-Easter preaching of the apostles, to a stone rejected by the builders that becomes the corner stone of a new construction (Mt. 21.42; Mk 12.10-11; Lk. 20.17; Acts 4.11; 1 Pet. 2.7). The Old Testament text referred to is Psalm 118(117).22, an idea found also in Isaiah 28.16. Those who belong to Christ are, therefore, parts of a building, living stones built into it (1 Pet. 2.5).

We have seen that the Book of Revelation speaks of the Church as a city that is also a bride adorned to meet her husband and Ephesians speaks of the Church as the household of God. A third set of images for the Church is therefore drawn from *human relationships*, *marriage* and *family life*. The Jerusalem above is a city, but is also our mother (Gal. 4.26; Rev. 12.17). Once again, this New Testament image has roots deep in the Old Testament where Jerusalem is imagined as a mother suckling her young (Isa. 66.7-14). That God and the people would be thought of in terms of lover and beloved was not new either. So, the Church is the

Bride of the Lamb (Rev. 19.7; 21.2; 21.9; 22.17) whom he loved
and for whom he has given himself (Eph. 5.25-26). She is united
to Christ who is both lover and mother, nourishing and cherishing
her (Eph. 5.29), joining her to himself in love and fidelity, filling
her with heavenly gifts so that she might know the love of God
and of Christ for her (Eph. 3.19). It is from the Father, Saint
Paul says, that every family in heaven and on earth is named
(Eph. 3.14-15). There is also a note of exile and pilgrimage in
the experience of the Church. Here and now, on earth and in this
time, she journeys in a foreign land, seeking what is above where
her true citizenship is, her true life hidden with Christ in God
until she appears in glory with him, her spouse (Col. 3.1-4; Phil.
3.20; Heb. 11.9-10, 13-16). This note of exile and pilgrimage
in the experience of the Church is of particular relevance today
and is one to which we shall return. For now, let us simply refer
finally to the text of Revelation 11.19–12.17, the great vision
of a woman clothed with the Sun and with the Moon under her
feet. She represents the Church and her experiences dramatically
portrayed there express figuratively the spiritual warfare in which
'her offspring' are inevitably caught up.

Lumen gentium thus gathers the most important biblical
images for the Church drawn from agriculture, building and
family life. An English Dominican, Geoffrey Preston (1936–77),
in a book entitled *Faces of the Church*, gives an extensive list
of New Testament images for the Church itself or for various
aspects of its nature, life and mission.[4] His text deserves quoting
in full as the book is not now easily found. He writes, on page 3:

> The New Testament boasts a wealth of imagery where the
> Church is concerned. There is the salt of the earth, a letter from
> Christ, fish and fish net, the boat and the ark; unleavened bread,
> one loaf, the table of the Lord, the altar, the cup of the Lord,
> wine, branches of the vine, vineyard, the fig-tree, the olive-tree,
> God's planting; God's building, the building on the rock, the
> pillar and buttress. Again, there is the mother of the Messiah,
> the elect lady, the bride of Christ, virgins; the wedding feast;

wearers of white robes or a choice of clothing. To this we can add: citizens, exiles, the dispersion, ambassadors, the poor, hosts and guests, the people of God, Israel, a chosen race, a holy nation, twelve tribes, the patriarchs, circumcision, Abraham's sons, the Exodus, the house of David, the remnant, the elect; a flock, lambs who rule; the holy city, the holy temple, priesthood. One can continue with: sacrifice, aroma, festivals; the new creation, first-fruits, the new humanity, the last Adam, Son of Man, the kingdom of God, those who fight against Satan. Nor does the list stop here. It would include also: the sabbath rest, the age to come, God's glory, light, life and the tree of life; communion in the Holy Spirit, the bond of love, the sanctified, the faithful, the justified, followers, disciples; the road, coming and going; confessors, slaves, friends, servants, the witnessing community. Finally, we may add: the household of God, sons of God, the brotherhood, the body of life, members of Christ, the body and the blood, the diversities of ministries, spiritual body, head of cosmic spirits, the body of which Christ is head, the unity of Jews and Gentiles, the growth of the body and the fulness of God. Not all these are strictly or exclusively images of the Church; but all are in some way ecclesial images, ways of speaking about the life of the Church, before God, in this world.

This is wonderful poetry, but what are we to take from it? Are any of these images to be preferred? Are there images that, either in their original or in their subsequent use, have taken on greater theological significance? The answer to this last question is, of course, yes, there are a number of these images that carry much greater theological meaning than others. At the same time, all of these images teach us something about the Church.

PRIMAL METAPHORS AND MODELS

From these dozens of images, Preston picks out what he terms 'primal metaphors', the most powerful images. He identifies ten of these, and the first part of his book consists in a more detailed consideration of each one: *ekklesia* (pp. 3–10), the people of God (pp. 11–22; *LG* 9–17), brotherhood ['fellowship'] (pp. 23–35), temple (pp. 36–47), flock (pp. 48–57), kingdom (pp. 58–67; *LG* 5), the poor of the Lord (pp. 68–75), the bride of Christ (pp. 76–84), the body of Christ (pp. 85–92; *LG* 7) and new creation (pp. 93–102).

We can make the list even more manageable, because among these primal metaphors three stand out for having attracted most attention in recent times, whether in the writings of theologians or in the teachings of the Church: 'people of God', 'kingdom' and 'body of Christ'. These are the richest images representing the Church that have also been the most influential in recent thinking about the Church within the Church itself. They are all solidly biblical in their origins.

Avery Dulles identified five 'models of the Church', but the term 'model' brings certain difficulties with it. The term has a particular meaning in sociology that was not intended by Dulles but may have influenced the way in which many of his readers received his work. Phrasing things in the way he did led to people, inevitably expressing preference for one model to another, against the explicit desire of the author, it needs to be said. It also generated a kind of 'models of the Church' industry where people felt the need to be creative and to propose alternative models, sometimes with little regard for any biblical or theological justification. Sociology and business organization tended to take over. This industry became even more productive if you dropped the definite article and went looking for 'models of church'. The truth is, however, that in spite of his warning, Dulles's own five original models already invited this kind of consideration, with only two of them having clear biblical roots, that of *herald* (1991, pp. 76–88) and of *servant* (pp. 89–102). The other three, *institution* (pp. 15–33), *mystical communion* (pp. 34–62) and *sacrament* (pp. 63–75; cf. *LG* 8), are not without theological pedigree and have some basis, however remote, in biblical revelation, but they do not take us to the heart of that revelation as do many of the more picturesque images on Geoffrey Preston's list.

It seems wiser to bunch Dulles's models together and to say that here are different but complementary ways of imagining the Church. If preferring one means ignoring another, or even ignoring more than one of them, then something crucial has been lost to our understanding. It is central to the argument of the present book that any hope of doing justice to the reality of what the Church is requires holding together a set of perspectives, a palette of images, a number of hermeneutical keys. Dulles's proposal of a mega- or meta-model, 'the community of disciples' (1991, pp. 204–26), obviously an important way of thinking about the Church, led some to speak of the need for 'super-models' – and that at a time when the term was normally used to describe those super-models of catwalk and fashion business terrain!

As we proceed, we will return to many of these images for the Church, to Preston's primal metaphors, to the three richest images picked out from those, and even to Dulles's models and super-model. For now, let us turn first to that way of describing the Church that came to dominate Vatican II's presentation in *Lumen gentium*, understanding the Church in the first place as 'the people of God'.

THE PEOPLE OF GOD

One of the most talked-about events at Vatican II was its rejection of the initial *schema*, or draft document, on the Church and its decision that the participants in the Council themselves would prepare a fresh draft. Central to this fresh draft, and to the final document, was the decision to make the idea of 'the people of God' the primary and fundamental description of what the Church is. That final document, *Lumen gentium*, contains the main teaching of the Council on the nature of the Church. It considers first the mystery of the Church and next the biblical theme of the people of God. In the third chapter it considers the hierarchical character of the Church, and for many this ordering (or reordering as it was in effect) carried great significance: 'the people' were to be considered before 'the hierarchy'.

It is important not to underestimate the significance of the debate about this. It is also important not to misunderstand who 'the people of God' are. Even today, sixty years after the Council, one sometimes hears people using the phrase 'people of God' as if it refers to everybody in the Church except the members of the hierarchy (in much the same way as in secular politics one might talk about 'the people' over against 'the parliament' or 'the government'). It may seem that this is what the ordering of the chapters of *Lumen gentium* implies: first the people, then the hierarchy. Well, yes, it is a significant change, as long as we do not forget that the members of the hierarchy also belong to the people of God. The point is not to distinguish the mass of ordinary Christians from those among them who become bishops (and priests and deacons). The point is to start with a biblical understanding of the Church that includes all its members equally and, as we will see, seeks also to include in that understanding not only other baptized Christians but their relationship with the whole of humanity.

Thus, the preacher who begins his preaching by saying 'my dear people of God' may be in danger of perpetuating a misunderstanding. For he too is a member of that people. People and hierarchy are not two classes within the same category. All belong to the people whether they are members of the hierarchy or 'lay' people, the technical term in canon law for members of the Church who are not ordained.

The notion of a 'people of God' has its roots deep in the Old Testament, right from the moment when history began for the Hebrew people. God called Abraham and promised that he would be the father of a great people (Gen. 12.1-2). The call is particular but with a universal significance, since in Abraham all the families of the earth will come to be blessed (Gen. 12.3). God sealed this promise in a series of covenants with Abraham and his descendants. The Bible is the record of this relationship in which, over and over again, God promises to be with his people on condition that the people show forth, in how they live, what their God is like. In other words that they show forth that they really do belong to God.

It is in the Book of Exodus, with the leadership of Moses, in the time of the liberation of the Hebrew people from slavery in Egypt, that we hear about God beginning in earnest to mould a people as his own. 'If you will obey my voice and keep my covenant, you shall be my own possession among all peoples', the Lord says to them through Moses, 'you shall be to me a kingdom of priests and a holy nation' (Exod. 19.5-6).

The covenant with Israel – 'I will be your God and you will be my people' – is a golden thread running through the whole of the scriptures. 'You shall be called the priests of the Lord', says the prophet Isaiah (Isa. 61.6). It is a privilege granted to God's chosen people, but also a mission entrusted to them in service of all the peoples of the earth whose worship will be led by Israel: 'nations shall walk by your light' and 'the wealth of the nations shall come to you ... they shall come up with acceptance on my altar' (Isa. 60.3, 5, 7). For a Christian reading of this history, the climax comes as expressed in the First Letter of Peter, where the disciples of Jesus understand themselves as the continuation of this history of the Hebrew people, the next chapter in this covenant story, a new and re-formed Israel. There we read:

> you are a chosen race, a royal priesthood, a holy nation, God's own people, that you may declare the wonderful deeds of him who called you out of darkness into his marvellous light. Once you were no people but now you are God's people; once you had not received mercy but now you have received mercy. (1 Pet. 2.9-10)

It is clear how this text echoes those cited from Exodus and Isaiah. It ends with a reference to another of the prophets, Hosea, who promises a renewal of the people in which the Lord will have pity on those called 'Not pitied' and will say to 'Not my people', 'You are my people', to which they will say 'You are my God' (Hos. 2.23).

The point here is this: that the Catholic Church, in its most authoritative recent statement about how it understands itself,

32

positions itself within this covenant history and says, 'This is where we believe ourselves to belong, this is who we believe ourselves to be, this is the grace and mission we believe ourselves also to have received.' So, the Church in its history reaches as far back as Abraham (at least: some of the Fathers of the Church speak of it beginning with Abel, described in the Roman liturgy as 'just' and honoured in some places as a saint, and Noah's ark was to become another image for the Church dear to some Christian teachers). In its reach, therefore, the Church believes itself to belong to the people God has chosen as his own, a particular community of people by whom all the families of the earth shall bless themselves.

On one hand, therefore, the Church is very particular, embedded in a particular history, made up of identifiable individuals and communities, with its own history of light and darkness to be considered further on. On the other hand, it understands itself as universal, 'catholic' in its original meaning, and so having something to do with, and for, all the people of the earth. 'The Church is the sacrament of the unity of humankind' is how Vatican II put it (*LG* 1). It is Jesus Christ who is 'the light of the nations', *lumen gentium*, but this light shines out visibly in those who believe in him. It is what a sacrament means: a visible sign of invisible grace, another point to be considered further on.

There are many places in the New Testament where the early Christian communities define themselves in the same terms as were used to describe God's chosen people in the Old Testament. They are children of Abraham (Gal. 3.7, 29; Rom. 4.16), they are the new circumcision (Phil. 3.3), they are heirs of the promises made to the patriarchs (Rom. 15.8), they are a new branch grafted on to an old olive tree (Rom. 11.17), they are the Israel of God (Gal. 6.16), twelve apostles are called to be judges of the new twelve tribes of Israel (Mt. 19.28; Lk. 22.28-30), they are sons and daughters of God (1 Jn 3.1), God's friends (Jas 2.23; 4.4), God's servants (1 Pet. 2.16), they are even God's slaves (Rom. 6.22). They believed in a new work of the same God, a fulfilment of God's earlier promises, and so they continue to this day to read those same sacred scriptures not simply as a historical record but as their story also.

MEMBERSHIP?

So how are members of the Church best described? As well as the list of Old Testament terms just mentioned, the New Testament adds further possibilities. Most famously, the name 'Christian' began to be used early on, at Antioch (Acts 11.26). On a superficial level it means simply a follower of Jesus Christ, one who has come to believe that Jesus, the teacher from Nazareth, is the Messiah, the 'Christ', or anointed one who was promised and expected.

But the term 'Christian' has always had more profound meanings besides simply identifying who belongs to the Christian movement. The Christ is the anointed one, and so the Christian is one who belongs to the anointed one, who belongs to the messianic people and so is himself or herself an anointed person. There are many references to this in the New Testament, not just to the fact that Jesus is anointed and so he is the Christ, but also to the fact that those who believe in him are anointed, they have come to share in the same Holy Spirit who is the power of God who anoints men and women for particular tasks.

Christians are, therefore, people who have received the Holy Spirit as a pledge or guarantee of the fullness of life that is promised (Eph. 1.13-14). They are anointed with the Spirit and so they do not need anyone to teach them (1 Jn 2.27), for they have abiding within them the Spirit who keeps them in the truth and enables them to abide in the Son and in the Father. Paul puts it dramatically in his Letter to the Galatians: 'It is no longer I who live but Christ who lives in me' (Gal. 2.20). We are to live by the Spirit, he says further on in the same letter, and to walk by the Spirit, enjoying the fruits of the Spirit: 'living by the Spirit' and 'belonging to Christ Jesus' are two ways of saying the same thing (Gal. 5.16-25). 'By one Spirit we were all baptized into one body and all were made to drink of the one Spirit' – it is once again a mixing of metaphors, but the meaning is the same (1 Cor. 12.13).

The disciples were first called 'Christians' at Antioch. But that piece of information also tells us that their earliest title was simply 'disciples'. This is the most common description of them in the Gospels: people who follow Jesus Christ, learn from him, and try to live in the way he taught and in the way he himself lived. 'Come, follow me' is a regular conclusion from the lips of Jesus to a miracle, an encounter or a discourse about the kingdom.

In other parts of the New Testament other terms are used for the disciples, who are now called Christians. They are 'confessors' because they bear witness by their words to the faith they have come to share (see, for example, Mt. 10.32; Rom. 10.9; 1 Jn 2.23; 4.15). They are also, therefore, 'the faithful', who must persevere in that faith even through times of difficulty and persecution, supported in that perseverance by the fact that God is faithful (see, for example, Acts 11.23; 16.15; 1 Cor. 1.9; Col. 1.2; Rev. 2.10; 17.14).

In considering the question of justification and salvation, Paul refers to Christians as 'the called [or elect]', 'the foreknown', 'the predestined', 'the justified', 'the glorified' (Rom. 8.28-30). Jesus speaks of 'the elect' in Matthew 24 (vv. 22, 24, 31) and in Luke 18.7. Paul speaks of election in relation to God's choice of Israel and how that election continues into this new moment of the Church in which God does a new thing while remaining faithful to the original election (see, for example, Rom. 9.11 and 11.7, 28). There are further references to Christians as 'the elect' in 2 Timothy 2.10 and 2 Peter 1.10. The term is used of individual Christians in 2 John 1.1, 13, unless these are personifications of Christian communities, in which case 'the elect lady' and 'the elect sister' refer to local churches.

I was startled one Sunday morning by a lady telling me, without batting an eyelid, that her uncle was a saint in a Christian community down the road from where we were. Coming from an Irish Catholic background I baulked at the presumption that any living person might already be described as a saint. But on reflection I remembered that Saint Paul frequently uses the term when speaking to or about members of the churches to whom he wrote. Sometimes it is qualified by 'called to be saints' – Romans 1.7 and 1 Corinthians 1.2, for example – but more often he simply calls them saints – 'to the Church of God which is at Corinth, with all the saints who are in the whole of Achaia' (2 Cor. 1.1), 'all the saints greet you' (2 Cor. 13.12), 'to the saints who are also faithful in Christ Jesus' (Eph. 1.1), 'to all the saints in Christ Jesus who are at Philippi, with the bishops and deacons' (Phil. 1.1), 'to the saints and faithful brethren in Christ at Colossae' (Col. 1.2).

Christians are people who have been 'sanctified' by the Holy Spirit. Many New Testament authors refer to members of the Church as those who have been, or are being, sanctified – see, for example, Acts 20.32; 26.18; 1 Corinthians 1.2; 6.11; Hebrews 2.11; 10.10, 14; 1 Peter 1.2. It is no moral achievement on their part, nor any successful observance of a law, that entitles them to be called 'the sanctified'. It is the whole purpose of their attaching themselves to Christ, in order that they might be sanctified and become members of God's holy people.

The only letter of Paul's that does not begin in this way is Galatians, where Paul's anxiety and anger about the issues he needed to address with them led him to ignore formalities and get straight down to business. His anxiety and anger were precisely in the face of forces that he felt were pulling them away from the holiness – the freedom of life in the Spirit – to which he had introduced them through the preaching of the gospel.

Christians, disciples, followers, confessors, the faithful who are justified, sanctified and glorified – we can add witnesses, the elect, a remnant, those called to be saints – there is for now no distinction of gift or status, of office or ministry, but all who are members of the Church share the same call to holiness of life. This litany of New Testament texts and references supports what Vatican II named 'the universal call to holiness': people who have undergone the same baptism and have received the gift of the same Spirit are called to share in a common destiny and to witness to what they have received. To be holy means simply to live one's life in accordance with the great commandment, loving God with all one's heart, soul and might, loving our neighbour as ourselves (Mt. 22.34-50; Mk 12.28-34; Lk. 10.27), in other words loving as Jesus loved his disciples (Jn 13.34-35). To be sanctified means to be enabled by God's grace to love in this way. Once again, a lot more about this as we go along.

We must hold our horses, though. This all seems too much, too soon. Hermeneutical keys, images, symbols, models, metaphors, a particular people chosen to carry a blessing for all people: what is the reality supporting what, after all, might be simply poetry and myth? To answer that question, we must speak about Jesus Christ, the icon of God (2 Cor. 4.4), bearing the very stamp of God's nature (Heb. 1.3), the only Son, closest to the Father's heart, who has made God known (Jn 1.18). At first, so it seems, the spirit of Catholicism is all about the Church. But the Church is all about Christ and Christ is all about God. At first, we experience the Church as an institution and then as a people. But at its deepest core it is a bearer of the mystery of God. It is to that mystery, the reality that supports everything that is said, that we now turn.

PART TWO

CHRIST, IMAGE AND SACRAMENT OF GOD

Around one of the doors of the great cathedral at Chartres are sculptures of Adam and of Christ and they have the same face: they are identical twins. It was a tradition in some places that Jesus had the same physical features as Adam. It is another way of speaking about the first human being created in the image of God and of Jesus restoring that image in humanity. Saint Paul contrasts them frequently, the first Adam and the last Adam, a first creation with a history of sin that is now overtaken by a new creation with a history of grace. There is renewal and a new beginning in Jesus Christ, more radical than the restarting that took place after Noah's flood. 'The same God who said, let light shine out of darkness' – the creator God in other words – 'has shone in our hearts to give the light of the knowledge of the glory of God in the face of Christ' (2 Cor. 4.6). Jesus Christ is the human being as originally intended, the image of the invisible God, making the Father known and calling all human beings to the renewal of their true nature by becoming conformed to him. Here we consider these histories of the two Adams and God's work of establishing within creation the human being who would be God's perfect image, icon or sacrament.

THE FIRST ADAM

In the first account of creation, Genesis 1.1–2.3, we are told that the human being is made in the image and likeness of God (Gen. 1.26). The statement that follows immediately – 'Let them have dominion over the fish of the sea and over the birds of the air and over the cattle and over all the earth and over every creeping thing that creeps upon the earth' – is so closely attached to 'being made in the image and likeness of God' that it seems simply to make explicit what that fact means: to be in the image and likeness of God simply is to have such dominion. Or at least it means being a creature of such a kind that such dominion can be entrusted to it, which is what God does two verses later (Gen. 1.28).

So, the human being is made in God's image, male and female (Gen. 1.27). God blessed them and said, 'Be fruitful and multiply, and fill the earth and subdue it; and have dominion over the fish of the sea and over the birds of the air and over every living thing that moves upon the earth' (Gen. 1.28). The human being is in charge of the creation, is God's steward within the creation. He and she are given all plants and trees to be their food, this vegetarian diet being also the diet of every beast of the earth, every bird of the air, everything that creeps on the earth, everything that has the breath of life (Gen. 1.30). The only creatures that are eaten by other creatures are the trees and plants and their fruits. And God saw everything he had made and it was very good.

How are we to understand this 'dominion' that God the Creator entrusts to the human being? When we think about the human being's exploitation of the natural world, legitimate questions arise about how this particular text has been used in the history of Christianity. Whatever it means, however, two things are clear. One is that the human being is being recognized as unique, standing out from all the other created realities. The other is that the human being is entrusted with a position of responsibility within creation. It must therefore be a creature whose nature allows it to undertake the tasks that come with such a position. Traditionally this is taken to mean that the human being has three qualities: *understanding*, *freedom* and *initiative*. These are not found in any comparable way in any other known creature in the universe even if some animals show some rudimentary capacity for knowing, deciding and acting. As God is creator – intelligent, free and acting – so the human created in God's image is creative within the creation – intelligent, free and acting.

Another suggestion as to what being in the image of God might mean is the simple, we might say primitive, interpretation that the human being is *the animal that stands erect*, with head held high and so able to survey the creation and oversee it, in a very concrete way. Other animals are preoccupied with what is on the ground, sniffing their way through the woods, across the fields, or along the floor of the ocean. The human being lifts up his head and is, literally, an over-seer.

Another, more significant, interpretation is that, as the only creature who is said to be created male and female, the human being is the *relational animal*. Presumably the other animals are also male and female, although this is not mentioned until later, when they are pairing off to go into Noah's ark (Gen. 6.19; 7.2-3, 9, 16). From the moment of their creation, however, the human beings are said to be male and female, and this is sometimes taken to mean that being in relation with each other is fundamental to their nature. In the minds of some Christian thinkers, in view of the understanding of God revealed by Christ, it does not come as a surprise that the creature made in the image of God, who is a relational God, is itself a relational creature. Knowing and loving another person is fundamental to what this creature is, just as we understand God's being and action to consist in knowing and loving. But even before the Christian revelation, being in relationship is at least implied in this ancient Hebrew text about the creation of the human being.

A final suggestion is that to be in the image of God means to be the *linguistic animal*, the animal that has the capacity for speech. God does only two things in the first chapter of the Bible: he speaks and he sees. God says, 'Let there be light', 'let the waters be gathered together', 'let the earth bring forth living creatures' – and things happen in accordance with his words. We can say, figuratively speaking, that God does not need to get his hands dirty in this first account of creation. It all happens simply by him uttering his word. It is not surprising, therefore, that the creature most like God would be understood to be a creature that speaks.

In fact, it is in the second account of the creation, Genesis 2.4-25, that the human being, now called Adam, or 'earth creature', does precisely this. He is introduced to all the other animals to see if there is among them a partner suitable for him, and as they pass before him he decides what each should be called (Gen. 2.19). He is already exercising his function as steward of the creation and partner with God in its management. To be the one who says what things are to be called is to exercise responsibility: this is what being in the image of God entails.

To say that the human being is created in the image and likeness of God is also a way of saying that the human being is *God's child*. This is clear from the passage where we read about the first child of Adam and Eve:

> When God created humankind, he made them in the likeness of God. Male and female he created them, and he blessed them and named them 'Humankind' when they were created. When Adam had lived for one hundred and thirty years, he became the father of a son in his likeness, according to his image, and named him Seth. (Gen. 5.1-3)

The human being is the image and likeness of God, Seth is the image and likeness of Adam. Clearly, then, another way in which we can translate 'being in the image and likeness of God' is to say it means being a child of God, or, as male and female, being a son and a daughter of God.

There are rich traditions, then, about the meaning of this phrase, 'the image of God', traditions about stewardship and oversight, about relationship and speech, about being children of God. The capacities that make all these things possible – intelligence, freedom, creativity – are taken also to mean that this creature has a unique status or dignity within the creation. For Thomas Aquinas, for example, this is the foundation of moral responsibility, since alone among the animals the human being is an agent in the full sense, a true source of action, entitled to credit and blame for what he does, rather than being simply an animal that reacts and responds to stimuli from without and from within. The inherent dignity that is recognized as the basis of human rights, in the United Nations declaration, for example, is linked with this conviction, whether the theological roots of it are acknowledged or forgotten. Without those roots how else can an 'inherent' dignity be recognized?

Another aspect of this is quickly apparent in the Book of Genesis, however, for these same capacities that give the human being a special dignity are the capacities that make sin possible. Only a creature with such capacities can be held responsible, in the full sense of the term, for what he does. He can therefore be praised for loving but must accept responsibility for killing.

When, after the Flood, God makes the covenant with which the creation is restarted, he recalls the fact that the human being is the image of God. But now the circumstances are less serene and less peaceful. Things have become fraught, there has been much violence, all the relationships that were harmonious at the beginning have been damaged by sin as God predicted. But the story is to continue with God accepting certain realities about this human creature, allowing them now to become meat-eaters, for example. The tendency to sin is strong, often expressing itself in violence. But once more God recalls the dignity and status of this creature when he says that 'whoever sheds the blood of a human, by a human shall that person's blood be shed; for in his own image God made humankind' (Gen. 9.6).

It is a poignant moment, for it is the last time in the Hebrew Bible, and in a context of violence and murder, that we are reminded of this fact: the human being is the image of God. All subsequent uses of the term 'image' in relation to God or the gods in the Hebrew scriptures refer to idols, phantoms or ghosts (see, e.g., Isa. 44.9-17).

There are two references in the Greek literature of the Old Testament that repeat what we have seen in Genesis. One is the Book of Sirach, Chapter 17, which recounts the history of God's dealings with Israel beginning with the creation of the human being in the image of God. The ability for understanding, freedom and action that goes with that status is expounded at length in that chapter, but so too is the fear that the rest of creation experiences in relation to the human being precisely because of the power those abilities give him. The other text is in the Wisdom of Solomon, Chapter 2, a reflection on good and evil in human relations, marked as they often are by resentment and envy. The good person excites opposition and provokes people to violence, and it is really God who is being put to the test in the testing of the good person. But death is not the last word, the author says, it is not part of God's plan, 'for God created us for incorruption, and made us in the image of his own nature' (Wis. 2.23).

THE LAST ADAM

The question of where a true image of God might be found only arises again in the New Testament. Other texts in the Old Testament speak about the possibility of knowing God through the works of creation and through God's actions in history. In other words, there are traces, later called 'vestiges', of the Creator's presence and work within creation and its history that should be enough to lead people to know something of God's reality and nature. But when we come to the Christian scriptures the original teaching returns, and it is tempting to say that it returns with a vengeance. It certainly returns with a new significance. For we are told, by Saint Paul, that it is Jesus Christ who is the image of God, literally the icon of God (2 Cor. 4.4). The same term is used in the Letter to the Colossians which describes Christ as 'the image of the invisible God' (Col. 1.15), and the Letter to the Hebrews tells us that Christ 'bears the very stamp of God's nature' (Heb. 1.3).

One New Testament appeal to the fact of the human being's creation 'in the image and likeness of God' is close to the kind of practical moral wisdom we find in earlier Hebrew writings. This is in the Letter of James, which appeals to this teaching in support of a simple moral exhortation. That Letter is a practical, straightforward and concrete handbook about the challenges human beings face in living and working together. As part of his critique of how we use our gift for speech, James laments that while 'with (the tongue) we bless the Lord and Father', with the same tongue 'we curse men, who are made in the likeness of God' (Jas 3.9).

Most of the New Testament references to the human being as the image of God have to do with human beings becoming linked with Christ, who is the image of God in a unique way. This is how human beings are restored to a likeness with God, with sin not only tarnished but effectively removed. Thus in 1 Corinthians we find a beautiful phrase in which man is described as 'the image and glory of God' (1 Cor. 11.7). The text is immediately problematic, however, because the term 'man' is exclusive in the context. The term used means male, not humankind. The next phrase is one not immediately beautiful to our ears: that 'the woman is the glory of the man'. Read on and you will see that Paul himself is in a spot of bother trying to explain what he means. Or is he trying to explain what someone else means? Or someone else trying to explain what Paul must mean? What seems like an inequality between man and woman has to be corrected by additional sentences such as, 'In the Lord woman is not independent of man nor man of woman; for as woman was made from man so man is now born of woman. And all things are from God' (1 Cor. 11.11-12). Something has crept in from somewhere to distort the original equality that is emphasized so clearly in both accounts of the creation (Gen. 1.27 and Gen. 2.20-24). That equality, according to other texts of the New Testament, is now restored through the work of Christ. And so all human beings, men and women, created in the image and likeness of God, are restored to that image and likeness 'in the Lord', in Christ. To be baptized into Christ is to put on Christ, Paul says in the Letter to the Galatians, which means 'there is neither Jew nor Greek, there is neither slave nor free, there is neither male nor female, for you are all one in Christ Jesus' (Gal. 3.27-28).

Within a few chapters of 1 Corinthians 11 we hear Paul saying that all who have been baptized come to bear the likeness of 'the man of heaven' (1 Cor. 15.49). All are conformed to the image of God's Son (Rom. 8.29), and all have put on 'the new man' who is being renewed in knowledge after the image of the creator (Col. 3.10). Another powerful text speaks of the transformation of the image of God in the human being that is brought about by faith in Christ: 'We all, with unveiled face, beholding the glory of the Lord, are being changed into his likeness from one degree of glory to another; for this comes from the Lord who is the Spirit' (2 Cor. 3.18). We become like the one we see: 'we shall be like him for we shall see him as he is' (1 Jn 3.2). It is Christ who makes it possible for us to see God and so be restored in our likeness to God.

Another important text on this point is to be found in the account of Paul's preaching at Athens. We read about this in Acts of the Apostles, Chapter 17. It is Paul's opportunity to preach to the intelligentsia of the city, Stoic and Epicurean philosophers among them. He does it on the Areopagus, a place in the city where important issues were treated. His discourse goes well at first. He speaks about their openness to different philosophical and religious opinions. He speaks about the gods and about the unknown God for whom they also left space. This is the God I want to talk about, Paul says, who created all things and who, in creating human beings, gave them a desire to seek after and to find God. He quotes some of their own thinkers and poets. Remember that Paul probably strengthened his classical and philosophical education during the silent years he spent in Tarsus after his first attempts to be a Christian preacher had collapsed. Tarsus, Paul's home town, was an important intellectual centre of the Roman empire.

Paul gets to a point where he begins to talk about repentance, about judgement, and about a man being raised from the dead to be that judge. There is a crescendo of disbelief as he expresses these last three points and the sermon ends in some confusion. Implied in Paul's sermon earlier, however, is a clear proclamation that if people want to find an image or representation of God within creation, then it is to be found in the human being. He rejects all worship of idols – 'God does not live in shrines made by man, nor is he served by human hands' (Acts 17.24-25) and 'we ought not to think that the Deity is like gold, or silver, or stone, a representation of the art and imagination of man' (Acts 17.29). Why not? Because we are ourselves God's offspring. Being God's offspring, literally 'coming into existence from God', we only have to look at ourselves to find within the creation the closest image and likeness of God, the source of our existence, 'in whom we live and move and have our being' (Acts 17.28). The art and imagination of man are wonderful things and many wonderful objects are created through human art and imagination. But we ought not to think that we are making God. It is rather the other way round: we are God's offspring, the ones created in his image and likeness, God's children, and restored to that dignity by the work of Jesus Christ who is the perfect image of the invisible God.

CHRIST: IMAGE AND SACRAMENT

Here is how the First Letter of John introduces the apostolic preaching of the first followers of Jesus:

> That which was from the beginning, which we have heard, which we have seen with our eyes, which we have looked upon and touched with our hands, concerning the word of life – the life was made manifest, and we saw it, and testify to it, and proclaim to you the eternal life which was with the Father and was made manifest to us – that which we have seen and heard we proclaim also to you so that you may have fellowship with us; and our fellowship is with the Father and with his Son Jesus Christ. And we are writing this that our joy may be complete. (1 Jn 1.1-4)

The ones who were with Jesus 'during all the time he went in and out among us' (Acts 1.21) are qualified to speak as eye-witnesses of the events recorded in the Gospels. They are people who have seen and heard and touched. Joined later by Saint Paul, whose call to be an apostle comes along a different route, they are people who can speak out of personal experience of Jesus. They have seen, heard and touched the one they describe as the Word, the Son, the perfect image, of God. Even Paul, in spite of his strange way of becoming an apostle, is to be a witness of what he has seen and heard (Acts 22.15).

They still needed faith in order to see the eternal life that was present in the one whose human life they shared. Even doubting Thomas, insisting on seeing and touching the wounded body of the Risen Lord, was still asked to believe. His eyes told him it was the Lord, his faith told him it was his God (Jn 20.28). It was always possible for other eye-witnesses of the same events not to believe and to put a different construction on what was happening among them. During the public ministry of Jesus, many who had been disciples 'drew back and no longer went about with him' (Jn 6.66).

Over the course of time the Church found the term 'sacrament' useful, even essential, as a way of speaking about this aspect of faith, that the life God wishes to share with His people must reach them through their seeing and hearing, smelling, tasting and touching. It may seem banal, obvious. If it is to reach human beings, then this message, this life, what the First Letter of John calls 'fellowship with the Father and with his Son Jesus Christ' (1 Jn 1.3), must be accessible in a way that human beings can understand, receive and use. *Sacramenta sunt propter homines* is an old theological saying: sacraments exist not because God needs them but because human beings need them. They coincide with our way of experience and knowledge.

Christ is the perfect image of the Father and so can manifest divine love to human beings. Christ is also the perfect created image of God and so can manifest human love to God. These realities – the grace of God to human beings and the worship of human beings towards God – become visible, audible and touchable in him. It is in this sense that he has been described as 'the primordial sacrament', the sign in both directions we can say, giving grace to human beings and giving true love to God.[1]

Christ humbled himself, Saint Paul says, by taking the form of a servant and being born in the likeness of human beings (Phil. 2.7). He humbled himself even further by undergoing a shameful death (Phil. 2.8). And he went yet further because, in words attributed to the Welsh poet David Jones, he 'placed himself in the order of signs'. Jesus himself, the image and icon of God, may also be described as a sacrament, and as *the* sacrament, of the human being's encounter with God. To speak of him as 'the sacrament of God' is to use a phrase not found in the scriptures but one that has emerged in the course of theological reflection on the scriptures. He makes God known and he opens the way for human beings to a life shared with God: that is the mighty claim of the Christian gospel. He is the Last Adam and as such the source of a new history, a history of grace, which reaches human beings through the community of the Church. The Church, continuing Jesus's message and mission, may also therefore be described as a sacrament. It is a place in which we may now come to know God and share in God's life: this is the mighty claim of the Church.

Clearly, we need to stop and reflect a bit more about the term 'sacrament'. The catechism from which the present author was taught the Catholic faith answers the question 'what is a sacrament?' by saying 'a sacrament is a sensible or outward sign instituted by Christ to signify grace and confer it on our souls'.[2] Herbert McCabe (1926–2001) in his catechism answers the same question in this way: 'a sacrament is a sacred sign by which we worship God, his love is revealed to us and his saving work accomplished in us. In the sacraments God shows us what he does and does what he shows us.'[3]

The simplest definition of a sacrament is to say that it is a visible sign of invisible grace. The term is used in the first place for those ritual celebrations of the Church that constitute its characteristic life, the 'mysteries' that are celebrated in the liturgies of the Church. The main sacraments are Baptism and the Eucharist, and Catholicism counts among these principal celebrations others that are related to those two. Confirmation completes Baptism, and the Anointing of the Sick and the sacrament of Penance strengthen believers in times of moral, spiritual or physical weakness. The sacraments of Holy Orders and Marriage sanctify the two main ways in which the common life of the community is articulated. These are all symbolic actions involving words and elements of the natural world, things visible, audible, touchable and even to be tasted and smelled, which serve a higher meaning and a new level of life.

The terms 'sacrament' or 'sacramentality', however, are sometimes used more widely, to refer to anything and everything that can be experienced as giving visibility to the invisible mystery of God. And not just visibility, but any translation of spiritual reality into material expression – sounds and tastes as well, things that can be touched and handled, even smells, as we will see, have their place in communicating the divine presence and action.

It means, therefore, that anything and everything in nature, in the human world or in historical events, can be given, or can take on, a 'sacramental' meaning. 'The world is charged with the grandeur of God', says Gerard Manley Hopkins (1844–89). His poem, 'God's Grandeur', sees God's presence around and within everything, 'the dearest freshness deep down things', a freshness preserved by the brooding Spirit in spite of the passage of time and human exploitation. An Irish counterpart, the executed poet Joseph Mary Plunkett (1887–1916), in his poem 'I see his blood upon the rose', speaks of nature as somehow containing now the suffering and death of Jesus, the death of Jesus transcribed into nature: 'carven by his power / Rocks are his written words' and 'His cross is every tree'.

To speak of sacraments and sacramentality is to speak of the Divine Poet. Thomas Aquinas says that God, as the maker of all things, can be creative with things in the way that human poets can be creative with words. We have seen that in the first chapter of the Bible God does only two things: he speaks and he sees. But the word from God's mouth is creative. Similarly, God can take things – and persons too, institutions and events – and give them a significance and a power beyond their original and innate significance and power. They can become the language with which human beings and God communicate with each other, sharing not just information but life and love and everything. The definition of a sacrament quoted above from an old catechism says it is a sign 'instituted by Christ'. Herbert McCabe's definition says that through these signs 'God's saving work is accomplished in us as God shows us what he does and does what he shows us'. The conviction is, therefore, that these particular signs, this particular language system, these symbols that carry God's life and establish us in communion with God, originate with Christ and are the means by which he continues his work. If they are a kind of poetry, it is the work of the Divine Poet who, as we said, can play not just with words but with things and events, institutions and people.

To refer to Christ himself as a 'sacrament' is another way of speaking about him as the visibility of God, and this is something that is expressed in many different ways in the New Testament. Some we have noted already, but there are more we can add. 'God was in Christ reconciling the world to himself' (2 Cor. 5.19). 'To have seen me is to have seen the Father', Jesus says to Philip (Jn 14.9). In the liturgy of the Christmas season, we find ourselves proclaiming that 'in Christ we see our God made visible, and so are caught up in love for the God we cannot see' (Preface of Christmas I).

It is important to stress that a sacrament belongs within a relationship of communication and communion. It belongs therefore to the world of symbols, those things in the human world that serve communication and communion. The first such system of signs is language itself. The characters being put on this page serve not only to communicate something to another mind but also to establish a relationship of shared interest between the one who is placing the characters on the page and the one who is reading them. Think of how many other systems of signs there are in the human world, from traffic signals to music, from works of art to theatre, from the many languages that there are to the many ways of celebrating life across different cultures: there are countless ways in which we can put words and other signifiers at the service of a shared life.

The terms 'sign', 'symbol' and 'sacrament' all belong to the same family but they are used in different ways in different contexts. It is not only believers who will see a deepening of meaning as we move from sign to symbol and from symbol to sacrament, but also a deepening along the same route, moving in the same direction. The importance of this for our purposes is well summed up in the opening verses of the Letter to the Hebrews: 'In many and various ways God spoke of old to our fathers by the prophets; but in these last days he has spoken to us by a Son ... through whom also he created the world. He reflects the glory of God and bears the very stamp of his nature, upholding the universe by his word of power' (Heb. 1.1-3).

The real challenge to faith in those verses is not that God might choose a human being to be a witness to God's life: there are many and various teachers of life and truth and love. The stumbling block is in the phrase 'through whom also he created the world'. And in the final phrase, 'upholding the universe by his word of power'. How could such a thing be, that this man would be a kind of cosmic Atlas, powerful enough to uphold not just this planet but the entire universe?

God continues to speak in many and varied ways – through all the works of human art and imagination, we can say. But there is one Word that is unique, complete and irreplaceable. There is one image of God that is likewise definitive, authentic and paradigmatic. There is one 'sacrament' instituted by God to seal the relationship with his people in an eternal covenant. This Word, image and sacrament is Jesus Christ. We read in John 6 that, following his discourse about the Eucharist, many of Jesus's disciples drew back and no longer went about with him. But not long afterwards we read that 'many of the people believed in him; they said, "When the Christ appears, will he do more signs than this man has done?"' (Jn 7.31).

We will turn next to speak of the Church too as a 'sacrament', not in exactly the same sense as Christ is so described but clearly in dependence on him. Pope Leo the Great (c.400–61) wrote that 'the visible presence of our Redeemer passed over into sacraments'.[4] The Church believes that through celebrating these sacred signs, human beings continue to be restored to their true nature and are introduced to their eternal destiny. For through these signs too, Christ continues to work.

3

THE CHURCH, SACRAMENT OF CHRIST

THE MYSTERY OF THE CHURCH

The Church is obviously an institution and, in a broader sense, a people. But when it came to speak about itself in *Lumen gentium*, the Catholic Church chose to speak first of 'the mystery of the Church'. Alongside all the images and metaphors drawn from the Bible, the most satisfying definition theologically is the succinct one from Saint Cyprian of Carthage that we have seen already, namely that the Church is 'a people brought into unity, from the unity of the Father, Son and Holy Spirit'.[1] This identifies very neatly the central and essential things about it: the Church is a people, it is a people who belong together and are united on some basis, and the basis on which they are united is the communion that Christians believe God to be and that they believe God to have shared with them. This is what is meant by 'the mystery' of the Church, its theological meaning.

This Trinitarian understanding provides the structure for the opening paragraphs of *Lumen gentium* where the relationship of the Church to the different Persons of the Trinity is considered, its relationship to God the Father (*LG* 2), to the Son (*LG* 3), and to the Holy Spirit (*LG* 4), culminating in Cyprian's summary description. We can relate the three most potent metaphors identified earlier with this Trinitarian account of the Church. It is the 'people of God', animated and united by God's Spirit. It is the 'body of Christ', somehow the continuation of the Son's presence and life in history. It is therefore, in anticipation, the 'kingdom' that is coming and that will be fulfilled in the house of the Father.

We have already noted the various ways in which the New Testament speaks of Christ, as the icon of God, as the perfect stamp of God's nature, and as the only Son who is closest to the Father's heart. It has also been stressed already that the Church is all about Christ and Christ is all about God, a line of dependence identified by Saint Paul writing to the first Christians at Corinth when he tells them 'all things are yours, and you are Christ's, and Christ is God's' (1 Cor. 3.21, 23).

This whole purpose of the Church is to point to Christ, to teach people about him, to inspire belief in him and so bring people to him. One of the best-known things he said about himself is his claim to be 'the way, the truth and the life' and that 'nobody comes to the Father except through me' (Jn 14.6). To speak of him as 'the Word made flesh' is to quote the scriptures once again. That phrase marks the climax of the prologue of the Gospel of John: 'the Word became flesh and dwelt among us' (Jn 1.14) and his mission was to make the invisible God visible. A number of New Testament authors refer to Christ as the image, or icon, of God, and in the last chapter we considered what it means to use that phrase, 'image of God', first of all human beings and then in a particular way of Jesus Christ.

Already we have spoken not only of 'images' but of signs and symbols, of models and metaphors, and of sacrament as a term that can be aligned with these others while being given a special meaning. The notion of sacramentality is preferred here as indicating some characteristics of Catholicism that are not necessarily exclusive to it but that serve to give it much of its distinctive shape.

SIGN, SYMBOL, SACRAMENT

Sign, symbol, sacrament: these terms belong to the same family but indicate a deepening of meaning in the order in which they have just been named. A sacrament is a visible or outward sign of an inward and in itself invisible grace. What the term sacrament catches is this point: that the invisible grace indicated by the visible sign is not just pointed to by the sign – the sign is here and the grace is somewhere else – but that the invisible grace is actually present and effective in and through the sign. The sign for the airport is not yet the airport – you might still be ten miles away from it – whereas the sign of the Eucharist is the presence of what is signified by it. In Herbert McCabe's words, in a sacrament 'God not only shows us what he does but also does what he shows us.'[2]

We can say that any symbol, as distinct from a sign, already does this to some extent. What we ask of a symbol is that it should 'stand in for' the thing it symbolizes, not just point towards it, but make present already its power and significance. A national flag is a good example of this: a piece of cloth is treated in an extraordinary way when it is saluted, sung to, put to bed at night and treated with great honour. All of this is because the piece of cloth has been designated by a community to represent the community's life and values, its history and its very existence. Human beings are symbol-making animals, and it is something we do in all kinds of contexts and for many different reasons. It is not strange to us, for it is implied in our being linguistic animals that we make signs and symbols and that we know what we mean by them.

What is added when we speak of certain symbols as 'sacraments?' What was Flannery O'Connor getting at when she said of the Eucharist that if it is a symbol (by which she clearly meant *only* a symbol) then to hell with it? Every symbol gets its meaning within a particular community for which that symbol functions as a vehicle of communication and communion. To speak the same language as another person is already to share a whole panoply of symbols that make communication and communion possible. The point of calling some symbols 'sacraments' is to say that these particular symbols have been designated by Christ, 'instituted' by him in the words of my old catechism. Sacraments are the symbols of a particular community, which, that community believes, were given to it rather than being symbols that it has itself devised. If we stay with thinking in terms of a language, then the sacraments are a language invented by Christ, in which he takes up realities of this creation, already full of symbolic potential at their own level, and puts them at the service of realities beyond this creation. Remember, the Divine Poet can be creative not just with words but with things (persons, events, institutions). This is the claim, then: that these particular symbols that we call sacraments serve communication and communion with God; they are not simply part of our seeking after the divine mystery but they belong to God's reaching out to share life and communion with us. As the Word made flesh Jesus revealed God to us, made God present among us and shared God's life with us. The sacraments of the Church continue that mission, making the knowledge, presence and life of God accessible to us in all our different times and places. The Bible has been described as the word of God in human words. The sacraments might then be described as the grace of God in human signs and symbols.

Catholicism is a physical religion, a matter of things being said, done and used by human beings united in the practice of those things and in the conviction that a certain kind or level of life is made possible by that practice. We have been using the term 'grace' to name the gift or life, the communication or communion, which is carried by the sacraments. It is among the most important terms in Christian theology. We can take it for now to refer simply to the whole impact in us of God's disposition of love towards us: it is a more abstract term for the covenant relationship of God being our God and we being God's people. Grace is the gift that enables us to appreciate and to live that relationship.

We have spoken of Christ himself as a sacrament of God, more precisely as the sacrament of the human being's encounter with God. 'No one has ever seen God', the Gospel of John tells us, 'but the only-begotten Son, the Word made flesh and dwelling among us, Jesus Christ through whom have come grace and truth: he has made God known' (Jn 1.14, 17-18). The Church may in turn be described as a sacrament of Christ. It is referred to from the beginning as a body, as in body politic, a society or community, but it is also from the beginning described as the very body of

Christ (1 Cor. 12.12-28; Eph. 4.4-16). The Church meets the definition of a sacrament because it is a visible sign of an invisible grace. What is the reality to which it not only points but which it also makes present and effective in the world? In the words of Thomas Aquinas, the purpose of the Church is the communion of human beings, the unity of the human race. That may sound like a call to universal fraternity and it is that. But the call is established on a very particular source for that unity, namely the unity of the Father, the Son and the Holy Spirit. *Lumen gentium* in its opening paragraph describes the Church as being 'in Christ, in the nature of a sacrament – that is a sign and instrument of communion with God and of unity among all human beings' (*LG* 1). We have seen already that the explanation *LG* gives of why that is so culminates in the declaration of Cyprian of Carthage, that the Church is 'a people brought into unity from the unity of the Father, the Son and the Holy Spirit' (*LG* 4).

THE MOON, A SYMBOL OF THE CHURCH

The distinction between a sacrament and what is 'only a symbol' can be brought out by considering one of the things often appealed to by early Christian teachers as a way of symbolizing the Church's relationship with Christ and its mission on behalf of the world. This was to speak of the Moon as a symbol of the Church.

Selene was the Greek goddess of the Moon, the sister of Helios who, as god of the Sun, provided her with all the light she had. In fact, she had no light to call her own, only light reflected from the Sun, to illuminate the night on one side of the earth while the Sun was shining on the other.

It was an imagery quickly taken up by the Christian Church. Christ is the Son, the light of the world (Jn 8.12), the light that enlightens every man and woman who comes into this world (Jn 1.9). This Son is also the Sun of Justice, an image from the prophet Malachi (Mal. 4.2), expanded in the New Testament to include not just the Messiah, to whom this title will properly belong, but also those illuminated by Christ's holiness.

61

The only light the Church can hope to share with the world is light received from Christ. As the eternal Son of the Father and as the anointed one of God, he is a source of light in himself, the 'light of the world' (Jn 8:12). The community of those who believe in him have a light to share with the world, but it is always his light that they share. Jesus himself says that the righteous will shine like the Sun in the kingdom of the Father (Mt. 13.43) so that they too can be given the title that belongs properly and principally to Christ: 'You are the light of the world' (Mt. 5.14). This too is anticipated in the prophecy of Daniel who, in speaking of the resurrection of the dead, says that the wise will shine like the brightness of the firmament and that those who turn many to righteousness will shine like the stars for ever and ever (Dan. 12.3). But the source of that light is always Christ and as it shines from the Church it is always, like the Moon's light, a reflected light.

Writing about why he is still in the Church, Joseph Ratzinger added a striking note to this ancient symbolism of the Moon. It has now been visited by human beings, he says, and has been studied in detail by scientists as rock, desert and mountains. But it has never been explored as light and yet it continues to shine. Applying this to the Church he says that it too has its rocks and deserts, and it has its appalling dust as well. But alongside all of that it still retains its radiance. 'In the night of our estrangement from God', he says, the Church still shines with the radiance of Christ.[3] So our attention and our interest cannot stop at the Church. We must see through the Church, to the One to whom the Church bears witness, the One who gives it the only significant meaning that it has, the One who is the source of any light or life, any grace or holiness, which the Church has.

DO YOU BELIEVE IN THE CHURCH?

Another way in which to see the difference between a symbol and a sacrament is this: it would be absurd for a believer to say 'I believe in the Moon' even if the Moon is a symbol of the Church, whereas in the creed we do say 'I believe in the Church' because the Church is a sacrament of God's dealings with humanity.

In what sense, though, are we asked to believe in the Church? Is it in the same sense in which a person might have faith in another human being, or in an institution of government? Is it in the same sense in which I believe what is said by people who are expert in an area of knowledge of which I am ignorant but whose authority in that area I have good reason to trust? Is it in the same sense in which a person is invited to believe in God?

If someone says 'I love the Church', what kind of love is involved? Looked at from certain angles there are many reasons not to love the Church, so to speak of 'love' rather than 'faith' might serve to bring out more clearly the potentially scandalous nature of saying 'I believe in the Church'.

Are we supposed to love the Church? You sometimes hear people saying 'I love my Church', and it seems like a good thing. But what kind of love ought we to have for the Church? Some people love Manchester United, some people love Dublin, some people love their political party and some people love the coastline along the west coast of Scotland. What kind of love ought we to have for the Church? Sometimes it is simply one of those more natural loves that people are talking about, connected with a sense of identity and belonging, of indebtedness for good things received through the Church, something that gives me a sense of who I am, perhaps over against others who do not share that identity. Is it because the Church can function, or be used, in this way that we might speak of loving it, believing in it, trusting it?

Here is another way of putting the question to get at what I am trying to get at: does the Church fall within the object of the theological virtues of faith, hope and love? Is it not towards God alone that we exercise these virtues of faith, hope and love, so that in thinking and writing theologically we should reserve these gifts or virtues for God alone? Is it not one of the reasons why they are called 'theological' virtues, because they have God as their direct object? Where does the Church fit in this? Does it come within the reach of the theological virtues, so that we can say, 'I believe in the Church, I hope in the Church, I love the Church' and that is with the same faith, hope and love with which I believe in God, hope in God and love God? It seems that the answer must be yes, that the Church comes within the reach of the theological virtues insofar as it is 'the church of God', as Paul says in the opening verses of his letters to the Corinthians (1 Cor. 1.2; 2 Cor. 1.1). The Church as a work of God falls within the reach of the theological virtues.

When we recite the creed, we express our faith not just in the Father, in the Son and in the Holy Spirit but also in the Church. Does it mean that the creed has four parts rather than three: Father, Son, Spirit and the Church? It can seem like that, and we will look more closely at the text in a moment. But it seems more correct to think of it in this way: the creed expresses faith in the Persons of the Blessed Trinity and lists for each one the particular works in creation and redemption that are appropriated to that Person. We believe in the Father ... and we list the most important things we assign to the Father: power and creation. We believe in the Son ... and we list the most important things to be said about his relationship with the Father, as well as the most important things we believe about his earthly career: that he 'came down from heaven, was born, suffered, died and rose again, that he ascended to heaven, is seated at the right hand of the Father and will come again in glory to judge the living and the dead'. For the Holy Spirit likewise ... we list the most important things to be said about the Spirit's relationship with the Father and with the Son, as well as the most important things the Spirit has done, and in the first place that 'he has spoken through the prophets'.

Is that it? Then we move on to what looks like a fourth part of the creed, which in the present English translation begins, 'I believe in one, holy, catholic and apostolic Church', and continues by listing baptism for the forgiveness of sins as something we confess, and the resurrection of the dead and the life of the world to come as things to which we look forward. It seems as if the only thing we have to say about the Holy Spirit is that he spoke through the prophets. Which is interesting, to say the least, because it seems to assign the work of the Holy Spirit to the time of promise and prophecy, whereas much of the New Testament is about the work and presence and power of the Spirit coming about as a result of the work of Christ. The Gospel of John even gives us this intriguing verse: 'as yet the Spirit had not been given because Jesus was not yet glorified' (Jn 7.39).

Here is the English translation of the creed currently used at Mass; notice the punctuation between what is said about the Spirit and what is said about the Church:

> I believe in the Holy Spirit, the Lord, the giver of life,
> who proceeds from the Father and the Son,
> who with the Father and the Son is adored and glorified,
> who has spoken through the prophets.
> I believe in one, holy, catholic and apostolic Church.
> I confess one Baptism for the forgiveness of sins
> and I look forward to the resurrection of the dead
> and the life of the world to come. Amen.

The Latin text of the creed speaks as follows of the objects of our faith:

> *Credo in unum Deum, Patrem omnipotentem ...*
> *Et in unum Dominum Jesum Christum ...*
> *Et in Spiritum Sanctum Dominum et vivificantem ...*

When it comes to the Church, we get, curiously, a 'sentence' with no verb:

> *Et unam, sanctam, catholicam et apostolicam Ecclesiam.*

We must presume that this phrase, in the accusative case, is governed by the preceding principal verb which is '*credo*', 'I believe'. But whereas in the case of the Son and the Holy Spirit it is clear that the meaning is *credere in*, to believe into the Son and into the Holy Spirit (more about what that means in a moment), the 'in' is missing when we come to speak of the Church.

Although it might seem like a minor grammatical question, many have seen in it an important theological distinction: do we believe in the Church in precisely the same way in which we believe in God? Does the Church belong to the object of theological faith, a virtue whose direct object is God? On the other hand, if we take this phrase introducing the Church as the object of a different kind of belief (the Latin being taken as *credere* rather than *credere in*), then belief in that sense is an expression of faith that is much weaker than the context of the creed seems to require. Up to then we have been expressing the strongest possible faith, in God as Father, as Son and as Holy Spirit. The creed is a kind of love song in which we list the great deeds of the one to whom we are giving our hearts. Now it would seem to change character and we give a list of doctrines: I believe that the Church is one, holy, catholic and apostolic, I confess baptism, I look forward to the resurrection.

However, things get curiouser and curiouser, as Alice put it. While the Latin follows the original Greek faithfully, with the same implications to be drawn about various senses of believing, the new English translation, as we have seen, translates the Latin as follows:

> I believe in one God, the Father almighty ...
> I believe in one Lord Jesus Christ ...
> I believe in the Holy Spirit, the Lord, the giver of life ...
> I believe in one, holy, catholic and apostolic Church ...

Begging my reader's patience for just a bit longer, let me say what I think is at stake here. On the one hand, we do not believe that the Church is the 'fourth person' of a Blessed Quaternity – clearly not. On the other hand, the English translation has detached from the Holy Spirit precisely those things that we believe to be the most important works of the Spirit: the Church itself, born at Pentecost; baptism for the forgiveness of sins, which is Jesus's gift of the Spirit to the apostles at Easter; the resurrection of the dead, which is a further marvellous work of the Spirit of life in Christ Jesus; and the life of the world to come, since the Spirit and the bride say 'Come' so that that life may be inaugurated (Rev. 22.17).

Better to think of it this way: the English translation is misleading in separating what is said of the Holy Spirit and what is said of the Church. The Latin and the Greek confirm that the English translation is misleading. It means that the great works of the Holy Spirit, to whom we give our hearts in the third part of the creed, include not just his speaking through the prophets, but also his creation of the Church, his power working in baptism, the resurrection of the dead and the life of the world to come.

In the way the creed is structured, therefore – the Father and his work, the Son and his work, the Spirit and his work – it is clear that our faith in 'one, holy, catholic and apostolic church' belongs within our faith in the Holy Spirit.[4] The Spirit of creation and sanctification works throughout creation but particularly in animating the body of Christ and filling the people called into the kingdom of the Father. The creed is not just a list of dogmas to be believed: it is a love song in honour of the one whose great deeds on our behalf it lists. Those lists can vary between the earliest creeds that survive, but putting together the two forms that are used regularly, the Nicene Creed and the Apostles' Creed, we say the following: that we believe in the Father who is maker of heaven and earth, of all that is visible and invisible; we believe in the Son who is begotten of the Father, through whom all things were made, who for us and for our salvation came down from heaven, was born of the Virgin Mary, suffered and died under Pontius Pilate, was buried and descended into hell, rose from the dead and ascended in glory to the right hand of the Father; we believe in the Spirit who spoke through the prophets (always guiding the history of God's people therefore) and whose works now are listed as 'the holy catholic church, the communion of saints, the forgiveness of sins, the resurrection of the body and life everlasting'.

In passing I have mentioned different levels or kinds of belief, and will conclude this chapter with a comment about these. In Latin there are three uses of the term 'to believe'. When it is followed by words in the accusative case it means to believe something to be true – I believe that there is a God, for example, *credo Deum*. When it is followed by words in the dative case it means to believe somebody when they say something – I believe God, for example, *credere Deo*. The third use of the term, with the word 'in' and the accusative case, *credere in*, took on a much deeper and richer meaning, which could be translated literally as 'I believe into God', *credere in Deum*. This is the phrase we find in the creed when it refers to the Father, to the Son and to the Holy Spirit. Thomas Aquinas proposed the etymology 'to give one's heart', seeing in the term *credere* a conflation of the two words *cor*, heart, and *dare*, to give. To believe, followed by the preposition 'in' and the accusative case, means more than just believing that something is true in the way a proposition is accepted as true: 'I believe there is a God', for example, or 'I believe Apia is the capital of Samoa'. It also means more than believing that another person is speaking the truth in what he or she says: 'I believe the prime minister when he says ...' or 'I believe the news reporter when she says ...' There is this third, and deeper, meaning in the Latin phrase *credere in* when it is followed by the accusative case. A literal translation is 'to believe into'. It is related to the first two but goes deeper than either of them, for it means, as Augustine and Aquinas point out, that we 'give our hearts' or 'we entrust ourselves' to the one in whom we express this kind of faith. We could translate it literally as 'I believe into the Father ... into the Son ... into the Holy Spirit'. What is then said of Father, Son and Holy Spirit can be understood not just as facts about the Person in whom we so believe but also as reasons why we entrust ourselves as we do to that Person.

This slightly strange translation, 'to believe into', also brings out what it means to call faith a theological virtue. It is an act of our understanding and freedom that carries us into the object in which we believe, hope and love, so that through the theological virtues we are united with God, sharing God's understanding and freedom.

We express our faith in the Church as the work of the Holy Spirit, as the operation of the Spirit in human history sustaining the life, knowledge and presence of Christ among us and bringing the work of Christ to completion. The Holy Spirit had already 'spoken through the prophets' to prepare the people for the coming of Christ. The same Spirit, poured out anew through the glorification of Christ, continues to work in human history. The final part of the creed lists these new and transforming works of the Spirit: the Church, baptism, the forgiveness of sins, the resurrection of the dead, and the life of the world to come.

To return to our question, then: if we believe in the Church, in which of these meanings of the term *credere* do we do it? To believe that the Church is 'x', 'y' or 'z' is one kind of faith. To believe the Church when it says 'a', 'b' or 'c' is another kind of faith. What about the third meaning? Is the Church a fitting object of our faith in that sense? This is what is meant by the question raised here, whether or not the Church comes within the object of the theological virtue of faith. It also helps to underline the distinction between what is 'only a symbol' and what qualifies as a 'sacrament' in the sense that Catholic Christianity seeks to give to that term.

We can only believe in the Church, hope in the Church and love the Church in that strongest possible meaning of faith because we believe it to be the Church of God. It is the assembly of human beings gathered by Christ and held together by his Spirit. To repeat the words of Cyprian of Carthage yet one more time, we believe it to be a people brought into unity from the unity of the Father, the Son and the Holy Spirit. At one and the same time we are a crowd of sinners (a people struggling) and we are the body of Christ (already somehow blessed with the unity to which God calls humanity and of which the Church is a sacrament at the service of that unity). It is this double identity that, in the end, explains the grammatical uncertainties, for the Church in its divine origin belongs to the One to whom we entrust our hearts, while in its human fragility it can easily undermine other kinds of faith that we would want to place in it. And yet it is this same earthen vessel that has carried to us the knowledge of Christ and that hands on to people this possibility of giving their hearts to the Trinitarian God. So, our love for God and our faith in God include the Church within their object insofar as it is the body of Christ and a work of the Holy Spirit.

Every time we celebrate the Eucharist, we ask the Lord to 'look not on our sins but on the faith of the Church'. Look not on our weaknesses and limitations and on the pettiness of our lives, but on the baptism we have received, the calling, the grace we have received that makes us members of the Church. Can we love the Church? Yes, we can love the Church, not for its human mistakes and sinfulness that are easily picked out when we look back across the history of Christianity and that shout at us as we survey its situation today. This is not why we love the Church, of course not, but because it is the Church of God. But – and here is the mystery – it is the Church of God not apart from sinful humanity but within that humanity, the humanity that is at one and the same time a crowd of sinners and the body of Christ.

Someone tells me: 'I believe in Christ but not in the Church.' Mahatma Gandhi is said to have expressed a similar view: he admired Christ but not Christians, whom he experienced as obsessed with wealth and power. It is an understandable sentiment in the sense in which it is intended and in the experience from which it comes. But none of us alive today would know anything about Christ were it not for the Church. It is the Church that wrote the New Testament. It is the Church that transmitted the necessary information about Christ across the centuries. It is the Church that continues to tell the story and to proclaim the message, the good news that is about Christ in the first place and not in the first place about the Church itself. Catholic Christianity takes this further step, believing that it is not just information about Christ that is transmitted by the Church but his presence and his life, his grace and his Spirit. This is what is offered to those who participate in the life of the Church. This is what is meant by saying that the Church is a sacrament of Christ, a sacrament of the unity of the human race, and not only a symbol of him or of that unity.

4

EMBODIMENT MEANS LIFE AND STRUCTURE

It has been common enough in church circles in recent decades to find people setting up an opposition between life and structure, sometimes using terminology such as 'values' and 'structures', 'spirit' and 'body', 'charism' and 'institution', sometimes theologizing it as a contrast between 'the prophetic' and 'the priestly', or between the 'lay style' and the 'clerical style', sometimes even psychologizing it into an opposition between 'heart' and 'head'. It seems strange that at such a late date, in the last decades of the twentieth century, there would have been this outbreak of what looks like a form of Cartesian dualism in Catholic circles. We need to challenge it in the name of a more holistic and a saner understanding of the human person, of human communities and relationships, and of the Church in particular.

We saw that most of the metaphors used to refer to the Church in the Bible are drawn from three areas of life: cultivation and husbandry, building and architecture, and human relationships. These categories do not exhaust the long list of images noted by Geoffrey Preston, but they contain most of them. We have given special attention to a more abstract and technical term, sacrament, a term not found in the Bible, because of the significance it took on over the course of the centuries. But many of the characteristics that are implied by that term are found also in many of the metaphors that are used.

The theme of this chapter, as indicated in its title, is that embodiment implies both life and structure. And it will apply this to the Church, as another characteristic that it is essential to think about in order to understand Catholicism. This combination of life and structure is clear in most of the metaphors already presented. In cultivation and husbandry, for example, we are obviously talking about living and growing things – sheep, vineyards, fish, trees of different kinds, and so on. Because they are organisms there is always also a structure to support their life, a structure without which it would not be possible for them to go on living. In the case of human relationships, the same is true. Whether we talk about friends, followers, disciples, servants, brothers and sisters, bride and bridegroom – once again we are talking about realities of our experience in which we find both life and structure. This is perhaps not as visible as it is in the case of metaphors taken from the natural world, but these two aspects are undoubtedly also present. We want our friendships, for example, to be living, developing and responsive to what is happening in and around them. At the same time every friendship quickly establishes some kind of structure of communication, encounter and sharing that is the basis and the life of the friendship. In the case of metaphors taken from the world of architecture and construction, it is easy to see that there is structure and more difficult to see that these are living things. But, once again, a little reflection assures us that the house, the temple or the city are only fully what they are because of the way in which they support a life that is taking place within them.

INSTITUTIONAL CHARISM

In a wonderful book about the life and mission of Saint Dominic, the French Dominican historian Guy Bedouelle proposed the phrase 'institutional charism' as a way of capturing something essential about the mendicant movement of the thirteenth century.[1] That century saw a revolution in preaching across the

Christian world. Not only is it the case that from then onwards we have a huge number of tracts and treatises dealing with the 'art' of preaching the gospel. There was also the phenomenon of many groups of Christians presenting themselves, with some kind of spontaneity and on personal initiative, as movements of the Spirit in the Church, manifestations of what today we would call a 'revival', a 'charismatic renewal', a 'new evangelization'. In fact, it is difficult to think of another development in the history of the Church that would meet, as fully as this mendicant moment does, the definition John Paul II gave to a new evangelization: that it would be new in ardour, methods and expressions.

There are many aspects to this moment in medieval Christendom, artistic and cultural, social and political, as well as theological and spiritual, but our focus is on those groups within it that were recognized almost immediately by the Church as new groups of official preachers, specifically the orders of mendicant friars founded by Saint Francis of Assisi (c.1181–1226) and Saint Dominic (c.1170–1221). They represented a new form of religious life in the Church, keeping some aspects of monastic life but adapting to new circumstances and a new mission. We can say that they represented a new form of church life, new ecclesial communities within the greater Church, stimulated, as one of the popes of the time put it, by the Holy Spirit who is constantly doing new things in the community of the Church for the well-being of humanity.

Before Francis and Dominic, there were already institutionally sanctioned preachers whose preaching was proving ineffectual against some of the heterodox movements that were not only troubling the unity of the Church but also seriously distorting the proper balance of Christian teaching (regarding the goodness of the material world, for example). Alongside these official preachers there were groups of charismatic preachers and teachers, some of them in fact identical with those heterodox movements, whose enthusiasm, verging sometimes on the apocalyptic, was in danger of carrying them beyond the boundaries of 'sane teaching' in ways that confused and disturbed rather than clarified and strengthened.

As already mentioned, a familiar temptation, familiar at least from its prevalence in the decades immediately following on Vatican II, is to set up an opposition between institutional structure and charismatic life. Hence the desire of Bedouelle and other historians of the mendicant movement to indicate what is generally seen as the key to its success: the Franciscans and the Dominicans were charismatic movements, inspired by leaders responsive to new needs in the Church, originating in particular gifts of the Spirit to those leaders, gifts given alongside the already established routes by which authority and entitlement to preach were transmitted. But they were also, and very quickly, institutionally recognized and confirmed, acknowledged by the popes and other bishops of the day as a providential addition to the life of the Church, as an answer to a need already obvious to those in authority, that a fresh preaching of the Church's life and doctrine was needed.

Bedouelle's phrase – 'institutional charism' – points out this double strength in the mendicant movement: it was charismatic, of the Spirit, new, evangelical, energetic, characterized by the joy and freedom of early gospel preaching (poverty, simplicity, mobility). A contemporary chronicler commented that the way of life proposed by Dominic and his companions was 'new', but then refers for its justification to Jesus's missionary instructions to his disciples in Matthew 10 and Luke 10! The mendicant movement was at the same time officially established, institutionally confirmed, integrated from the beginning with the established structures of the Church, recognized by the body as a legitimate development, an extension of its capacities, a further application and adaptation of the apostolic life that continued to flow in those old veins, an infusion from the Spirit to extend and renew the life of the entire body.

To set up an opposition between 'charism' and 'institution' here would be to fail to appreciate what the organic life of a social body involves. It is clear from various things he wrote that G. K.

Chesterton considered the jellyfish and the crustacean as poor solutions to the challenges of life: one is floppy and the other is rigid. Think about such creatures for a moment. We can apply the image to the Church in this way: charism without institution and institution without charism are both poor solutions to the challenges of the Church's life. The organic life of an institution such as the Catholic Church clearly requires structures through which that life will flow, just as it requires life if it is to be something more than a dead thing, a skeleton, a valley of dry bones.

The most important theological point we can make about this is to say that the Church is the body of Christ animated by the Holy Spirit. To use the technical terms, if we have a Christological understanding of the Church without a pneumatological understanding, or vice versa, then we are failing to do justice to the reality.[2] Included in thinking of the Church as a sacrament is to see it as a creature of Christ, his body in history, as well as a creature of the Holy Spirit, a communion of love. An adequate ecclesiology, a satisfactory theology of the Church, will not feel obliged to choose between the models of the Church that are on offer, to include some and to exclude others. The particular conjunction of 'institution' and 'charism' is of greater importance than many of these images, precisely because keeping these together points us immediately to the Trinitarian origin of the Church: a people brought into unity from the unity of the Father, the Son and the Holy Spirit. If you wish we can assign to the Son the corporate, institutional and incarnate aspects of the Church and to the Holy Spirit the vital, energetic and creative aspects of the Church. But to separate these would be disastrous.

The collaboration of the Spirit of Life and the Son whose body we are is to be seen not just in the Church as a whole, the body with its organic life, but also in the central ritual celebrations that we call the sacraments. That we always pray through Christ and in the Holy Spirit is clearest in the Eucharist, but it is done in the other sacramental celebrations also. The

Eucharist is brought about through recalling the words of institution under the inspiration of the Holy Spirit, who is called down precisely so that the elements of bread and wine, over which those words are spoken, might become the body and blood of Christ. After which the Spirit is called on again, to fill those who participate in the sacrament, that they might become 'one body, one spirit in Christ'.[3] The Church as a whole, always institutional and always charismatic, is itself a sign, a pledge, a sacrament, making present in time and space a reality originating from beyond itself. It is a work of the Father active in the always complementary missions of the Son and of the Holy Spirit.

THOMAS AQUINAS ON THE CHURCH

Let us stay with the 'mendicant movement' for now and consider how Thomas Aquinas, perhaps the greatest in a century of extraordinary Christian theologians, spoke about the Church as the body of Christ. Before the early modern period there was no sub-section of theology, or particular treatise within that subject, that was called 'ecclesiology', theology of the Church. Thomas Aquinas has no treatise with this name among the many parts, questions and articles of his voluminous writings. If one sets out to construct from his writings an ecclesiology – to find his answer to the question 'what is the spirit of Catholicism?' – the places in his works to which one will be drawn are those dealing with the sacraments and with the spiritual life that is shared within the communion of those who believe in Christ. It is there that he speaks of how faith in Christ is received, what it means to receive that faith, and what the rights and obligations are that follow on the reception of that gift. The thought that the Church itself should be a matter for explicit and systematic theological consideration seems not to have entered his mind. Which does not mean that he does not speak often about the Church, particularly where he is commenting on biblical texts that speak of it. Thus, we find Aquinas doing with the writings of Saint Paul what we must do with the writings of Aquinas: constructing from them a more systematic account of the Church than Paul himself presents.

There are a number of places in his letters where Saint Paul speaks of the Church as the body of Christ: Romans 12.4-8; 1 Corinthians 12–14; Ephesians 1.22-23; 4.1-16; and Colossians 2.19. In his commentaries on these texts, Aquinas takes Paul at his word and spells out how the characteristics of an organic animal body are to be seen in the life of the Church. In some of these texts Paul identifies the entire body with Christ – Romans 12.4-8 and Ephesians 4:1-16 – whereas in others Christ is described as the head of the body, ensuring its coordination, inter-connection and mutual support – Ephesians 1:22-23 and Colossians 2.19. The text of 1 Corinthians 12–14 deals with the articulation and variety of functions that is found in any organic body. Here we will review Aquinas's commentary on texts in which Paul speaks of the Church as the body of Christ. In Chapter 7 we will review his commentary on 1 Corinthians 12–14 on the variety of gifts in the Church, and in Chapter 10 we will see how he receives those texts in which Paul speaks of Christ as head of the Church.

THE MYSTICAL BODY OF CHRIST – ROMANS 12 AND EPHESIANS 4

If 'people of God' became the preferred first way of referring to the Church at Vatican II, the metaphor of the 'body of Christ' dominated Catholic thinking about the Church in the earlier part of the twentieth century. In the encyclical letter *Mystici corporis Christi* (*On the Mystical Body of Christ*, 1943), Pope Pius XII gave an authoritative presentation of this metaphor as applied to the Church, a metaphor that clearly has significant biblical authority to support it, particularly in the letters of Saint Paul.

79

After the majestic symphony of the first eight chapters of his Letter to the Romans, and the detailed reflection on the meaning of Jesus Christ for Judaism in Chapters 9 to 11, Paul brings his longest letter to a close with five chapters, Romans 12–16, in which he speaks about various concrete aspects of the way of life that the Roman Christians have received and that they have been called to live out in practical and concrete ways.

Near the beginning of this last part of the letter is a section – Romans 12.4-8 – detailing the variety of gifts, here specifically 'functions', that God has given to the Church. The image of the body comes immediately to Paul's mind – 'as in one body there are many members, and not all the members have the same function, so we, though many, are one body in Christ, and individually members one of another' (12.4-5).

In his commentary, Aquinas notes how Paul so easily uses the likeness there is between the 'mystical body', the Church, and the 'natural body'. For his part, Aquinas thinks first of the unity of a body, supported in this by Paul's text, for the Greek here has 'as in *one* body' and not just 'as in a body'. After that, Paul talks of diversity, necessary if something is to be truly a body, and then of the diversity of functions that is found in the mystical body, the Church. There would be no point, Aquinas says, in a diversity of members if they did not have different operations to perform. As a living reality the Church has an articulated structure.

There is the temptation to stop there and to say that in Romans 12–16 it is only 12.4-8 that contains material relevant to a reflection on life and structure in the Church. But all five final chapters of Romans are concerned with the lifestyle of a Christian community, with the life underway in and through the structures that sustain it. If our eyes are drawn to particular images, and how they articulate the unity and diversity of the body, it does not mean that the rest of those chapters – concerning the virtues of the Christian life as lived out in a whole variety of situations and relationships – are not also relevant. We can say that Romans 12–15 gives us an 'identikit' portrait of the person and of the community being formed by the grace of the Holy Spirit. The wonderful theological portrait given speculatively and systematically in Romans 1–8 is made explicit and concrete, is explained more practically, in these final chapters. It even reaches the most ordinary level of human relating, with Paul asking, in Romans 16, to be remembered to a long list of friends and acquaintances and sending his good wishes to them.

A community living by 'the law of the Spirit of life' will be characterized by love in the first place, but also by zeal, hospitality, joy, blessing, forgiveness, hope, love of enemies, not passing judgement, preferring the other to oneself, and so on. It is a familiar list found in other letters of Paul, but only here, in Romans, is it given such a magnificent context and justification. The particular emphasis on the union of Jew and Gentile in the Church, considered at length in Romans 9–11, is a chord in this great work that is sounded again, and very beautifully, in Romans 15.7-13.

The other main text in which Paul speaks of the Church as the body of Christ is Ephesians 4.1-16. Once again Aquinas sees Paul as primarily concerned with the unity of the Church, exhorting the Christians of Ephesus to remain in that unity. As members of Christ, they all belong in one body, a unity that is not just social or political but that is also 'in the Spirit', spiritual, because it is established on the faith and the love that they share. This is how he interprets Ephesians 4.4, the 'one body' referring to the faith that they share and the 'one Spirit' referring to their mutual love. The Church's unity is therefore a union with God in the first place, through faith and charity, a spiritual unity that comes to us from Christ (see also Rom. 8.9; Jn 17.2-3).

But the unity of the Church is complex, Aquinas continues, more like that of a city, at once unified and diversified. It is interesting that he moves easily from the metaphor of the body to the metaphor of the city, each of them central to New

THE SPIRIT OF CATHOLICISM

Testament imagery for the Church. The text of Ephesians continues by speaking first of what is common to the whole Church (4.5-6) and then of what is distinctive of different parts within it (4.7-13).

Aquinas presses the image of the city, with the same preoccupation regarding unity, saying that its unity is confirmed in four ways, by having one head, one law, its own 'insignia' and one end. This is what he finds in the famous declaration of Ephesians 4.5-6: 'There is ... one Lord, one faith, one baptism, one God and Father of all who is above all and through all and in all'. The one head is Christ and the one law is faith, faith understood to refer both to what is believed and to the disposition of the heart that believes. It is this unity in faith, Aquinas says, that makes the Church catholic, universal. The 'insignia' of the Church are the sacraments of Christ, in particular Baptism, which is the door to the other sacraments and which is therefore the only one mentioned here by name. And the end of the Church is God: it is to the Father that Christ leads us, fulfilling the faith of Israel in the one God and Father who is transcendent ('over all'), powerful ('through all') and immanent in all things ('in all'). These qualities of the one unique Godhead are suitably appropriated, Aquinas says, to the Father, the Son and the Holy Spirit respectively.

In Ephesians 4.7 Paul begins to speak of the diversity of gifts that is found along with this unity, whether the Church is imagined as a body or as a city. The fruit of these gifts of Christ is, in the first place, the work of ministry itself that they make possible, then the work of strengthening believers in their faith, and third the work of building up the Church by adding new members to it. All of that work is towards the ultimate fruitfulness in the kingdom of heaven, to bring all to a unity in faith and in the knowledge of the Son of God. It is in such knowledge, Jesus tells us, that eternal life consists (Jn 17.3).

Is this third fruit, building up the Church, to be expected in this world, within history, or is it something that belongs to the end of time? Aquinas thinks the Ephesians text can be read both ways. It can be understood to refer to the full adulthood of Christ's body in the resurrection of all people, each one at the perfect age of thirty-three years, a quaint tradition that he is happy to record. It can also be understood to refer to the maturity of the Church itself, when it reaches a spiritual fulfilment that resembles the mature adulthood of Christ (Eph. 4.13).

Taking it in this second way we can then imagine the Church reaching such fulfilment or maturity not necessarily everywhere simultaneously, or once and for all, but from time to time along the course of history, and also from place to place, in holy individuals and flourishing communities, when they live generously and courageously the life of faith and love in which God's grace establishes them.

Continuing the theme of maturity, Paul says that the Church is called to be a community of adult believers, of people called to grow up in their faith and to leave behind childish things (Eph. 4.14; 1 Cor. 13.11). It is a call to be stable in believing (1 Cor. 14.20; Jas 1.6) and not to be blown around by every wind of doctrine that emanates from the cunning, the crafty and the deceitful (Eph. 4.13-14). The reference to wind might have given Aquinas the opportunity to speak of the Holy Spirit, who is an alternative wind to that emanating from the false teachers. The reference to 'speaking the truth in love' (Eph. 4.15) strengthens the opportunity, since the Holy Spirit is the Spirit of truth (Jn 14.17) and the Spirit's name is love (Rom. 5.5). But Aquinas does not take this opportunity, speaking instead about being truthful in action and not only in words or in teaching. This 'speaking of the truth' in action is to be done in love, love being the form of all the virtues – an idea very dear to Aquinas – and love is the gift or power that brings the life of faith to maturity (1 Cor. 16.13-14). We must continue to grow, Aquinas concludes, for 'to stand still in the way of God is to retreat'. This latter is a saying that was growing in popularity in Aquinas's day, though it seems like a piece of wisdom that needs to be freshly discovered by each generation of human beings.

Aquinas thus develops Paul's metaphor of the body, but one wonders whether he would press it as far as including some aspects of the inevitable fate of organic animal bodies. Including these aspects, the church community would need to be considered as susceptible to illness as well as open to growth, susceptible to regressing as well as to maturing, susceptible to corrupting as well as open to flourishing, all of these things potentially happening in different parts of the church community in different places and at different times. We shall consider this question in our next chapter.

We saw how Aquinas moves easily from the metaphor of the body to that of the city. For him both metaphors speak of unity and diversity. But our focus in this chapter is structure and life. We turn next, therefore, to consider those biblical metaphors, taken from the world of architecture and construction, the metaphors in which it seems most difficult to see this theme of structure and life together.

THE CHURCH AS A BUILDING, A CITY, THE TEMPLE

Reviewing this set of metaphors for the Church we see that sometimes it is referred to simply as a house or a household, sometimes as a pillar or a buttress or a building, sometimes more specifically as a temple, perhaps as an altar, or even as the Temple. It is spoken of also as a city, once again sometimes more specifically as the City of God, or Mount Zion, or the city of Jerusalem.

It might seem strange to include this set of metaphors in a consideration of life and structure, for they seem to be all structure. They are images of strength and security, of settlement and establishment, but also of a community and its shared life being given a local habitation and a name. A building is something like the skeleton of the body, giving it structure, strength and support, as a kind of internal scaffolding. It says nothing about what kind of life might thereby be supported or about what might go on in the building or in the city. Images of natural things seem to speak more directly about the Church, especially those images drawn from living organisms.

At the same time, within the context of Israel's historical experiences and covenant faith, the city of Jerusalem and the Temple in that city were already charged with profound symbolic and spiritual meaning long before the time of Jesus or the birth of the Church. It is not surprising that the city of Jerusalem and the Temple should figure prominently in the teaching of Jesus, in the climax of his mission and in the earliest Christian writings. The City and the Temple were already 'sacramental' realities and it was unavoidable that the Church, seeing itself as the fulfilment and continuation of God's promises to Israel, should feel the need to understand its own relationship to that city and to that building. This was to become the conviction that the Church itself is now the City of God and the Temple in which God dwells.

The ark of the covenant, referred to also as the ark of the Lord, indicated the physical location of God's presence with the people. The *shekinah*, the presence of God, was in the empty space above the ark. The ark itself was initially housed in a tent and travelled with the people on their desert wanderings (Exod. 25–26). When King David consolidated the settlement of the people in the kingdoms of Judah and Israel, he picked Jerusalem for his capital, a city outside both of those territories, and it was there that he planned to build a temple as a permanent and more worthy dwelling place for the glory of the Lord (2 Sam. 7). It fell to his son Solomon, however, to build the temple, although David at least had the joy, flamboyantly expressed, of bringing the ark of the covenant into the city (2 Sam. 6).

The dedication of the first temple in Jerusalem is movingly described in Chapter 8 of the First Book of the Kings. It was there that the Lord had chosen to make his home. It was the focus of prayer and the place of sacrifice. The great feasts, recalling the historic events by which God had bound the people to himself, were all celebrated in the Temple. These became linked with the seasons of the year so that the record of historical events in linear time, and the celebration of seasonal change and fruitfulness in cyclical time, came to be celebrated together. The Torah, the first five books of the Bible, gives much space – in Exodus, Leviticus and Deuteronomy – to explaining the reasons for these celebrations as well as the rubrics and rituals to be followed in carrying them out.

The sacred character of the Temple was extended to include the whole of the city of Jerusalem, often referred to as Mount Zion, the principal hill on which the city was established. These physical and geographical realities, the City and the Temple, came to represent most powerfully the faith of the people of Israel. There God dwelt among them. There prayer was effective. There the sacrifices were offered. There the king was enthroned. There the High Priest entered the Holy of Holies on the Day of Atonement, coming into the very presence of God's glory, in order to confess the sins of the people, offer the blood of the sacrifices in atonement, and beg forgiveness and reconciliation from the Lord.

It is only by appreciating the place of the Jerusalem Temple in the faith and religious practice of Israel that we can hope to understand two later events in the people's history. One is the Babylonian Exile, which meant the loss of the land, the loss of the city and the loss of the temple. This was total devastation, a collapse of catastrophic dimensions. It meant, in effect, the death of God for them, for the glory of the Lord abandoned the temple and departed from the city (Ezek. 10). They had therefore lost all those things that had been given to them as guarantees of God's special favour towards them: the land, the city, the temple itself.

Many centuries later, after many other vicissitudes undergone by the city of Jerusalem and by its restored temple, the prophet Jesus of Nazareth enacted as the signature tune of his mission, a cleansing of that building (Mt. 21.12-13; Mk 11.15-17; Lk. 19.45-46; and Jn 2.13-17). His sustained critique of the temple system, as well as a crazy promise to rebuild it in three days if it were to be destroyed (Jn 2.19), constituted a large part of the evidence that led to his conviction, condemnation and execution.

There is no avoiding Jerusalem or the Temple in the Gospels. Luke centres his two-part work, the Gospel of Luke and Acts of the Apostles, on the city of Jerusalem. His Gospel begins and ends there. The mission of Jesus enters its decisive stage from the moment he set his face resolutely towards Jerusalem (Lk. 9.51). The Holy Spirit brings the Church to birth in Jerusalem and it is beginning from there that the gospel message will be preached, in Jerusalem, Samaria, and to the ends of the earth (Acts 1.8).

The Gospel of John presents the ministry of Jesus in relation to the great Jewish feasts. His visits to the city, the signs he gives and his great discourses all take place in the city, often within the temple itself, and always at the time of the great feasts. The idea is that those feasts and what they represented for the relationship of the people with God are all fulfilled in the life and work of Jesus. The temple that will be rebuilt in three days is Jesus's body, something the disciples only remember after he had risen from the dead (Jn 2.22).

The Gospel of John teaches in other ways that the latest form of the temple is actually the physical body of Jesus. It is there that the sacrifice acceptable to God is now offered. When John says 'we have seen his glory, as the only Son from the Father', he is referring to the death of that only Son (Jn 1.14; 3.16; 1 Jn 4.9). The link between Cana, the first sign in which he revealed his glory (Jn 2.11), and Calvary, the climactic sign of that glory (Jn 12.17-33 and 19.26), confirms it: his glory is that of an only son, seen in the moment of that son's death. The acceptable sacrifice is the body of Jesus itself (Heb. 10.10). His is the blood that now seals the repentance of the people and the renewal of the covenant on the great and universal Day of Atonement. He is the priest, the sacrifice, the one who offers the prayer that pierces the heavens and calls down the grace and blessing of God on a sinful and struggling

THE SPIRIT OF CATHOLICISM

people. Strangely too he is the scapegoat, the Lamb of God, who carries away the sins of the people. His side, opened by a soldier's lance, corresponds in his body to that place in the temple precinct from which Ezekiel saw the waters of the river of life flowing from the right side of the sanctuary (Ezek. 47.1-2). The fountain opened in the heart of Jerusalem, of which the prophet Zechariah spoke (Zech. 12.10), is the wound in the side of Jesus, from which, Catholic Christianity believes, flows the sacramental life of the Church, Baptism and the Eucharist, the water and the blood (Jn 19.34; 1 Jn 5.6-9).

We find an intriguing reference to Jesus as a builder in the Letter to the Hebrews. He is being compared to Moses, who was 'faithful in God's house' (Heb. 3.2). In line with the argument of Hebrews, Jesus is identified not just as a greater occupant of the same house but as its builder (Heb. 3.3; cf. 1.2). He is there not just as a servant but as the son, not just as an occupant but as the builder of the house. And that house we are, the text concludes, 'if we hold fast our confidence and pride in our hope' (Heb. 3.6).

It is not surprising, then, to find Paul saying 'we are the temple of the living God' (2 Cor. 6.16-18). This is found in a section of 2 Corinthians where Paul contrasts the worship of idols with the worship of the living God. We are the temple of the living God, he says, meaning not that we have a better temple alongside other temples, one in which the living God is worshipped as compared with idols. What he says is that we ourselves, the community of believers, are the temple of the living God. He quotes those words that echo through all parts of the Bible: 'I will be your God and you will be my people.' Paul supports his case by quoting from the prophets Hosea and Isaiah. We belong to that people with whom God involved himself and we join them in becoming the temple, the dwelling place of God in the world, where God's presence ought particularly to be seen and experienced. It is a very daring claim – to some it will seem exaggerated and even scandalous, to say not just that 'I go to the temple to worship the living God', which might seem arrogant enough to be going on with, but that 'I and those who share my faith *are* the temple of the living God': we are the place where the world ought to find Christ.

5

FORMS OF CORRUPTION IN THIS BODY

Embodiment means life and structure. In thinking about this we focused particularly on the metaphor of the living organic body for which embodiment means finitude and limitation, and inevitably also corruption. When we speak of a 'body politic', using the analogy of an animal body to understand the life and structure of a human community, we are obviously speaking metaphorically. In the case of the Church, as we have seen, it has a particular character, for which we use the term 'sacrament': a reality of the visible and tangible physical world that at the same time becomes the bearer of a level of life, communion and communication far beyond its original level of existence. Saint Paul, Thomas Aquinas and many others have not hesitated to push the analogy of the organic body as a way of speaking about the Church, and they have drawn many conclusions from the details of that analogy.

We now turn to considering the forms of corruption that are possible in this body that is the Church, another aspect of this rich imagery. We speak of corruption, not because it is the body of Christ, but because it is a body of human beings living in a world that presents them with many challenges, a body of sinful human beings living in a world that tests their faith from many directions.

An important work of Aristotle's natural philosophy is entitled *On Generation and Corruption*. All that comes to be can also perish. It is particularly and most obviously true of animals, including the human animal. They are brought into being by 'parents', they feed and develop, they grow to maturity and, at least potentially, flourish as the kind of creature that they are. They become capable of reproducing and continuing the cycle by bringing into being 'children' of their own. But none of them individually is immortal, and there is no gap between the moment of their full maturity and the beginning of their decline. In the same moment in which they achieve their prime they begin to weaken, grow old, and then older, until inevitably they die. In the meantime, as physical and corporeal beings, they are subject to a multiplicity of circumstances and agents that can cause them to suffer illness, to lose some of their capacities and even to die prematurely.

In terms of a body's generation and corruption we talk about the Church coming to birth. We have seen how Aquinas, following Paul, identifies different senses we can give to the notion of the Church reaching its maturity. Church historians and historians of doctrine will speak about its development across the centuries. But we must talk also about its weakness, its loss of health and the ways in which as a body it has in the past, and might again in the future, become ill or disabled. We must speak also of ways in which it might corrupt, losing, at least temporarily, some of its energy and life, subject as it is to a variety of circumstances and agents capable of disturbing and distorting it, of interrupting the flow of that life.

The creed speaks of the Church as one, holy, catholic and apostolic. While it cannot lose the apostolicity of its foundation or the catholicity of its mission, its unity must always be worked for and sometimes defended. Its holiness in particular is always vulnerable, not in the saints who have already followed Christ and Mary as they did: the communion of the saints guarantees the Church's enduring holiness. The vast majority of its members, however, including its leaders, are all too prone to 'the lust of the flesh, the lust of the eyes and the pride of life' (1 Jn 2.16; cf. Gen. 3.6), the temptations of exploitation, power and possession. These are common to all human beings, but they take on a particular character and force when they conflict with the purpose and way of life presupposed by the Church's holiness. Holiness simply means observing the great commandment of love for God and for our neighbour, loving as Jesus loved his disciples. Sin means turning away from that love to prefer something less than it that also militates against our own true flourishing.

TREASURE IN EARTHEN VESSELS

The phrase that gives this section its title is found in 2 Corinthians 4.7. In this second part of his correspondence with the Christians of Corinth Paul frequently speaks about his own struggles and weaknesses. It is a passionate letter, in which he defends his work among them in the face of criticism coming from the Church there as a whole, it seems, as well as from the leaders of a number of factions that had already come to exist among them. There is 'fighting without and fear within', he says (2 Cor. 7.5). The two letters to the Corinthians give us a list of problems that had already arisen in this community as it began to grow and mature, and how familiar that list will seem: sexual immorality, arguments about liturgy, arguments about authority, who is entitled to preach and teach in the Church, questions about the relationships between men and women in the Church, questions about the handling of money, tensions between some attached to tradition and others enthusiastic for new spiritual things. They are questions that have beset the Church in every age and they are all there, right at the beginning.

Paul also expresses a sense of personal weakness in the face of such problems. His writings are all occasional letters, addressed to particular individuals and communities, usually in order to confront specific problems that had arisen among them. He reminds the Corinthian Christians that not many of them were rich or powerful, not many came from noble families (1 Cor. 1.26-31). God chose rather what is weak and foolish, low and despised, he says, so that it would be clear that the transcendent power belongs, not to the vessels that carry it, but to the treasure that nevertheless is carried by those vessels (2 Cor. 4.7). The Church coming into existence is made up of ordinary people with the aspirations and limitations of ordinary people.

Humility was a central theme of the gospel of Jesus – 'everyone who exalts himself will be humbled, but the one who humbles himself will be exalted' (Lk. 18.14) – and so we might be tempted to think that Paul's references to his struggles are somehow obligatory for a preacher of that gospel. Is it not, after all, the gospel of a man who, so Paul had been brought to see, had humbled himself even to the point of death (Phil. 2.8-9)? But as we read on in 2 Corinthians, it is impossible to doubt the sincerity of Paul's own struggles, particularly in those passages of powerful rhetoric in which he lists the experiences that honed and strengthened him in his work of preaching and church-building.

Let us revisit those passages. First, the one in which he refers to the treasure carried in earthen vessels:

> For what we preach is not ourselves, but Jesus Christ as Lord, with ourselves as your servants for Jesus' sake. For it is the God who says 'Let light shine out of darkness', who has shone in our hearts to give the light of the knowledge of the glory of God in the face of Christ. But we have this treasure in earthen vessels, to show that the transcendent power belongs to God and not to us. We are afflicted in every way, but not crushed; perplexed, but not driven to despair; persecuted, but not forsaken; struck down, but not destroyed; always carrying in the body the death of Jesus, so that the life of Jesus may also be manifested in our bodies. For while we live, we are always being given up to death for Jesus's sake, so that the life of Jesus may be manifested in our mortal flesh. So, death is at work in us, but life in you. (2 Cor. 4.5-12)

He returns to the theme in this 'litany of hardship':

> We put no obstacle in any one's way, so that no fault may be found with our ministry, but as servants of God we

commend ourselves in every way: through great endurance, in afflictions, hardships, calamities, beatings, imprisonments, tumults, labours, watching, hunger; by purity, knowledge, forbearance, kindness, the Holy Spirit, genuine love, truthful speech, and the power of God; with the weapons of righteousness for the right hand and for the left; in honour and dishonour, in ill repute and good repute. We are treated as imposters, and yet are true; as unknown, and yet well known; as dying, and behold we live; as punished, and yet not killed; as sorrowful, yet always rejoicing; as poor, yet making many rich; as having nothing, and yet possessing everything. (2 Cor. 6.3-10)

And writing with even more passion towards the end of the letter, provoked by the criticisms of those whom he refers to as 'pseudo-apostles' and 'super-apostles', he gives us this wonderful crescendo:

Are they servants of Christ? I am a better one – I am talking like a madman – with far greater labours, far more imprisonments, with countless beatings, and often near death. Five times I have received at the hands of the Jews the forty lashes less one. Three times I have been beaten with rods; once I was stoned. Three times I have been shipwrecked; a night and a day I have been adrift at sea; on frequent journeys, in danger from rivers, danger from robbers, danger from my own people, danger from Gentiles, danger in the city, danger in the wilderness, danger at sea, danger from false brethren; in toil and hardship, through many a sleepless night, in hunger and thirst, often without food, in cold and exposure. And, apart from other things, there is the daily pressure upon me of my anxiety for all the churches. Who is weak and I am not weak? Who is made to fall, and I am not indignant? If I must boast, I will boast of the things that show my weakness. The God and Father of the Lord Jesus, he who is blessed for ever, knows that I do not lie. At Damascus, the governor under

> King Aretas guarded the city of Damascus in order to seize me, but I was let down in a basket through a window in the wall, and escaped his hands. (2 Cor. 11.23-33)

These texts are the work of a skilled rhetorician, but one who mocks himself since, in concluding that passage, the classical presentation of the acts of a hero is turned upside down, for it comes to a climax not with the most impressive of his achievements but with the most humiliating of his experiences, escaping from a city by being let down along the wall in a basket.

In 1 Corinthians he is generally more restrained, although there are flashes of anger there too. Once again stung by his critical opponents among the preachers of the gospel and by the fact that the Corinthians are being taken in by them, Paul says this:

> For I think that God has exhibited us apostles as last of all, like men sentenced to death; because we have become a spectacle to the world, to angels and to men. We are fools for Christ's sake, but you are wise in Christ. We are weak, but you are strong. You are held in honour, but we in disrepute. To the present hour we hunger and thirst, we are ill-clad and buffeted and homeless, and we labour, working with our own hands. When reviled, we bless; when persecuted, we endure; when slandered, we try to conciliate; we have become, and are now, as the refuse of the world, the offscouring of all things. (1 Cor. 4.9-13)

So even a quick review of Saint Paul's letters, especially those written to the Corinthians, shows us that the drama of sin and holiness is already well underway in the first decades of the Church's life. There are factions and jealousies, there are scandals about sex and disagreements about liturgical practice, there are questions about orthodoxy and leadership, there are power struggles and concerns about money ... the whole gamut of what falls under 'the lust of the flesh, the lust of the eyes and the pride of life' are present in the life of the infant Church, with the added edge that comes when disagreements are theological. Paul talks about difficulties coming from natural disasters and from opponents beyond the Church. He speaks of problems arising within the community, between individuals and factions, into which he is inevitably drawn. But he speaks frequently also of his personal weakness, for example in the following text, which has given us a number of phrases that have become proverbial:

> to keep me from being too elated by the abundance of revelations, a thorn was given me in the flesh, a messenger of Satan, to harass me, to keep me from being too elated. Three times I begged the Lord about this, that it should leave me; but he said to me, 'My grace is sufficient for you, for my power is made perfect in weakness.' I will all the more gladly boast of my weaknesses, that the power of Christ may rest upon me. For the sake of Christ, then, I am content with weaknesses, insults, hardships, persecutions, and calamities; for when I am weak, then I am strong. (2 Cor. 12.7-10)

Nobody knows what the 'thorn in the flesh' was, whether a moral weakness, a difficulty in his personality, a physical or psychological illness. It is not the only place in which he talks about his personal struggle. Romans 7 is another such place in which he says that he experienced the common human experience of struggling with temptation, seeing what is good but doing the opposite, finding himself unable to do what he wants and instead doing the very thing he hates (Rom. 7.15, 19).

One could continue – there are similar passages in 1 Corinthians 15.8-11, 30-34 and in 2 Corinthians 1.3-11. Let us keep in mind just a few things from all these texts. One is the image of the earthen vessel that carries a great treasure, for this is what we believe the Church to be, each member individually and the Church corporately. Another is his celebration of God's grace 'made perfect in weakness' (2 Cor. 12.9). Another is Paul's reference to the daily pressure of his anxiety for all the churches – it is how he understood what was entailed by the call that came with his conversion, and the way in which he honoured that responsibility made him the greatest church-builder of the first generation of believers.

In fact, these realities of human weakness and conflict, 'the lust of the flesh, the lust of the eyes and the pride of life', temptation and succumbing to it – all this will seem to be even more present in Catholicism than in other communities of human beings. This is the shocking assertion coming, not from a critic or opponent of Catholicism, but from Cardinal John Henry Newman, the most important religious thinker of the nineteenth century and now a canonized saint of the Church.

NEWMAN ON CORRUPTION

Newman offers a very interesting reflection on corruption in the Church and why it will be the case that the Catholic Church will seem to be more corrupt even than other Christian bodies.[1] He is not saying it is necessarily more corrupt – his 'conversion' would have been perverse if that was what he meant. So why does he think it will seem more corrupt? In the first place, Newman says, it is because the Church is the bearer of a great treasure. It is the earthen vessel that carries a treasure by comparison with which the Church's weaknesses, failures and limitations will stand out more clearly. The light of the glory of God on the face of Christ that Paul speaks about (2 Cor. 4.6) is what the Church carries, the reality to which it bears witness. We have spoken of the Church as the sacrament of Christ, symbolized by the moon, with no light of its own. But considering the source of the light that it does reflect, its own failures, blemishes and limitations will be all the more obvious. Newman's argument is an application to the Church of what Jesus is recorded as saying in Luke 12.48, 'from everyone to whom much has been given, much will be required; and from one to whom much has been entrusted, even more will be demanded'.

This may seem like an apologetic argument *ex corruptione ecclesiae*, that the Church's survival in spite of the failures and perversions of so many of its members is a sign that it must somehow belong to Christ and be sustained by the Spirit. Otherwise, it would surely have disappeared long ago. People's criticisms of Catholicism can sometimes seem to be in tune with this point. Those criticisms are often marked by great anger, an anger more often than not fully justified. But they are also often marked by notes of regret, sadness, disappointment and disillusionment, as if people are also saying, 'We expected more', 'we thought this would be a better place than it is', 'we feel betrayed for having placed our trust there'.

Newman's thought, as a believing member of the Church, is that whatever darkness appears in it will be darker because the light the Church carries is so much brighter. *Corruptio optimi pessima* is an old saying: the corruption of the best will be the worst corruption. It means that at times the Church's aspiration to live up to what it has received is confirmed more by the failure of its members than by any success. Evil appearing so close to what is good, evil operating under the cloak of goodness, will be illuminated more powerfully by the good it seeks to pervert and corrupt. We might also suppose that the attention of Satan, with all that that word entails, will be particularly drawn to the Church, as it is to any person who seeks to serve goodness and truth in the world.

CONGAR ON REFORM

The most important study of this question in the twentieth century was undertaken by the French Dominican Yves Congar (1904–95) and published under the title *True and False Reform in the Church*.[2] It is a careful, well-documented, reflection on those aspects of the Church that are essential to its fidelity to Christ and those aspects in which it will regularly need reform. When it was first published, Congar's work was condemned by many in the Church. There is no need to waste time now pointing out how absurd that condemnation was. Congar distinguished the forms, practices and habits of historical Catholicism from its dogmas, hierarchical structure and what he calls 'Christianity in itself'.

The first will be constantly in need of reform, the second remain foundational and fundamental. More recent developments in church life, and revelations about corruption in many supposedly 'Catholic' countries, make it almost obligatory to revisit Congar's work. His comment that there were at the time he wrote 'hardly any abuses to reform'[3] will raise many eyebrows: he thought instead that it was simply a question of 'renewing structures', and then not any of the structures he regarded as essential and untouchable.

One aspect of Congar's analysis that deserves renewed attention is his point that if the Church thinks of itself as giving to the world, it must also recognize how and what it receives from the world. 'The world' here means all that is outside and around the Church, secular powers and movements in thought and culture. It is the same world in which the Church and its members must of necessity live and experience, so a simplistic opposition serves no purpose. The relationship of the Church with all that is 'outside' is something to which we must return, but for the moment it is helpful to note Congar's list of what he regarded as the most important aspects of what the Church receives from the world:[4] first, it receives from the world the context for its life and the conditions in which it lives; second, it receives questions from the world and partial answers, as well as receiving some of its own treasures back, the fruit of seed sown by the Church at an earlier time; finally, the Church sometimes receives from the world God's judgement on its own disobedience. It means that the Church will, from time to time, need to humble itself and be called to order by the world, be summoned back to its proper service of the world and acknowledge that the kingdom of God – grace – is to be found outside the Church also. Congar concludes that the Church's energy must synchronize with the energy of the world, although not to follow or accept just anything, nor to pretend to be in sympathy where it is not. On the other hand, the Catholic Church would find it very difficult to regard itself as a 'sect', a kind of counter-culture insulated within the bigger reality of humanity. Because it understands itself as the sacrament of the unity of the human race, it is obliged by its own self-definition to clarify its relationship with all human beings and the relationship of all human beings with it. And, as in any relationship, it cuts both ways.

TENSION AND CONFLICT

Henri de Lubac was a contemporary of Congar and his classic work *Catholicism* has already been mentioned.[5] Like Congar he was for some years forbidden to teach, but, again like Congar, he lived long enough to see much of his work enshrined in the documents of Vatican II as 'official church teaching'. While Congar spent the time of his suspension writing a book on the Temple, de Lubac spent it writing a book on the Church.[6] It is a book that is very valuable in its own right, but also fascinating in that it already contains so much of what was to appear ten years later in *Lumen gentium*. The fifth chapter of *The Splendour of the Church*, entitled 'The Church in the World', is among the most helpful texts for reflecting on the particular question of the relationship between the Church and the world. Its conclusion coincides with what we have seen in Congar: a kind of fruitful synergy is constantly being sought in the relationship of the Church and the world. De Lubac is thinking in the first place of the relationship between the Church and the State, a relationship that he argues will never be fully satisfactory during the Church's earthly pilgrimage. There will always be points of tension, if not – and this is a point that is clearer in de Lubac – open conflict.

Was the year 2000 the last year of the twentieth century or the first year of the twenty-first century? It was certainly celebrated as the beginning, not just of a new century but of a new millennium. After the nineteenth century's Newman and the twentieth century's Congar and de Lubac, there is a book published on that threshold of 2000, by Nicholas Healy, which also deserves mention again at this point.[7] Healy argues that, instead of focusing on what he calls an epic or blueprint account of the Church, ordered around a particular ideal model, it is better to apply the idea of the theodrama as proposed by Hans Urs von Balthasar (1904–88). This means accepting that the story of salvation is marked by those things that make drama dramatic: tension and suspense, creativity and loss, conflict and resolution. De Lubac hints at this also, and Healy gives two reasons for it. The first is that the Church needs to be considered concretely and practically rather than idealistically, and the epic or blueprint approach inevitably encourages abstraction and idealization. The second is that the epic or blueprint approach tends to undermine the distinctiveness of the Church, failing to do justice to its concrete reality in favour of regarding it as an example of a more generalized spirituality or religiosity.

We can develop that second reason by repeating something said earlier: the epic or blueprint approach tends also to a kind of Platonizing of the Church, seen in the tendency to use the term 'church' without the definite article, as in expressions such as 'how to be church'. It is as if the term 'church' refers in the first place to some essence that can be instantiated in different ways and to different degrees. It is a way of speaking that fails to recognize the Church as a particular subject or agent in history, which is how Catholicism understands itself, the Church being more like a person than an essence.

Pope Paul VI made the same point in his first encyclical letter *Ecclesiam suam* (1964).[8] He writes there:

> We must love and serve the Church as it is, wisely seeking to understand its history and to discover with humility the will of God who guides and assists it, even when he permits human weakness to eclipse the splendour of its countenance and the holiness of its activity. It is precisely this holiness and splendour which we are endeavouring to discover and promote. (n. 46)

We are endeavouring here to avoid the limitations of an epic or blueprint approach by applying the tools identified in our introduction: a strong sense of the Church's sacramental character, as a physical, social and historical reality, as well as a readiness to use all the images, metaphors, analogies and models for the Church given in the scriptures, particularly those concerned with living organisms, their qualities and their vicissitudes. We will see in the next chapter how a balance of elements is essential if Catholicism is to remain healthy. This balance, like the proper relationship between the Church and any civil power, or the 'synergy' between the Church and the world of which de Lubac and Congar speak, is never perfectly achieved in the time of the Church's earthly pilgrimage. It is rather something that must always be worked towards. That might sound like a new kind of idealization, but rather than focusing on the form of the Church in its perfection at the end of time we want to focus on the Church in its concrete and practical present life.

Healy puts the question in this way: how are we to acknowledge the concrete sinfulness of the Church while maintaining the conviction that it is 'a better way' to truth and salvation? The epic or blueprint approach will tend to idealism and abstraction when what is needed is an understanding of the Church that will be, in Healy's terms, 'practically and prophetically effective'. An approach such as the one he takes from Balthasar – or the one being followed here – seeks to hold together a number of elements that otherwise may be confused, separated or treated one-sidedly: the divine and human constitution of the Church; reflection on the Church in its concrete life; the presentation of a distinctive identity for Catholicism that will not collapse it into a general form of spirituality or religiosity; and the scandal of particularity, the claim that from my limited perspective within the unfolding history of salvation, and in spite of my sins, my sharing in the faith of the Church orients me to the truth of God. In his consideration of faith as a theological virtue Aquinas stresses the latter point: that our assent to the articulations of faith, to the terms in which we express what we believe, does not terminate in the articulations themselves, limited and particular as they must necessarily be, but reaches beyond them, to the truth they convey (*Summa theologiae* II.II 1 2 ad 2).

The most striking part of Healy's argument is that it leads him to highlight the Church's need for others who are different, different not just in a pluralistic kind of way, as others among a range of possibilities from which one might choose, but different in a way that is conflictual: 'conflicting traditions are a necessity for truth-seeking', he says.[9] Congar and De Lubac make the same point, and it is what puts the drama in Balthasar's theodrama. Where different bodies make genuine truth claims – and this is happening all the time, even where the only truth claim made seems to be that there is no truth – then they must engage with one another in relation to these conflicting truth claims. The same is true in relation to the secular world, which promotes its own truth claims even when it claims some kind of neutrality.

At first it seems that to think in terms of a 'pluralistic society' is a helpful way forward, a way that will free the world from certain kinds of fundamental (and fundamentalist) conflict. Only later, perhaps, is it realized that the phrase is contradictory, for to have a society simply is to have a community of people sharing life on the basis not of a multiplicity of fundamental values but on the basis that some particular values are accepted as the criterion, in law for example, against which ways of living and practice within the society are to be evaluated, permitted or forbidden. Following different sports clubs will not usually cause fundamental conflict in a society, whereas disagreements about the good for human life, or about the common good, continue to generate such conflicts, especially when we want to get down to concrete norms and practices.

A possible response in the face of potential conflict is to identify the Church's task with the humanist project in general. In other words, if it becomes clear that the pluralist way is not sustainable, an alternative is what Healy calls 'inclusivist'. But this is where the concrete particularity of the Church can be lost, eliminated by accounts of the Church's life and mission that seek to be acceptable across the board, spiritualizing and universalizing what is at the heart of the Church. But at the heart of the Church is a Person and therefore particularity, a concrete history, unique characteristics, a history of sin and holiness. Stimulated by Healy's questions, the response offered here will be in terms not so much of Balthasar's theodrama as of von Hügel's understanding of the elements of religion and the characteristics of the idea of Christianity in Newman's sense. This is not idealistic or abstract, but rather seeks to be what Healy says is needed today: 'a theological narrative of the concrete identity of the Church over time'.[10]

Before we leave this chapter, however, let us return to its main theme, to offer some further thoughts on the question of corruption in the body that is the Church.

SINNERS CALLED TO HOLINESS

The parish that puts a notice in the church porch saying 'Sinners only need apply within' has a precedent in the teaching of Jesus himself, who said that he had come not for the healthy or the righteous but for the sick and for sinners (Mt. 9.13; Mk 2.17; Lk. 5.31-32; 7.34, 47). We have this treasure in earthen vessels, Paul says, to show that the transcendent power belongs to God and not to us (2 Cor. 4.7). Paul is not just saying, 'take a little bit of consolation from the fact that we are only human'. It will seem like a cop-out for the Church to say this too readily about itself. What Paul is saying is something more mysterious, however. He is saying that we carry the treasure in earthen vessels *in order to show*, so that it might be clear, that the transcendent power belongs to God and not to us. This reasoning can seem puzzling.

The English mystic Julian of Norwich (1342–c.1416) makes a related argument in saying that 'sin is behovely'.[11] This old word means that sin is somehow appropriate, has a certain convenience, is fitting, and brings a certain advantage. What she means is that, by God's providence, what the Easter liturgy calls the 'happy fault' of human sin makes it possible for us to see more clearly the merciful love of God in response, so that our sins actually, and strangely, can strengthen our love for God. Does it mean we should sin more so that God can show his mercy more powerfully? Of course not, Julian says, just as Saint Paul says the same thing in response to the same question: 'are we to continue in sin that grace may abound? By no means' (Rom. 6.1-2). His answer carries the sense of 'don't be ridiculous' or 'don't be absurd'. As Julian says also, to think that we should set out to live in a corrupt way, or be blasé about such a thing, in order to give God opportunities to show mercy, means failing to understand the reality of sin: the damage it does, the suffering it causes, the ways in which it destroys the lives of people, of families, of communities, how it ruins their well-being and their happiness. The corruption that results from sin is all too real, as has been incontrovertibly seen in the Church in recent decades. For Julian, the reality of the crucifixion of Jesus shows clearly the reality and the destructive power of sin, the price it exacts from humanity.

Our faith is in God and in the Church only because, as we saw in Chapter 3, it is the Church of God. Amazingly, Paul's preferred way of addressing the Corinthians is with this precise title, 'the Church of God' (1 Cor. 1.2; 2 Cor. 1.1). This is how he addresses them even as he faces and engages with the scandals, conflicts, divisions and corruption that characterize the lives of those very same people. In spite of all that, they are 'the Church of God'.

Human beings continue to react in primitive ways to the experience of loss, suffering and death. By 'primitive' I mean fears and anxieties that are deep in us and that only emerge in situations of loss and suffering, particularly in the face of death. A cousin, diagnosed with terminal cancer in her mid-thirties, said to me, 'I must have done something really bad to have ended up like this.' In the midst of the Coronavirus pandemic many voices spoke of it as a punishment from God, or at least a warning allowed by God. Is that experience the result of our sin? And if it is not a punishment from God, if we think that such a view expresses a pagan understanding of God rather than a Christian one, then is it still some kind of *karma*, the inevitable fruit of our betrayals of nature, of others, of justice, of truth? In some circumstances it is easy to see that certain kinds of loss follow directly from certain kinds of sin. In Ireland, Austria, Germany and Australia the steep decline in attendance at Catholic liturgies in recent years, for example, clearly testifies to disillusionment, disappointment, anger, humiliation and disgust in many people when confronted with the sins of the abuse scandals. In some places and at some times, therefore, the experience of loss is a direct consequence of identifiable sins committed by individuals, whether sins of action or omission. Most people will know this from personal experience also.

But in other circumstances the connection is not at all clear as we grapple with what we call 'innocent suffering'. Frequently in the Bible we come across this debate about the connection between sin and suffering. What is the calculus by which to understand it? The most sustained reflection on it is the Book of Job. Most of the book is given to Job's friends, who pour energy and time into trying to convince him that there must be a just proportion between what he is experiencing and what he must, therefore, have done to deserve it. Job remains forever a champion of the perplexed human being, the one who refuses to accept pious solutions that seek to justify God, because Job knows in his heart of hearts that these solutions are based on falsehood.

To return to the question of sin and holiness in the Church, one might wonder at the steady stream of people who become Catholics each year. Why do they do it? There is so much negative publicity about the Church, much of it brought on by the Church itself, and there are so many questions about faith and objections to it from scientists and philosophers, that sometimes it seems the problems, difficulties and questions will inevitably overwhelm faith. It can seem like too fragile a flame to withstand all this. Why do people continue to come to the Church? Why do they come to believe in Christ at all? And why do those who are Catholics remain Catholics, at least for the most part? Every now and again a book or article appears with that title, 'Why I remain a Catholic'. It seems as if, like Paul's ministry, it is something that needs explanation and defence. It is a challenge to present any such explanation or defence, because to be faithful to the heart of the matter one must speak of the weakness and foolishness of God revealed in the death of Jesus and continued in the life of the Church.[12] It means embracing a paradox of fear and love (2 Cor. 5.11, 14), of affliction and joy (1 Thess. 1.6), of death and life (Rom. 6.11), preferring God's weakness and foolishness to any alternative power or wisdom (1 Cor. 1.18-25).

It is essential to recall that we are speaking in the first place of a community of people in history, 'the Catholic Church', rather than of 'Catholicism' as a philosophy or movement or ideology. Remember that the Corinthian Christians were, in one and the same moment, 'the Church of God' and riddled with problems. It can only be that people came to believe that this community, in spite of its obvious limitations and failures, was where they could encounter Jesus Christ, not just to learn about him but to share in his life, to be in communion with him through being in communion with these others who also believed. Catholic Christianity will not be understood if we think of it in the first place as adherence to a theory or a set of beliefs and practices. It is only because people believe there is something of personal significance to be found there that they attach themselves to it. 'Personal significance' means not just something in it for me – salvation, eternal life – but that these gifts come from the Person of Christ into whose presence and life, into whose love and wisdom, we are introduced in the Church.

The fact that the vessels are earthen, though it is an obstacle to some, is actually – this is Paul's argument – a demonstration to others that any truth or love or holiness found there can only be from God. Do we see the earthen vessel or the treasure it carries? Some will see the earthen vessel but not the treasure. We live in times where it is very easy to see the earthen vessel and very difficult – to the point of impossibility for many – to see the treasure. Is it not the case, some reasonably ask, that the vessel shows itself to be so earthen – and not at all in any wholesome sense that this term might carry – that it is better to go elsewhere to seek the treasure?

Is it not a strange kind of arrogance to claim that the treasure that Catholic Christianity claims to carry cannot be found, or cannot be as effectively accessed, elsewhere? So where? There are other Christian denominations and other great religious traditions, there are philosophies and spiritualities. It seems reasonable to conclude that what the Church carries for the world is carried also elsewhere. If it is a question of doctrines, rituals and moral teaching, then there are many cultures, traditions and schools to choose from. Surely from among all of those it will be possible to find the same treasure – doctrines, rituals, moral guidance – without the egregious obstacles that Catholicism inevitably presents for many?

While many people see first, and to the exclusion of all else, the 'earthiness' (corruption, crudeness, banality, kitsch) that excludes this institution from carrying any unique treasure of value to humanity, there are still many who see first, and fundamentally, the treasure that it carries, however deeply obscured it may be for others. Such people will find themselves saying, like Peter in John's Gospel, 'Lord, to whom shall we go? You [Jesus, and now here, this earthen vessel] have the words of eternal life' (Jn 6.68).

PART THREE

6

CHRIST'S THREEFOLD MISSION AND THE CHURCH'S THREEFOLD NATURE

When Saint John Henry Newman wrote about the 'idea' of Christianity he meant by this that it is a phenomenon, a historical community, an undeniable social and cultural reality. He did not mean an idea in somebody's head – what Nicholas Healy would call an epic or blueprint model of the Church – but rather the reality with the spirit that gives it its distinctive character and life. In a small way we are seeking to follow in Newman's footsteps, and have done so in the first chapters of this book by focusing on the notion of sacramentality, or embodiment, considering some of the consequences that follow from that.

Newman gives us a second hermeneutical key for thinking about the mystery of the Church, one that, as we shall see, has its origins in the Bible itself. Although this key is developed further in the work of Friedrich von Hügel, von Hügel himself acknowledged his indebtedness to Newman, who helped him, as he helps us, to see how deeply rooted it is in Jewish and Christian traditions.

The three essential 'elements of religion' are variously described by von Hügel as the institutional or historical, the intellectual or doctrinal, and the mystical or active. He acknowledged that Newman was one of his sources for this tripartite distinction. In a sermon he gave in 1840, Newman had spoken about these three as aspects of all human experience.[1] Human living always involves endurance, thought and active life, he says. These characterize the life of every human individual, distributed in different ways according to people's gifts, personality, interests

113

and profession. He assigned these three also to different groups of people, speaking of one group as those who predominantly suffer or endure, a second group those who are predominantly studious or intellectual, and a third group those who are for the most part involved in government and administration. They are found also in religion, specifically in Christianity, Newman describing knowledge, power and endurance as the three privileges of the Christian Church.[2] In his later writings he changed the terminology somewhat, speaking then of devotion or passion in place of endurance, of philosophy or science in place of knowledge, and of party adherence or fellowship in place of active life.[3] Christianity, he wrote, is at once a philosophy, a political power and a religious rite.[4]

Nicholas Lash (1934–2020) immediately pointed to two facts about this threefold distinction: one is that each of these aspects of human experience, because it is the experience of a finite nature prone to weakness and even to sin, contains within itself the seeds of its own corruption. In other words, each of these aspects has the potential to become ill or to go mad. The second fact to be underlined immediately is that the best protection against such illness or madness is the coincidence of each one with the other two. In other words, the balance of these three aspects is what keeps them healthy, whether individually or all together.[5] We will look at this in more detail when we come to consider von Hügel's presentation of these 'elements of religion'.

But first let us look back, across the centuries, beginning with the Bible. Newman linked these three privileges of the Christian Church with the three 'offices' of the Messiah, who was to be a priest, a prophet and a king. The priest is concerned with the mystical, the active, the pastoral and the devotional. The prophet is concerned with teaching, with thought, with doctrine and with meaning. The king is concerned with administration, with government, with order and with security in a community.

At Vatican II this threefold office of Christ moved to the centre of the Church's consideration of its own identity and life. In its second chapter, on the theme of the people of God, *Lumen gentium* speaks of the messianic people as being 'priestly, prophetic and kingly' because Christ is priest, prophet and king (*LG* nn.9–13). For the moment, note that the royal or kingly office is understood in relation to the 'kingdom' that Jesus announced and initiated. Belonging to Christ means participating in a life that has these three characteristics. This is appealed to so often in the documents of Vatican II that it can be regarded as a kind of 'gene' or Christian DNA that is to be found not just in the organism of the Church as a whole but in every individual member of the body that is the Church. Everybody in the Church is priestly, prophetic and royal by virtue of their initiation into its life. Each of the particular ministries, works of service, gifts, vocations, states of life – all have this same DNA within them. It does not mean that we are all clones, however. In certain groups and individuals within the one body we find these three elements balanced in different ways depending on the particular gifts and vocations of the people concerned. What is crucial for the moment is to appreciate the origins of this idea as well as its importance for thinking about the health of the Catholic Church.

PRIEST, PROPHET, KING

In the moment of its calling Israel was identified by God as 'a kingdom of priests and a holy nation' (Exod. 19.6). Moses was the prophet called by God to lead and to organize this community, giving it moral, ceremonial and judicial laws. Its life was to be structured by a certain moral wisdom, by particular liturgical practices, and by a system of justice modelled on God's own holiness. The early Christians understood themselves as the heirs of this relationship with God. The Jews among them were Jews who had come to believe in the fulfilment of a new covenant that had been foretold (Jer. 31.31). The former pagans among them understood themselves as a wild branch grafted onto the old tree (Rom. 11.17). They did not hesitate therefore to describe themselves in the same terms, even quoting verbatim the text from the Book of Exodus: 'you are a chosen race, a royal priesthood, a holy nation, God's own people' (1 Pet. 2.9).

The life of God's people was overseen, guided and nourished, by priests, by prophets and by kings. As we read through the Hebrew Bible, the Christian Old Testament, we come across these figures all the time. The historical experiences of the people are an essential part of the story of their relationship with God. The judges and kings who ruled them are regarded as put in place by God to fulfil the social, political and economic aspects of their life under the covenant. The prophets worked with the political leaders and often in conflict with them, their main task being to bring the light of God's word to bear on historical events and situations as they unfolded. The priesthood was the third essential element, offering the sacrifices and leading the prayers of the people.

In a time of exile and abandonment the prophet Daniel lamented that there was 'no ruler, or prophet, or leader, no burnt-offering, or sacrifice, or oblation, or incense, no place to make an offering before God or to find mercy' (Dan. 3.38 [= Prayer of Azariah, verse 15]). In other words, the people's life had been emptied of its essential content, with no king, no prophet and no priest. Jeremiah, too, lamented the loss of everything, the king in exile, while 'the prophets and priests ply their trade through the land, but without knowledge' (Jer. 14.18).

This people is made up, therefore, of kings and prophets and priests and its significant life is royal, prophetic and priestly. Not surprisingly, the Messiah, a figure who was to represent the people before God, was also expected to be a king of the house of David, a prophet like Moses, and a priest, or at least someone who would act in the place of the priesthood in offering a sacrifice and leading the prayers of the people.

If we jump forward to the Christian Middle Ages, we find Thomas Aquinas describing Jesus as 'priest, king and legislator'. Legislator has taken the place of prophet for the moment because Aquinas hesitates to call Jesus a prophet (*Disputed Questions on Truth* 20, 6). This will seem strange to our eyes but is connected with the particular understanding of prophecy that Aquinas had, as well as his particular understanding of the knowledge that

Jesus had, a knowledge that, as it were, reached beyond the need for a special gift of prophecy.

But in other contexts, more central to his account of the work of Christ, Aquinas says that the mysteries of the life of Jesus are to be understood according to the pattern of priesthood, prophecy and kingship (*Summa theologiae* I.II 102ff.; III 41). For Aquinas these offices are linked with the different parts of the law given to the Jewish people. The gift of the law was a first incarnation of the Word. Calling it 'the way to knowledge' – the divine wisdom, in other words – the Book of Baruch says that 'she appeared on earth and lived with humankind' (Bar. 3.37). Baruch is referring to the giving of the law to Moses on Mount Sinai. For Aquinas this divine wisdom was articulated in precepts that were ceremonial, moral and judicial. Here is how he applies this pattern to Christ:

- *That Christ is a priest* is revealed in his being baptized and tempted, in other words in his work of sanctifying and praying. It is revealed also in how he fulfilled the ceremonial or liturgical precepts of the law and in his work of enabling access to God. As a priest he offers the new and eternal sacrifice that seals the new and eternal covenant. He does this in his own flesh and blood and his body is now the temple, the place of God's presence and power (*Summa theologiae* III, 39; III, 41).
- *That Christ is a prophet* is revealed in his lifestyle as a poor preacher, teacher and miracle worker sharing life with sinners (*Summa theologiae* III, 40; 41; 43–4). It is revealed also in how he fulfilled the moral precepts of the law and in his work of publishing the truth. As a prophet he is the one who reveals the Father, he is the teacher of Israel. It is part of Jesus' own teaching, that he is a king and a prophet.
- *That Christ is a king* is revealed to all kinds of people in the infancy narratives of Matthew and Luke, to shepherds and to wise men, to civil and religious leaders. It is seen also in how he fulfilled the judicial precepts of the law and in his work of freeing people from sin. As king, Jesus

is Lord of the Sabbath, and he enters Jerusalem, the royal city, acclaimed as a king. 'Yes, I am a king', he says to Pilate (*Summa theologiae* III, 36, referring to John 18.37).

For Aquinas this threefold office is in the first place the vocational grace of Israel, and for him it determines all further details of Christ's ministry in Israel. It is not Aquinas alone who sees Jesus as faithful Israel, the faithful servant of the Lord, an individual who at the same time represents the entire people, and as such therefore a priest, a prophet and a king. All comes to be focused in him so that he might fulfil what was promised and finally create a people fit for God, once again a royal priesthood, a holy nation, a people set apart (1 Pet. 2.9-10).

It is particularly in speaking of Christ as the end of the law that Aquinas appeals to the threefold ministry: he fulfils the law in its judicial, moral and ceremonial precepts, and therefore as king, prophet and priest.[6] But for Aquinas it is to be seen very clearly also in the Paschal Mystery, as Jesus frees people from sin, opens for them access to God, and bears witness to the truth. In the work of Christ, coming to its climax in the events of his passion, death and resurrection, the (royal) law and the prophets are fulfilled and true (priestly) prayer and sacrifice are offered.

We could stop at other points along the way across the Christian centuries. John Calvin (1509–64), for example, is often credited with bringing into sharper focus this threefold office of the Messiah.[7] However, as we have seen, it is rooted in the Bible and is already used in important ways by Thomas Aquinas. At the beginning of the twentieth century, Newman's application of this theme received an interesting and potentially very fertile development, in von Hügel's presentation of the elements of religion as institutional (royal), intellectual (prophetic) and mystical (priestly).

THE ELEMENTS OF RELIGION

Friedrich von Hügel was born in Florence in 1852, son of Baron Carl von Hügel, an Austrian diplomat, and Elizabeth Farquharson, a convert to Catholicism from Scottish Presbyterianism. He had an eclectic education from a variety of tutors and came to live in England in 1867. In 1870 he contracted typhus and this left him deaf. Shortly afterwards he experienced a serious spiritual crisis through which he was helped by a Dutch Dominican, Raymond Hocking.[8] In 1873 he married Lady Mary Herbert with whom he had three daughters. One of his daughters, whom he refers to as 'my True', pre-deceased him.[9]

Friedrich inherited his father's title of 'Baron of the Holy Roman Empire' as well as sufficient income to live comfortably without having to undertake paid work. He devoted himself to classical, historical, philosophical and religious studies. Around 1890 he met Henri Huvelin (1830–1910) in Paris, who introduced him to the great mystical writings of Christianity and helped him overcome depression and anxiety. Huvelin was confessor and spiritual director also to Charles de Foucauld (1858–1916), whose life and spirituality von Hügel recommends to his niece.[10] Von Hügel was a friend to many of the notable philosophical and religious thinkers of his day, including Norman Kemp Smith (1872–1958), professor of philosophy at Edinburgh, Wilfrid Ward (1856–1916), another leading lay Catholic, the French philosophers Henri Brémond (1865–1933), Maurice Blondel (1861–1949) and Lucien Laberthonière (1860–1932), the church historian Louis Duchesne (1843–1922), and central figures of the modernist controversy Alfred Loisy (1857–1940), George Tyrrell (1861–1909) and Ernest Troelstch (1865–1923). In 1905 von Hügel founded the London Society for the Study of Religion, a discussion group that developed into a society of Catholic scholars. He was never condemned as a modernist, but his admiration for and friendship with many modernist leaders caused concern when that movement of thought was condemned by the Holy See in 1907. Von Hügel died in 1925.[11]

Our interest is mainly in the first of his works, *The Mystical Element of Religion*, in which, following on what he found in Newman, he presents his understanding of religion's three elements. He sees these not only as structural but also as developmental elements that he refers to as stages, aspects or forces. The first is the 'institutional-historical', which he regards as the child's means of apprehending religion. This is not to disparage it. It involves sense, memory and imagination. Later he will speak of it as 'social Christianity', important for counteracting, for example, the individualism of the mystical. The second element is the 'intellectual-doctrinal', which he regards as the young person's mode of approaching religion. Once again it is not in order to disparage it: each of these elements is essential in the overall health of the mature religious sensibility. This element involves question and argument, analysis and synthesis, study and research, just as young people follow their desire to know and to understand what they are being asked to believe. Later, von Hügel speaks of the importance of science and says that 'the study of the impersonal' is necessary for purifying the personality. The final element he calls 'mystical-active' and it is the approach to faith of the mature human being. It involves emotion and experience, intuition and feeling, free decisions and action on the basis of evidence.

What von Hügel intends, then, is a developmental journey that includes two moments of crisis as the individual believer (or community, or parish, or Church?) grows from one stage to the next, integrating these elements as they go along. Each element is always accompanied by some measure of the other two, and the earlier stages are not to be abandoned but are to be taken up into the later ones. Each is necessary but any one of them becomes destructive where it ousts the other two, and yet each has a tendency to do just that. Crisis presents the possibility of growth, but it also carries the threat of tragic outcomes. As noted, there are two moments of crisis if one is to grow from one stage into the next.

The first moment of crisis is in the transition from the institutional to the intellectual. One temptation here is to cling exclusively to the existing, simply institutional, external position and to fight or to avoid all approaches to its reasoned, intellectual apprehension and systematization. If we give in to this temptation, the person's religion will contract and shrivel up. He will align his religion with economics and politics and assimilate it to external law and order, von Hügel thinks. The result is a religious sensibility that remains immature, being little more, in fact, than a form of superstition. The other temptation in this first crisis is to let the intellectual supplant the institutional completely. This will result in the person's religion growing hard and shallow; he will align it with science and philosophy, which may eventually come to replace it altogether. Giving in to this temptation will lead to rationalism, agnosticism and indifference.

The second moment of crisis is in the transition from the intellectual to the mystical, or to what he refers to elsewhere as 'emotional-experimental' life. This transition is also necessary if religion is to be complete. If one is tempted to revert to the institutional stage it may well be because one finds this mystical stage revolutionary, threatening disorder and confusion on account of its emotional power. For the one tempted to stop at the intellectual stage the mystical will seem like mere subjectivity or as sentimentality verging on delusion. Seeing things too much from the view of the mystical, on the other hand, a person will be tempted to sweep aside the external institutional element as so much oppressive ballast and to reject the intellectual as so much useless hair-splitting or cold rationalism. The triumph of the mystical, if it is not kept in balance by the other two, would mean what von Hügel describes as an all but incurable tyranny of mood and fancy. Its pathology would be fanaticism rather than superstition or indifference. It has even led in the past to what he ominously refers to as 'apocalyptic orgies', an observation in which he seems to anticipate the analysis of Ronald Knox's study of the pathologies of religion, which was not to appear until forty years later.[12]

Although it seems more logical to think of this development happening in the direction in which it is expounded – from institutional to intellectual to mystical – it could also be that a person of a particular temperament or experience might begin at any point in the story, beginning even from the mystical-active and needing to supplement their understanding with what is to be found at those points of the developmental journey that they have not as yet lived through.

Von Hügel is not only proposing a general 'theory of religion' or 'theory of cultural phenomena'. What he says can be applied in many areas, and he believes, following Newman, that these three elements or forces are distributed throughout all peoples of whatever age, gender, profession or race, and at all times in history. The three elements are to be found in all the great religions, but, as a believing Catholic Christian, he is convinced that this developmental journey, integrating philosophy, science and religion, will come to its fulfilment in the life, teaching and mission of the Church. 'It is in Christianity,' he says, 'and throughout its various vicissitudes and schools, that we can most fully observe the presence, characteristics, and interaction of these three modalities' (*The Mystical Element*, p. 61). They can be seen already within the New Testament, represented by the apostles Peter, Paul and John; they can be seen among the early teachers of the Church; and they help us to understand the different crises, transitions and tragedies in the history of the Church. Later, he says that the entire life of the human spirit, of which religion is for him the centre, is fruitful only with a vivid and continuous sense of God and of the cross of Christ.

Von Hügel does not envisage a simplistic journey from one element to the next but an organic, developmental maturing in religious faith and experience. Each element is always accompanied by some amount of the other two and the entry into a new 'stage' never involves the complete abandonment of the preceding one. There are difficulties in making the transition from one stage to another, just as there are difficulties for human beings making transitions in other areas of life: difficulties that are educational, psychological, social, intellectual, moral and spiritual. Von Hügel envisages dangers and opportunities within, and between, people depending on how these three elements are, to a greater or lesser degree, espoused or excluded. The transition from one stage to another, or, better, to a new balance of these three elements within the person or within a community, is always marked by crisis and therefore – it is worth repeating – must live with the threat of negative, as well as the possibility of positive, outcomes.

There are what von Hügel calls 'causes operative in all religion' that will seek to minimize or suppress one or other element or even deny the need of any multiplicity. One of these is the urge to simplify, which, he believes, is always part of the religious temper. Yet every truly living unity is constituted in multiplicity. We have emphasized this here already, speaking of the necessity of structure, and therefore of multiplicity, in any living organism.

There are special motives operating in each element towards the suppression of the other two. Von Hügel says that 'the three great constituents of religion ... each in its own way, tend continually to tempt the soul to retain only *it*, and hence to an impoverishing simplification'.[13] Sitting lightly to any consistency in terminology, but explaining clearly what he wants to say, he says the 'historical and institutional element' can set itself against all else; the mystical element, now called 'the emotional and volitional', can set itself against the 'historical and institutional'; and the 'emotional and volitional', singly or in combination with the 'historical and institutional', can set itself against the 'analytic and speculative', the intellectual, element. The institutional and the mystical would then be regarded as 'the two chief constituents', so that the intellectual would be relegated to some lesser place behind the other two. It is an interesting exercise to meditate on how each of the elements might challenge the other two, or how any pair might conspire to challenge the third. It is interesting also – and illuminating – to reflect on where you are personally in regard to these three elements. How are they balanced in your life? Or in that of communities to which you belong? Or in the Church today?

ECCLESIA SANA IN CORPORE SANO?

A healthy religious person or community will be one in which these three elements are in their proper balance. This is von Hügel's proposal, supported by its roots in the work of John Henry

Newman and further developed and applied by, for example, Karl Rahner (1904–84) and Nicholas Lash. Applying his analysis to the Catholic Church, then it too will be healthy when these three elements or forces are present and operative, keeping each other in their proper balance. Even if we do not accept von Hügel's philosophical analysis we can still say this, because it is based in the first place not on that analysis but on what we have seen about the threefold office of Christ as king, prophet and priest. Von Hügel himself links the institutional, intellectual and mystical elements of religion and the threefold office or role of Christ, and we have simply followed him here on this point.

It is also a better way of thinking about the Church than an approach based on various 'models of the Church'. One of the reasons for this is that the 'models' approach, almost inevitably, will pull people towards choosing among the models on offer, comparing and contrasting them in order to decide which is better and which is best. With the approach of von Hügel, however, you must accept all three elements. There is no pressure to choose, any more than there would be pressure to choose between the circulation of the blood and the nervous system, between the skeleton and the brain, between the times of childhood, adolescence and adulthood, if what we are thinking about is the healthy body and the healthy human being. On the contrary: if any one of his three elements prevails over the others, or if any two of them prevail over the third, in such a way as to distort their proper relationship, then the reality becomes unbalanced and there are problems.

We can return to the Corinthian letters of Saint Paul and see in them that there were already tensions threatening a proper balance of these elements. The threats to Paul on one side came from 'Judaizers', moved by the pull of the institutional, by concern for the law and for tradition. Threats to Paul on the other side came from Hellenistic-Jewish 'spirit people', people feeling the pull of the mystical and the charismatic, joined it seems by those given to the pursuit of wisdom and knowledge. We see it in the cries of these different groups. From one side we hear, 'I belong to Cephas (Peter)' (for the law, the tradition, the institutional) and from the other, 'I belong to Apollos' (the philosophical, the mystical, the intellectual). The problem was not the absence of any of the elements but some loss of the correct proportion and relationship between them. The challenge was to do justice to the truth of each of them, keeping them all present and in their proper relationship.

To what did the cry 'I belong to Paul' refer (1 Cor. 1.12)? Was he obliged, against one group, to stress the mystical and active, the liberating power of the Spirit, the element they were neglecting? Was he obliged, against the other group, to talk up the practical and the pastoral, the fact that we are called to live together as one body taking account also of the sensitivities of our neighbours? Was he defending the prophetic, intellectual element against a stress on either the institutional represented by Cephas or the mystical represented by Apollos? He is clearly uncomfortable not only with what they were saying and doing, but also with how they were evaluating him and where they were positioning him along this theological spectrum.

'I belong to Christ' is the cry Paul wants to hear from all of them. Was Paul crucified for you? Were you baptized in the name of Paul? Is Christ divided? (1 Cor. 1.10-13). You are still in the flesh, he says, as long as you are dividing things up in this way and assigning different elements to different church leaders. You are still infants in Christ, failing to grow to maturity in this faith, because you are dividing things that ought to be kept together under the single headship of Christ (1 Cor. 3.1-11, 21-22). Paul does not add 'Christ who is priest, prophet and king', but it would not be inappropriate to add it, for it is another way of saying what he does say, referring everything to Christ. If another Jesus is preached, a different spirit embraced, another gospel accepted, then there are inevitably problems (2 Cor. 11.4).

What he does say is that he decided to know nothing among them in their arguments and their divisions 'except Jesus Christ and him crucified' (1 Cor. 2.2). This is a stumbling block for the Jew – 'Cursed be every one that hangs on a tree', the old law had said (Deut. 21.23) – and it is foolishness for the Greek – witness the reaction of the intellectuals at Athens to Paul's preaching of Jesus's death and resurrection just before he arrived in Corinth (Acts 17). He returns to the same issues elsewhere, challenging on the one side those who would take away the freedom for which Christ has set us free (Gal. 5.1) and on the other those who would abuse that freedom by using it for anything less than love (Gal. 5.13-14).

For Paul the various distortions already taking place were ways in which the cross of Jesus was being emptied of its meaning and of its purpose, people finding their salvation in ways other than through that mystery, through law and tradition and institution on one side, through mysticism and philosophy on the other. 'But we preach Christ crucified,' he says, 'to those who are called, the power of God and the wisdom of God' (1 Cor. 1.23-24). For von Hügel the life of the human spirit is centred on religion, and religion remains fruitful through a vivid and continuous sense of God and of the cross of Christ. In this he is simply translating and transmitting the message of the gospel, from Paul and from Jesus: the cross is also the key that unlocks the mystery, revealing most fully those privileges of knowledge, power and endurance of which Newman spoke.

Somebody once said that Carl Gustav Jung did for the number 4 what Sigmund Freud did for sex – he found in it the key to all the mysteries of human experience. We might be in danger of doing the same with the number 3, becoming perhaps a little mesmerized by it. Is the idea of a threefold nature of the Church not somewhat arbitrary? Who is Friedrich von Hügel in any case and what authority does his way of thinking have? His account of the elements of religion is undoubtedly very interesting. It is a kind of anthropology and a kind of psychology, another way of thinking about the Church as a human reality. As such it is also potentially very useful for thinking about the health of the Church. But the real force of his approach comes from its association with the Bible's teaching about Christ as priest, prophet and king. The Messiah has these three offices and so too the life and activity of the messianic people takes this shape and has these characteristics, a threefold nature that the Church has as the body of Christ.

It has become popular in some places to speak about the fundamental tasks of the Church as (using the Greek terms) *kerygma*, *leitourgia* and *diakonia*, or proclamation, liturgy and service. It is easy to see how these continue the same threefold pattern: the proclamation is the prophetic aspect of the Church's life, the liturgical is its priestly aspect, and the service of its members and of all men and women is its 'royal' aspect in the sense of seeking to build the kingdom of God in human history.

In the next three chapters we will look more closely at each of these aspects of the Church's life, beginning with what we can call the Petrine aspect, the Church as a hierarchically organized institution; continuing with the Pauline aspect, the Church as a prophetic presence in human history; and finally considering the Church in its Johannine aspect, as a communion of love – where we will see that something further needs to be added, for Jesus entrusted the beloved disciple to the care of his mother and this is taken to mean that the Church will always also have a Marian aspect.

7

AUTHORITY, SERVICE AND LEADERSHIP

A story goes around about Jeremiah Newman, Bishop of Limerick in the 1970s, that in explaining Vatican II's preference for describing the Church as the people of God he said it meant that 'everybody in the diocese is equal, from me down'. The 'from me down' might be received with a chuckle or it might be taken to reveal the irredeemably hierarchical, authoritarian (later patriarchal) character of the institution that is the Catholic Church. It seems like another 'no brainer' when one thinks of Catholicism: think hierarchy, think authority tending to authoritarian and paternal tending to patriarchal.

The decision of Vatican II to speak first of the Church as the people of God (*LG*, Chapter 2) and only then of the Church as hierarchical (*LG*, Chapter 3) was regarded as a big deal at the time. Nowadays that ordering of things seems so obvious that one wonders what the fuss was about. But the term 'hierarchy' continues to have a particular association with the governmental structure of the Catholic Church and, where it originally meant something like a network of relationships, it has come to be used almost exclusively of one level in a network, in this case 'the bishops'.

There are hierarchies everywhere in life, although the term is not necessarily used everywhere. Any institution or major project undertaken collaboratively by human beings requires lines of authority, leadership, responsibility and accountability. If the institution is to flourish and the project is to be accomplished then there have to be such structures. The structures themselves can vary and the lines of accountability and responsibility can be organized in many different ways, but some such lines are indispensable. Workplaces, hospitals, schools and colleges, banks and supermarkets, families and societies and communities – any sharing of life and any common endeavour requires some hierarchy, a distribution of responsibility and a delegation of decision-making power. If it is not done, then what happens will be decided by the ones who shout the loudest and who bully the most.

In Chapter 4 we saw that embodiment implies both life and structure, and in the last chapter we saw how religion too must include a political, institutional element. Christ is a priest and a prophet, but he is also a 'king' and the domain of his influence is referred to as a 'kingdom'. We cannot immediately jump to any particular conclusions from that, for he is a very peculiar kind of king indeed. But we can say that if, among the apostles, Peter, Paul and John represent the elements of religion identified by John Henry Newman and the others, and link that with Jesus's roles as king, prophet and priest, then this present chapter is under the guidance of Saint Peter, the one to whom Jesus entrusted the keys of his kingdom.

But first back to Thomas Aquinas. He offers an interesting way of beginning to think about hierarchy, authority and articulation within the body of Catholicism. Always ready to ask the most radical question first, in his *Summa theologiae* (= *ST*) he considers whether it is even appropriate that there should be a diversity of offices (*officia*) or of states of life (*status*) in the Church.[1] Why should there be such a diversity? In the second article of *ST* II.II 183 he gives three reasons why it should be so.

In the first place, he says, there needs to be diversity for the perfection of the Church. There is a fullness of grace in Christ, but in him it is simple and unified whereas in the Church it is diversified. He compares it with how the goodness of God is simple and unified in itself but diversified across the creation. The whole array of the created world manifests the glory of

God, each thing manifesting some aspect of that glory, from the humming bird to the giraffe, and from the Pacific Ocean to the planet Jupiter. In a similar way, the grace that is concentrated in Christ is spread across the community of the Church in a variety of offices, states and – Aquinas now adds – activities. He refers to Ephesians 4 in support of this: the grace that is one and full in Christ is given to individual men and women according to the measure of Christ's gift (Eph. 4.7), meaning in practice that 'some are apostles, some prophets, some evangelists, some pastors and teachers' (Eph. 4.11).

The second reason for diversity is in order to serve the actions that are necessary for the life of the Church. Things need to be done, and they will be done more quickly and without confusion if responsibility for doing them is shared around. The text he relies on for this point is in Romans 12: 'as in one [human] body we have many members and all the members do not have the same function', so in the Church, which is one body in Christ, there are many members 'having gifts that differ according to the grace given to each one' (Rom. 12.4-6).

The third reason for diversity is for the dignity and beauty of the Church, which consists in a certain order. In the classical definition of beauty, order or harmony is one of its essential characteristics, but there is no order or harmony unless there are parts to be ordered and to be brought into harmony. The reference by Aquinas to 2 Timothy 2.20 is perhaps surprising – it says that 'in a great house there are not only vessels of gold and silver but also of wood and earthenware', and it continues by encouraging us to ensure that we will be vessels for noble use. The second biblical reference he gives is even more surprising, for it is to the First Book of the Kings, where we read that the sumptuous beauty of the court of King Solomon left the Queen of Sheba breathless: 'when she had observed all the wisdom of Solomon, the house that he had built, the food of his table, the seating of his officials, and the attendance of his servants, their clothing, his valets, and his burnt-offerings that he offered at the house of the Lord, there was no more spirit in her' (1 Kgs 10.4-5).

She was overcome by the variegated beauty of it all. For Aquinas it is a text that is useful for meditating on variety and beauty in the Church's life.

We have already considered Aquinas's commentaries on some of the texts in which Saint Paul speaks about unity and variety in the body of Christ. The one does not threaten the other, Aquinas says, and he returns to this point here in replying to various objections. Unity is not threatened where it is established on faith, charity and mutual service (*ST* II.II 183, 2 ad 1; Aquinas refers to Eph. 4.16). A body by definition has a diversity of parts, and so too in the case of the Church there will be kinds of diversity, which he now names as offices (*officia*), states (*status*) and grades (*gradus*: *ST* II.II 183, 2 ad 2). In spite of this diversity and variety the peace of the Church is maintained by the Holy Spirit (*ST* II.II 183, 2 ad 3; Aquinas refers to Eph. 4.3 and 1 Cor. 12.24-25).

What, then, is the basis for the distinction Aquinas makes between offices, states and grades? He considers that question in the following article, *ST* II.II 183, 3. He returns to the point that the Church's perfection requires different states, the actions it needs to do require different offices, and the beauty or adornment of the Church requires different grades. Ecclesiastical orders are especially distinguished, he says, according to diverse offices (*ST* II.II 183, 3 ad 3). In other words, for the different things the Church needs to do in order to express and develop its life, there needs to be a diversity of offices. But he sees two other kinds of diversity in the Church: a diversity of states for the perfection of the Church and a diversity of grades for its adornment. If we say that the kingly applies to the actions or to the government the Church needs, we can say that the prophetic applies to the perfection or full integrity of the Church, and that the priestly applies to the holiness of the Church in its life of prayer and sacrifice. Diversity of offices refers to government and organization. Diversity of states refers to vocations and ways of living. Diversity of grades refers to the degrees to which individual members of the Church live out the life of the gospel and grow in holiness. We can therefore detect in Aquinas's distinction of grades, states and offices the by now familiar biblical triad of priest, prophet and king about which he speaks more explicitly in other parts of his writings.

PUTTING HIERARCHY IN ITS PLACE

From what Aquinas says it is clear that even within the Church there is not just one hierarchy to be thought about, the hierarchy of offices, but at least two others: a hierarchy of what he calls states and a hierarchy of what he calls grades. Aquinas himself immediately points out that there can be overlap between these different varieties of gifts – such that a person who has an office (a bishop, say) may also live in a particular state (in the early Church he would have been married, in modern times bishops are celibate) and adorn the Church with a particular grade of holiness (he is a holy man or perhaps not so holy). Recalling this should help to loosen up a bit our thinking about hierarchy, in order to contextualize the particular understanding that is normally associated with the word. The almost exclusive link between jurisdiction in the Church and the ministerial priesthood raises a number of important questions, not least concerning the fact that the other kinds of diversity do not often register in people's minds as the important kinds of distinction in the structured life of the Church that they are. They refer to states of life and to degrees of holiness, and the absence of either would make of the Church a much poorer if not in fact a deformed body.

It seems as if the term 'hierarchy', meaning a 'sacred order', was invented by a Greek-speaking Syrian monk of the sixth century who published his writings under the name of one of Saint Paul's converts, Dionysius the Areopagite, mentioned in Acts 17.34. Because of this pious fraud, associating his writings with the era of the apostles, the writings of this anonymous monk took on a much greater authority than they would otherwise have gained. They proved to be hugely influential in Greek and later when translated into Latin, and influenced very significantly some of the great medieval theologians, including Aquinas, as well as most of the medieval and early modern spiritual and mystical writers (Eckhart and John of the Cross, for example), the author of *The Cloud of Unknowing*, and even the creators of masterpieces of Gothic architecture, who were also inspired by this anonymous author's consideration of the themes of light and darkness, mystery and revelation.

Pseudo-Dionysius, as he is now known, applied the term 'hierarchy' first to the relationships between the choirs of angels. Taking up biblical texts that refer to different groups of angelic beings – angels, archangels, principalities, dominions, powers, authorities, thrones, cherubim, seraphim – Pseudo-Dionysius gathered them into 'choirs' and set out to explain the mutual relationships between the different choirs. The lower choirs depend on the higher ones, he said, who mediate to them the light that they in turn receive from higher choirs. Thus, the notion of hierarchy is itself unavoidably hierarchical in our modern sense of the word: it is about higher and lower, up and down, service and dependence. (Can we imagine a seraph saying 'every spirit in these choirs is equal, from me down'?!) But an aspect of it that we may fail to see is that a hierarchy isolated from its above or from its below becomes meaningless. The term no longer applies because part of its original significance is closer to what we would include in a term like 'network'. It is a network in which each level constitutes the other: if the parent makes the child, the child also makes the parent; if the teacher somehow enlightens the student, the student somehow makes the teacher. The relationship is always mutual and the meaning of each level is only secured through its relationship with the levels above it and below it.

Pseudo-Dionysius uses another device that was also to become universal in later theology and spirituality: the idea of three stages of spiritual enlightenment – those of beginners, of people becoming proficient and of people achieving some kind of perfection. This allowed him to distinguish levels within the choirs of angels and to speak about the ways in which they depend on and strengthen each other. He then applied these ideas of hierarchy and stages of enlightenment to the community of the Church, in a work that speaks in this way of clerics, monks and those being initiated, as well as of the sacraments of Baptism, Eucharist and Anointing. Aquinas for his part applies the stages of enlightenment in the first place not to the hierarchy of office holders in the Church but to the hierarchies of grades or states – from which, of course, those holding offices are not excluded.

It seems reasonable to propose, then, that we think of three hierarchies in the Church: one of office holders, one of different states of life and one of grades of holiness. Can we make a further move and speak also of three *magisteria* in the Church, meaning three centres of authority in teaching and witnessing to the Christian faith? Just as the term hierarchy tends to be limited in use to the hierarchy of office holders it is normal practice to limit the use of the term *magisterium* to the teaching authority of the office holders. That use of the term is canonized, we can say, and plays an essential role in Catholic doctrine. In *Dei verbum*, for example, Vatican II's Dogmatic Constitution on Divine Revelation, the mutual relations between Scripture, Tradition and the Magisterium serve to explain the Catholic Church's understanding of how the truth revealed by God in Jesus Christ finds its way to you and to me.

To speak of a *magisterium* of theologians in the Church has, in fact, often been done. This refers to the authority to teach the truth revealed by God in Jesus Christ that belongs to those who give themselves to the study of that truth. Aquinas uses the term to refer to both teaching bodies: the *magisterium* of pastors and the *magisterium* of teachers. The question of the relationship between the two *magisteria*, that of the office holders in the Church and that of the theologians, has received a number of sustained considerations in recent decades.[2] Once again, these two categories are not mutually exclusive, since some theologians become bishops and presumably all bishops rely on theologians to advise and guide them in their teaching work. When push comes to shove, Catholic theologians will agree with Aquinas that there is no competition between these two *magisteria* and that the right to judge definitively in matters of doctrine belongs, in the end, to the *magisterium* of the pastors.

Office holders have authority, then, and so also do theologians and others whose expertise and commitment places them in particular states of life within the Church. It is perhaps less usual to think of a third *magisterium* in the Church, a third hierarchy. This would be the hierarchy, with its accompanying authority, of those men and women who are simply holy, the saints, people living the message and the life of the gospel in ways that are proficient and even perfect. Their knowledge of God and their wisdom about life may have come to them along a different route to that of the office holder or the theologian. But they speak from what Aquinas calls a 'connatural' knowledge of divine realities, as people attuned to those realities, who not only know about them but who, through their lives of faith, prayer and charity, have experienced those divine realities in a more direct and immediate way.

It is appropriate to mention here a group of women who belong to two of these hierarchies: that of the theologians and that of the saints. These are Hildegard of Bingen (1098–1179), Catherine of Siena (1347–80), Teresa of Avila (1515–82) and Thérèse of Lisieux (1873–97), Doctors of the Church. These women are renowned for their understanding of the faith as well as for their living of it, and their writings continue to exercise significant influence in many areas of thought and experience. Edith Stein (1891–1942) might perhaps join them some day and she has already been canonized as Saint Teresa Benedicta of the Cross. Other women to exercise very significant influence in Catholic life and beyond are Frances Cabrini (1850–1917), Saint Teresa of Calcutta (1910–97) and Dorothy Day (1897–1980), along with any number of foundresses of religious congregations that have worked extensively in education, health and pastoral care in every part of the world, particularly on behalf of the poor and of women. Many women grace these two hierarchies, then: those of theological wisdom and holiness of life.

So king, prophet and priest might be aligned, by some analogy, with bishop, theologian and saint as we have aligned them also with Aquinas's offices, states and grades. The points to be stressed here are, first, that we can identify a variety of hierarchies within the life of the Church (once more stressing that a particular individual might belong to two or even to all three) and, second, that the term hierarchy in its origins has something of the meaning of 'network' and therefore implies mutual relations. George Talbot, a Rome-based enemy of John Henry Newman, objected to his work on consulting the faithful in matters of doctrine. The laity's job, Talbot famously said, was to hunt, shoot and entertain. An English bishop, more well-disposed but still concerned by Newman's work, asked him rhetorically, 'Who are the laity?', to which Newman replied that 'the Church would look foolish without them'. The story illustrates well the point being made here: that hierarchy implies a network of mutual dependence and relationship. We have simply added the further thought that it is helpful to remember that there is more than one hierarchy within the life of the Church.

MANY GIFTS, MINISTRIES AND TASKS

This variety of hierarchies can be seen already in 1 Corinthians 12–14, three chapters that contain the fullest consideration by Saint Paul of the various gifts Christ gives to his body, the Church. We see there the foundation on which later Church teaching and theological reflection based their understanding. 1 Corinthians 12 deals with the gifts of the office holders. 1 Corinthians 13, the best known of these chapters, considers 'the way that is better than any other', the way of love, the gift *par excellence* of Christian holiness. 1 Corinthians 14 deals with certain more unusual charismatic gifts such as prophecy, interpretation of prophecy and *glossolalia* or the gift of tongues.

In 1 Corinthians 12 Paul spells out, in more detail than he does anywhere else, what the metaphor of the body means. He prefaces this explication with a summary of what is found in other places in his letters – there is one Spirit, one Lord, and one God, but a variety of gifts, of services or ministries, and of workings or actions. It is all for the common good, and a first list given here begins with wisdom and then names knowledge, faith, healing, miracles, prophecy, discernment of spirits, tongues and the interpretation of tongues (1 Cor. 12.4-11). Just as the body is one and many, so Christ is one and many. By one Spirit all are baptized into one body, in which there is multiplicity and diversity, and all drink of one Spirit, by which there is unity and integrity (1 Cor. 12.12-13).

In the following section, 1 Cor. 12.14-26, Paul says that a body needs members and no member can say of itself 'I am not needed', just as no member can say of any other member 'you are not needed'. A single organ is not a body because it has just one function; a body needs to be able to perform many functions. In fact, parts of the body that are more vulnerable, or that are considered less honourable, are treated with greater care and modesty. It is all so arranged by God, Paul says, that there is no discord between different parts of the body. Not only that, but the members also have a care not just for themselves but for all the other members as well. If one member is in pain, the body is in pain. If one member is honoured, the body is honoured.

'You are the body of Christ and individually members of it' (1 Cor. 12.27). This introduces a second list, this time a list of functions or offices, some new and some overlapping with the one given earlier: apostles, prophets, teachers, workers of miracles, healers, helpers, administrators, speakers in various kinds of tongues. The questions that follow apply what had been said already about the organs of the body: are all apostles, or all prophets, or all teachers, etc.? Is the body only a hand, or a foot, or an eye, etc.? (1 Cor. 12.27-30). But earnestly desire the higher gifts, Paul concludes, from where he begins to speak about the 'still more excellent way', which is love, the supreme gift (1 Cor. 12.31–13.13).

Aquinas highlights the role of the Holy Spirit in relation to the body. He sees it in the distinction made in 1 Cor. 12.4-6 where 'Spirit', 'Lord' and 'God' might refer to the distinct Persons of the Trinity – Spirit, Son and Father – or might be understood instead as being entirely about the Holy Spirit, who is also referred to as Lord and God. It may be because Paul speaks here of 'spiritual (gifts)', *pneumatika*, that Aquinas moves in this pneumatological direction, to highlight the work of the Holy Spirit as the Divine Person to whom is appropriated the work of establishing and sustaining the Church. All gifts, Paul says, are manifestations of the Spirit for the common good: this too encourages Aquinas in the pneumatological direction.

These manifestations are seen particularly in the charismatic gifts given to particular individuals for the sake of the community, graces distinct from the sanctifying grace that is a gift given to all who belong to Christ. The charismatic gifts show the presence of the Spirit in the Church, teaching and sanctifying. In another way they show the presence of the Spirit in the particular individuals to whom these gifts are given. It explains why the gifts are here first listed as operations, Aquinas says, referring to 1 Cor. 12.8-11, and then as offices or functions, 1 Cor. 12.28-30. The term *pneumatika* used by Paul could mean either 'spiritual gifts', as it is normally translated, or 'spiritual persons'.

Paul's talk about the foot and the hand are taken by Aquinas to refer to the least noble and the most noble of limbs, the foot, which touches the ground and carries the weight of the whole body, compared with the hand, which is the 'organ of organs'. A body in its integrity must have both. In the Church this means, for Aquinas, that there must be both prelates (hands) and subjects (feet), since in any organized society power and authority must be arranged in some way between the members. A body without one or the other will lack integrity and remain incomplete.

The reference to the eye and the ear Aquinas takes to represent in the Church the contemplative and studious on the one hand and those being instructed by them on the other. Just as nature produces the organic animal body and each part has its place and its contribution to the working of the whole body, so the articulation of offices and states in the Church is the outcome of divine providence whose will it is that there should be this diversity in unity.

If all were one thing the perfection and beauty of the body would be lost. That the eye cannot say it has no need of the hand lends itself to a quick comparison for Aquinas: Mary cannot say that she does not need Martha; the contemplative side of the Church's life is sustained by the active. Nor can the head, the 'prelates', say this about the feet, the 'subjects'. It anticipates Newman's comment that the Church would look very foolish without its lay members: it would be literally footless. To think of the clergy alone making up the Church is as odd as thinking that the eye or the hand alone makes up a complete body. Aquinas moves easily to the stratified structure of medieval society, in our eyes perhaps implying inequality and hierarchy in a pejorative sense, in which a mutual dependence across the different classes is recognized but at the same time has no hesitation in regarding people as being therefore more or less noble. But the point of Paul's text, endorsed by Aquinas, is that the body under consideration cannot function properly without this diversity. And across all of this cuts the virtue of charity and the Holy Spirit's gift of wisdom, the most important criterion of nobility in the Christian kingdom, a reminder that holiness may be found anywhere and everywhere, across all distinctions of activities, offices or states.

The thing to be guarded against above all is 'discord in the body' (1 Cor. 12.25). In Aquinas's Latin, 'discord' is *schisma*, division or separation, that thing which for a Catholic sensibility is the worst of disasters. A natural body is free of discord when the proper proportions and relationships of its members with each other are in place. So too the body that is the Church: its health, integrity and unity require that the appropriate balance and relationship are maintained between the different parts in their different offices and functions. This unity is preserved in the natural body by the inclination of each organ to protect not just itself but the other organs of the body as well. In the Church it is maintained by the care that each one ought to have for each of the others.

Is Christ himself a member of the body that is the Church? In the Letters to the Ephesians and to the Colossians, Christ is spoken of as the head of the body (we will consider the meaning of this more fully in Chapter 10). Here Paul says simply, 'You are the body of Christ and individually members of it' (1 Cor. 12.27). Aquinas's Latin has *membra de membro*, one interpretation of which could be that each member of the Church is such from his or her belonging to that member who is Christ, the head of the body. This is Christ in his humanity, Aquinas is quick to point out, since in his divinity he is not a member or a part of anything but rather the common good of the whole universe. Linked with this is the unusual phrase Paul uses in Romans 12.5, saying that we are 'individually members of one another'. In commenting on that phrase Aquinas says that whenever one member of the Church serves another by the gift of grace that they have received, they are said to be members of that other who is thus served, and he refers to Galatians 6.2 and 1 Peter 4.10 in support of this.

This leads, then, to the second list of spiritual gifts, now described as functions or offices, referring to the persons to whom those responsibilities have been entrusted rather than to the responsibilities themselves. Apostles come first with the threefold responsibility that the New Testament assigns to them: governing, teaching and working miracles to confirm that teaching (see, for example, Mk 16.20; Lk. 9.1-2; 22.25; Jn 15.16). As he does elsewhere, Aquinas speaks of the apostolic responsibilities being shared in by others who were not members of the original apostolic college. In the first place there are prophets and then other teachers: these are 'taken into the communion of the apostolic office', he says. Workers of miracles and healers also share in an aspect of the apostolic office: that of confirming the word of the Church's preaching. Other ministries in the Church see to particular tasks or geographical territories – these are the 'helpers' (for Aquinas these are senior advisory clerics) and 'administrators' (for Aquinas these are parish priests or pastors).

Finally, there are those who assist with the teaching aspect of the apostolic ministry as speakers in various kinds of tongues and interpreters of tongues. 'But earnestly desire the higher gifts', Paul concludes (1 Cor. 12.31) – and here is the most excellent of all: love, *agape*, *caritas*. So the Church is apostolic, not just in its origins but in the fact that the apostolic responsibilities continue in the Church where they are undertaken in a variety of ministries (see also Eph. 4.11-12).

Fundamentally, the call is the same for every member of the Church, to follow Christ by living according to his way and so grow in holiness. This is the topic of *Lumen gentium*'s fifth chapter, the universal call to holiness. To be holy means that in our thoughts, words and actions we live out the great commandment that Jesus gave his disciples: to love God with all our heart, mind and strength, and to love our neighbour as ourselves. That is how the Gospels of Matthew, Mark and Luke summarize the great commandment (Mt. 22.34-40; Mk 12.28-34; Lk. 10.25-37), which the Gospel of John phrases in a different way: 'Love one another as I have loved you' (Jn 13.34; 15.12). Holiness simply means doing that.

OFFICE HOLDERS INVESTED WITH SACRED POWER

Power is the most difficult thing to manage in human affairs and therefore the thing in which human beings are most keenly interested. Who has power over me and why? Over whom do I have power and why? Most of what counts as news each day is connected with power: politics, of course, with elections and coups from time to time, controversies and arguments about what is best for a society, stories about corruption and conflict, the rise and fall of big names, winners and losers in the power struggles of the world. Think of how important a person is as long as they have power and of how unimportant they immediately become as soon as they no longer have that power. Think of how much energy human beings give, and the sacrifices they are prepared to make, in seeking equality and freedom, the vindication of their rights and the doing of justice, the elimination of discrimination and the promotion of fairness.

These are all about the management of power and the prevention of its corruption, how to maintain a good distribution of authority, which any organized society requires. There is usually much in the news also about money and sex, but normally in their relation to power: money at the level of power in institutions and organizations, sex at the level of power in personal relationships. The counsels Jesus gave his disciples, if they wanted to live with the same freedom as he did, are directly connected with these three realities. They concern poverty (money), chastity (sex) and obedience (power), just as the roots of sin of which the Bible speaks are directly connected with them also: the lust of the flesh or physical satisfactions, the lust of the eyes or possessing desirable things, the pride of life or being autonomously wise (Gen. 3.6; 1 Jn 2.16). What is rooted most deeply in us, in our anxieties as in our desires, is power: to have control, to remain free, to decide for ourselves.

Perhaps that is enough to explain why the hierarchy concerned with jurisdiction in the Church is the one that gets most attention. Not that this is the exclusive preoccupation of that hierarchy, at least in principle, but it is the aspect of its authority that registers most quickly with people. So, when *Lumen gentium* considers the hierarchical character of the Church, it is the 'office holders invested with sacred power' (*LG* 18) that it has in mind. Most of its third chapter deals with the office and responsibilities of the bishop. It has sometimes been said that the First Vatican Council, held in 1869–70, was the Council of the Pope, for it was there that the prerogatives of that office were solemnly defined, whereas Vatican II was the Council of the Bishop, for it gave much attention to clarifying the function and authority of bishops in the Church. Priests and deacons were acknowledged also, of course, as were lay people, and religious women and men, those members of the Church who consecrate themselves in a further way to its life as nuns, monks, friars, etc. But more energy and time was given to clarifying the role and relationships of the bishop than to any other office in the Church.

There are always hierarchies within the hierarchies, and Vatican II was concerned to explain the relationship between the bishops of the Church, as individuals and as a group, with one particular bishop, the Bishop of Rome, the Pope. Together they make up a college that succeeds to the college of the apostles and that has supreme power in the Church. For centuries there had been tensions concerning this relationship, and Vatican II sought to resolve some of those by clarifying the authority of individual bishops as well as that of the bishops as a whole united with the Pope, whether they are together in one place for a council of the Church or they are teaching together while remaining in their own places throughout the world. In a carefully worded text, every phrase of which was subjected to careful scrutiny and debate, LG 22 speaks as follows about the relationship between the bishops and the Pope:

> The order of bishops is the successor to the college of the apostles in their role as teachers and pastors, and in it the apostolic college is perpetuated. Together with their head, the Supreme Pontiff, and never apart from him, they have supreme and full authority over the universal Church ... This college, in so far as it is composed of many members, is the expression of the multifariousness and universality of the People of God; and of the unity of the flock of Christ, in so far as it is assembled under one head. In it the bishops, whilst loyally respecting the primacy and pre-eminence of their head, exercise their own proper authority for the good of their faithful, indeed even for the good of the whole Church, the organic structure and harmony of which are strengthened by the continued influence of the Holy Spirit. The supreme authority over the whole Church, which this college possesses, is exercised in a solemn way in an ecumenical council. There never is an ecumenical council which is not confirmed or at least recognized as such by Peter's successor. And it is the prerogative of the Roman

Pontiff to convoke such councils, to preside over them and to confirm them. This same collegiate power can be exercised in union with the Pope by the bishops while living in different parts of the world, provided the head of the college summon them to collegiate action, or at least approve or freely admit the corporate action of the unassembled bishops so that a truly collegiate act may result.[3]

Famously, Vatican I defined the infallibility of the Pope when, in certain circumstances, he teaches in a particular way about certain matters. At the time and since, this definition provoked strong reactions, both within and outside the Catholic Church, but one might argue that the work of that council was important precisely in determining the criteria – setting the limits, in other words – by which an infallible definition by a Pope could be recognized. What is not so often mentioned is that the Pope is not the only organ of infallible teaching in the Church. The Church as a whole teaches infallibly and so too, in certain circumstances, does the college of bishops in union with the Pope.

All of this, however, is a consequence of our faith in the Holy Spirit's active presence in the life of the Church, a faith founded on things recorded as coming from the lips of Jesus. The Holy Spirit is the Spirit of truth, Jesus says, who will bring to the remembrance of the disciples all that he taught them as well as leading them into the fullness of truth (Jn 14.26; 15.26; 16.13). The disciples are to be consecrated in the truth so that the work of God achieved in Jesus might reach all those who, through the preaching of the apostles, would come to believe in him (Jn 17.17, 20).

If we believe that God is true and that in Jesus Christ God has revealed things about himself and done things for humanity in a final and definitive way, then it is not unreasonable to think that God will also ensure the safe travel of this revelation and of this work of salvation across time and space. To believe that the Church will not ultimately lose the truth it believes to have been entrusted to it, or to believe that certain organs of the body are equipped to teach that truth infallibly, is simply to express our faith in the Holy Spirit's active presence and continuing guidance of the Church. Because it is a body there must be organs through which this presence and guidance are articulated, which is why the Church speaks of the different ways in which it believes itself to be equipped to teach infallibly. This is not through any particular achievement of its own apart from the presence and guidance of the Holy Spirit.

Dei verbum, Vatican II's Dogmatic Constitution on Divine Revelation, speaks compellingly about what has been referred to as the Church's 'indefectibility' in what it has received, the belief that in spite of the vicissitudes of history and the mistakes and corruptions of human beings, this earthen vessel will continue to carry the treasure that has been entrusted to it. *Dei verbum* 8 says this:

> the Church, in her doctrine, life and worship, perpetuates and transmits to every generation all that she herself is, all that she believes. The Tradition that comes from the apostles makes progress in the Church, with the help of the Holy Spirit. There is a growth in insight into the realities and words that are being passed on. This comes about in various ways. It comes through the contemplation and study of believers who ponder these things in their hearts (cf. Lk. 2.19, 51). It comes from the intimate sense of spiritual realities which they experience. And it comes from the preaching of those who have received, along with their right of succession in the episcopate, the sure charism of truth. Thus, as the centuries go by, the Church is always advancing towards the plenitude of divine truth, until eventually the words of God are fulfilled in her.

The need for infallibility, if we can put it like that, is based on this conviction, that the Church will be maintained in the truth by the Spirit. Thus, in *Lumen gentium* 12 we read that the Church as a whole teaches infallibly:

The whole body of the faithful who have an anointing that comes from the holy one (cf. 1 Jn 2.20, 27) cannot err in matters of belief. This characteristic is shown in the supernatural appreciation of the faith (*sensus fidei*) of the whole people, when, 'from the bishops to the last of the faithful', they manifest a universal consent in matters of faith and morals. By this appreciation of the faith, aroused and sustained by the Spirit of truth, the People of God, guided by the sacred teaching authority (*magisterium*) and obeying it, receives not the mere word of men, but truly the word of God (cf. 1 Thess. 2.13), the faith once for all delivered to the saints (cf. Jude v. 3). The People unfailingly adheres to the faith, penetrates it more deeply with right judgment, and applies it more fully in daily life.

Further on we read about the circumstances in which the college of bishops as a whole is believed to teach infallibly:

Although the bishops, taken individually, do not enjoy the privilege of infallibility, they do, however, proclaim infallibly the doctrine of Christ on the following conditions: namely, when, even though dispersed throughout the world but preserving for all that amongst themselves and with Peter's successor the bond of communion, in their authoritative teaching concerning matters of faith and morals, they are in agreement that a particular teaching is to be held definitively and absolutely. This is still more clearly the case when, assembled in an ecumenical council, they are, for the universal Church, teachers of and judges in matters of faith and morals, whose decisions must be adhered to with the loyal and obedient assent of faith. This infallibility, however, with which the divine redeemer wished to endow his Church in defining doctrine pertaining to faith and morals, is co-extensive with the deposit of revelation which must be religiously guarded and loyally and courageously expounded ... The infallibility promised to the Church is also present in the body of bishops when, together with Peter's

147

THE SPIRIT OF CATHOLICISM

successor, they exercise the supreme teaching office. (*Lumen gentium* 25)

Finally, *Lumen gentium* 18 confirms the teaching of Vatican I that in certain circumstances the Pope can teach infallibly:

[The] teaching concerning the institution, the permanence, the nature and import of the sacred primacy of the Roman Pontiff and his infallible teaching office, [is proposed] anew to be firmly believed by all the faithful.

Note that it is 'the Church's charism of infallibility' that is present in the Pope in a singular way (*LG* 25). As soon as it was defined in 1870, this teaching about papal infallibility was quickly caricatured, as if the Pope was saying he could predict the winner of next year's Grand National or understand Einstein's theory of relativity without studying physics. Even a quick look at the conditions and circumstances required for an infallible definition is enough to head off such caricatures. The Pope can do it only as pastor of the universal Church, if he has been validly elected, if he is not in heresy or schism, if he is of sound mind, and is free of coercion. It can only be about certain matters, not the results of horse races or the details of physics, but only 'doctrine pertaining to faith and morals … co-extensive with the deposit of revelation' (*LG* 25). Finally, the act itself must be clearly and evidently intended as an act of defining.

It would be strange to write about the spirit of Catholicism without mentioning the terms 'hierarchy' and 'infallibility'. We have sought to do that here by reminding ourselves of the broader context to which these terms belong as well as the subject matter with which they are concerned. Note that any community living from a scripture that it believes to be revealed will also develop a tradition of interpretation of that scripture as well as identifying some authority whose interpretation is to be regarded as authentic.

CONCLUSION

One might wonder why one particular level of hierarchy in the Church – the one that is normally referred to as 'the hierarchy' – needs to spend time defending its right to teach and to govern. Because of what we have said about power, it will be clear that people rightly want to know the basis on which other human beings claim any power or authority over them. So, the basis of that power and authority in the Church will always need to be understood and justified. Is there more to it, however? Is it a symptom of that 'clericalism' that Pope Francis identified as one of the most pressing problems for the Church to resolve? There is undoubtedly much work to be done in understanding the phenomenon of 'clericalism' and recovering a healthy sense of the ministerial priesthood serving the common priesthood of all God's people.

Hans Urs von Balthasar made an interesting observation about this, precisely in writing about why he remained a Catholic. The apostolic structure of the Church, he said, is always only visible together with its humiliation. It may be another way of referring to the fact that this treasure is carried always in earthen vessels. More deeply, though, he was referring to the fact that the apostolic office is charged in the first place with 'preaching Christ crucified' (1 Cor. 2.2), a preaching that is done not only with words but with the lived experience of the preachers' lives.[4]

A non-Catholic friend once expressed admiration for the Catholic Church's capacity to live with its 'shadow' and to do so as overtly as it does. Others might argue that its shadow is so dark and pervasive that it has little choice but to do that. Nevertheless, the Church is overt in presenting itself to the world as a social and political reality, engaged as much as any other human organization in facing the challenges that come with managing power. It is even more directly engaged in facing those challenges because its mission is to witness to a Lord whose power was revealed in the weakness of the cross and whose wisdom was seen in its foolishness (1 Cor. 1.22-24). The apostles are 'fools for Christ's sake', Paul famously says in his argument with the Corinthians about the basis of his own authority (1 Cor. 4.10), an argument that drives him to the hyperbole of claiming that the apostles are in fact 'the refuse of the world, the dregs of all things' (1 Cor. 4.13).

It is the shocking scandal of Calvary that takes our breath away rather than the splendour of Solomon's court or even the drama of a solemn Roman liturgy. While acknowledging the authority of the Church's office holders, we end by recalling the third hierarchy of which we have spoken, the third *magisterium*: that of holiness, a hierarchy in which the one who is first is the one who, in love and obedience, has made themselves last of all and servant of all (Mk 9.35).

8

TAKE ALL THOUGHT CAPTIVE

In one of his novels the Irish writer Brian Moore (1921–99) refers in passing to faith as 'reason's opposite'. It is an unfortunate expression but reflects a view that has taken serious hold in contemporary culture. Science, philosophy, reason: these are the ways to reliable knowledge. Religion, theology, faith: these are the ways to – well, to anything and everything it seems: fairies at the bottom of the garden, the Moon is made of green cheese, and the world sits on the back of a stack of giant turtles. In the spirit of Catholicism, however, faith has never been regarded as reason's opposite. Faith, on the contrary, gives reason new things to think about, fresh mysteries to stretch its limbs upon and a reach beyond anything it could have attained just by itself. On the other hand, reason has been and is of great assistance to faith. Reason helps faith to articulate more clearly the mysteries it transmits. Reason prepares the way for faith through thinking about the world, about human nature and about the first causes of things. Reason accompanies faith every step of the way since faith remains restless, never fully content intellectually. Our hearts are restless until they rest in God, Augustine says. Our minds are also restless: in faith we assent while continuing to cogitate, Aquinas says.

There have been moments, and they are quickly recalled, when the triad religion-theology-faith has exercised a mistaken supervisory control over science-philosophy-reason. The case of Galileo is the most famous of these and it cannot be forgotten. On the other hand, there have been many more moments in which religion-theology-faith has encouraged reason, promoted science and even helped philosophy to develop. The latter point has been made by a philosopher, Anthony Kenny, who, in his history of Western philosophy, shows how the need among the Christians of the first centuries to develop a language for their new doctrines, and to strengthen the intellectual foundation of those doctrines, drove important developments in philosophy itself.

Much work is still being done by philosophers and theologians concerning the rationality of faith and even concerning the meaning of rationality itself. Some ways of understanding what it means to be rational sell the human being short, failing to take account, for example, of the moral and aesthetic dimensions of the human being's engagement with the world, or of the unavoidable situatedness of the human being (we can never have a view 'from nowhere'). One of John Paul II's most important encyclical letters was on the question of the relationship between faith and reason, which he describes in the encyclical's first sentence as two wings on which the human spirit rises to the contemplation of truth (*Fides et ratio*, n. 1).

To some it might seem ridiculous to claim not only that religion-theology-faith is not opposed to science-philosophy-reason but also that it actually champions them, but it is undeniably the case. From the beginning, Catholic Christianity was a defender and promoter of learning, emerging as it did within well-established traditions of Hebrew, Greek and Roman thought. There were always voices from within to raise doubts – what has Athens to do with Jerusalem, the second-century African theologian Tertullian famously asked – but these voices never prevailed. A slightly tongue-in-cheek book called *How the Irish Saved Civilization*[1] reminds us that at a crucial moment it was Irish (and British) monks who preserved a large part of ancient Latin culture and even brought it back to illuminate the continental 'dark ages' when they were in danger of losing it. From monastic schools to cathedral schools to the emergence of the university – these were all church institutions that encouraged the preservation of knowledge, the cultivation of learning and the pursuit of wisdom.

The twelfth century already saw a renaissance in Europe with the arrival of many ancient texts translated either from Greek or Arabic. These were not exclusively theological or even philosophical texts, but knowledge about everything, astronomy, music, medicine and so on. The beginnings of modern science can be seen in the work of medieval scholars like William of Conches, Hildegard of Bingen, Robert Grosseteste and Albert the Great, and who can deny that the 'founding fathers' of modernity – people like Descartes and Newton – were people living within the same atmosphere of learning and research encouraged by religion and faith?

PAUL'S ANTI-RHETORICAL RHETORIC

At the same time there are some texts in the New Testament that might be taken as encouraging a kind of anti-intellectualism, as if faith were purely a matter of will-power, some kind of blind leap into the darkness, a trust without sound reason. Tertullian has already been mentioned. His question – what has Athens to do with Jerusalem? In other words, what have science and philosophy to do with theology and faith? – is one that has been raised again from time to time. It seems as if the official line of 'modern culture' is that faith and reason are not just distinct but opposed domains – what has MIT to do with Rome? – an opposition that would lead to radical loss for both.

What are the texts in the New Testament that might support an anti-intellectual stance? Well, Jesus himself thanks his heavenly Father for hiding 'these things' from the learned and the clever and revealing them instead to infants (Mt. 11.25; Lk. 10.21). Elsewhere he encourages his disciples to become like little children (Mt. 18.3-4; 19.13-14; Mk 10.13-15; Lk. 18.16-17), meaning, it seems, to be humble and to have a kind of innocent trust that seems to exclude, at least in relation to 'these things', critical questions and hard intellectual work. In the Gospel of John, Jesus addresses his disciples as 'children' (Jn 21.5) and even as 'little children' (13.33). In response to criticism of how young people were excitedly welcoming him on his entry to Jerusalem, Jesus quoted Psalm 8.2: 'Out of the mouth of babes and sucklings you have brought perfect praise' (Mt. 21.16).

The terms for 'child' or 'infant' are used frequently in Paul's letters: all who believe in Christ are 'God's children' (Rom. 8.14-21; Gal. 4.28, 31; Eph. 5.1, 8; Phil. 2.15). Not only that, on occasion Paul refers to his correspondents as his own children (1 Cor. 4.14; 2 Cor. 6.13; Gal. 4.19) whom he has cared for as would a nurse or a father (1 Thess. 2.7, 11). He speaks about and even addresses Timothy, Titus and Onesimus as his children (1 Cor. 4.17; 1 Tim. 1.2, 18; 2 Tim. 1.2; 2.1; Tit. 1.4; Phlm. 10). The author of the First Letter of John also addresses his readers as 'children' (2.14, 18) and often as 'little children' (2.1, 12, 28; 3.7, 18; 4.4; 5.21). Paul is not the only New Testament author to speak of his converts as little children who are as yet unable for solid food, needing to be fed for the moment on milk (1 Cor. 3.1-2; 1 Pet. 2.2; and Heb. 5.13).

This chapter is under the guidance of Saint Paul as the last one was under the guidance of Saint Peter. Paul, however, not only regards his addressees as children, he seems at times also to disdain human learning in favour of a knowledge and wisdom that are sourced exclusively in faith. Knowledge puffs up, he says to the Corinthians, whereas love builds up (1 Cor. 8.1-3). 'When I came to you', he tells them in the same letter, 'it was not with any show of oratory or philosophy.' 'I was with you in fear and trembling,' he goes on, 'and my speech and message were not in plausible words of wisdom but in demonstration of the Spirit and of power, that your faith might not rest in the wisdom of men but in the power of God' (1 Cor. 2.1-5). The wisdom of this world is folly with God (1 Cor. 3.19). The weapons of our warfare, he writes in his Second Letter to the Corinthians, are not merely human but have divine power to destroy strongholds: 'we destroy arguments and every proud obstacle raised up against the knowledge of God, and we take every thought captive to obey Christ' (2 Cor. 10.3-6).

We could continue, but it is enough to make the point for now: an anti-intellectual interpretation of the gospel and of faith will find texts in the New Testament that seem to support it. It can bring together the preference of Jesus for a childlike response of faith, texts that speak of the poor and uneducated entering the kingdom before the sophisticated and the powerful, the fact that his apostles quickly click into a paternal attitude towards their fellow disciples, and Paul's series of comments that describe worldly wisdom as worthless by comparison with what is learned through faith: it all seems to strengthen Tertullian's question: what can Athens offer that could compare with what we receive from Jerusalem?

To be childlike, preachers will quickly tell us, does not mean to be childish. In a recent analysis of the collapse of Irish Catholicism, one of the reasons given for that collapse is the infantilizing textbooks through which the generation that is now adult were taught the faith when they were children. Children themselves do not want to be infantilized, never mind adults. Perhaps some catechetical programmes were so effectively adapted for younger children that their content and purpose seemed to belong only to the same stage of development as Thomas the Tank-Engine and Postman Pat – to be appreciated when we are children but left behind when we move on to serious study and face the demands of adult living.

It is clear from other passages in the Gospels, however, that Jesus wants adult disciples, people ready to shoulder the cross, to put their backs to the plough and to get down to the serious work of building his kingdom. The attitude of trust and humility necessary to enter that kingdom is best learned from Jesus himself, who is also described as the son and even as the child of God: it is from him that we ought to learn what he means when he tells us to be childlike. It clearly does not exclude the strength of courage, perseverance, generosity and love that characterized his life. Paul's comments contrasting God's foolishness with human wisdom are mainly in a particular context in which an intellectual group of Christian believers regarded themselves as superior by their wisdom and knowledge to other believers who were not so gifted. Paul is calling them back to the fundamental and universal need of all human beings for love and for the kind of enlightenment, accompaniment, forgiveness and healing that can only come through loving and being loved. Pride is one of the greatest obstacles to acknowledging that need, a pride that is easily solidified by the kinds of ability and achievement that the world rightly values but that, in the fuller context of the human situation, are never adequate to address the most radical needs that we have.

There are other texts in which the New Testament writers encourage us to be students, to undertake research, to develop arguments, to grow in our intellectual ability and understanding, and so to place everything at the service of Christ's kingdom of justice, love and truth. The First Letter of Peter tells us to be ready to give reasons for our hope (1 Pet. 3.15). Paul says we are to offer God a rational worship, our minds transformed and renewed (Rom. 12.1), and we are to have the mind of Christ (Phil. 2.5; 1 Cor. 2.16), which, once again, refers primarily to the moral and spiritual dimensions of human intelligence.

Paul himself is a bit of a contradiction, for in his writing he reaches heights of rhetorical power even, and particularly, in the many passages in which he seeks to downplay his own natural intellectual abilities. We have seen these more than once already: passages in the Corinthian letters where he stresses his own weakness and impotence as well as the foolishness of human wisdom and the poverty of human strength. He does it in powerful words that constitute some of the most stunning writings from the ancient world. Like other New Testament authors, he is well able to marshal rabbinic-style arguments, for he was trained not only in the Hellenistic schools of Tarsus but also in the Jewish schools of Jerusalem. He has been compared to Seneca for his moral teaching and to Gamaliel for his use of scripture. Not only is his style of writing rhetorically powerful but his mastery of sarcasm and irony is also nothing less than brilliant.

Clearly the call to become like little children is a call to develop certain moral and spiritual dispositions, to remain humble and trusting in relation to God, gentle and reverent in how we relate to others, even in argument (1 Pet. 3.15; 1 Cor. 13.4-7). In challenging those who regard themselves as superior in knowledge and wisdom, Paul hints that he does not want his converts to remain children for ever (1 Cor. 3.1-3). 'When I was a child,' he says of himself, 'I spoke like a child, I thought like a child, I reasoned like a child: when I became a man, I gave up childish ways' (1 Cor. 13.11). 'In thinking, be mature', he adds later (1 Cor. 14.20). They are to grow up and become adult in their faith, strong and wise in facing the challenges of life (Eph. 6.10-20). The Letter to the Hebrews says that solid food is for the mature, 'for those who have their faculties trained by practice to distinguish good from evil' (Heb. 5.14). For the mature we do impart a wisdom, Paul says, 'a secret and hidden wisdom of God which is revealed through the Holy Spirit' (1 Cor. 2.6-13). Grown up intellectually, they are to stand confident and secure, no longer infants tossed and blown about by every wind of doctrine (Eph. 4.14).

The call to holiness extends as much to the scientist and the philosopher as it does to the theologian or the priest. The knowledge, understanding and wisdom of which Jesus and Paul speak when they refer to things hidden from the clever and from human wisdom, things now revealed to 'mere children', are the divine things that none of us come to know except through encountering Jesus Christ and coming to believe in him. This is as true for the philosopher and scientist as it is for the theologian or priest. It is not so much about how people conduct research and pursue their studies as about how people live, which obviously includes the integrity with which they conduct research and study. Members of any profession can pursue their search for the truth accessible through their profession in a way that blocks access to the wisdom of God revealed in the cross. In the same way, members of any profession can live their lives – including their life of research and study – in a way that leaves them open to the wisdom of God revealed in the cross.

Any truth, no matter by whom it is said, is from the Holy Spirit: this was a saying handed down to the Middle Ages of which Thomas Aquinas was particularly fond. He had the strongest possible sense of the objectivity of the truth – it is strong in itself, he says, and nothing can prevail against it. This conviction enabled him to live with exceptional freedom and courage in his pursuit of the truth. There is no need to be defensive of the truth in a fundamentalist way – that is always a sign of a weak hold on the truth, a hold that is shrill and empty. The wisdom that comes from above, on the other hand, brings confidence in the objectivity of the truth as something beyond us and ahead of us. We can therefore serve the truth with courage and freedom. The Letter of James tells us that such wisdom is pure and peaceable, gentle and open to reason, full of mercy and good fruits, without uncertainty or insincerity (Jas 3.17). What about taking that as a list of the objectives of any teacher-training or pedagogical formation, not just in those disciplines that are closer to religion-theology-faith, but in any discipline whatsoever in any of the many ways in which science-philosophy-reason undertake research and seek truth?

THE LOVE OF LEARNING AND THE DESIRE FOR GOD

It is clear from its history that Catholic Christianity has never followed the 'anti-intellectual' interpretation of the New Testament texts we have just considered. The heir of Jewish, Greek and Roman traditions of education, as already noted, it was helped further in the early Middle Ages by resources and methods coming to it also from Islam. Some centuries later it encountered the great cultural traditions of India, China and Japan, and there were always Catholic scholars keen to be in dialogue with the teachers of these philosophical and religious traditions.

The encounter of religion-theology-faith with science-philosophy-reason has never been without tension and sometimes conflict. Academics will not be surprised, familiar as they are with tension and conflict even within the boundaries of a single discipline, working with an agreed subject matter and an agreed methodology. It is inherent in the nature of faith itself that there is room for disagreement in the interpretation of whatever evidence is put forward in support of it. In the time of Aquinas, the objection was raised by some that his project of putting the resources of pagan philosophy at the service of Christian theology meant he was 'watering down' the faith. On the contrary, he replied, far from watering down the faith what it means is turning water into wine, giving the water of philosophy a fresh direction and depth through its collaboration with theology. At the same time, he stresses that philosophy has its own way to truth and this must be respected, pointing out that if the philosophical arguments offered in support of the faith are clearly inadequate, it is not sufficient to say that theology will do the necessary correcting: what is needed in such circumstances, he says, is better philosophy.

Newman has been mentioned often in these pages, and he wrote one of the most sustained reflections on the rationality of faith in modern times – one of his last works – called *An Essay in Aid of a Grammar of Assent*. Using Aristotle's philosophy, as Aquinas had done before him, he develops a very interesting argument about the ubiquity of a form of prudential apprehension and assent in human affairs: that it is not only a matter of religious belief, but also something without which human life, communication, relationships and society would not be possible. We are equipped with a capacity that he called the 'illative sense', which enables us to recognize when it is reasonable to assent to the conclusion that must follow when probability reaches a certain point. The strength of our assent must follow the strength of our apprehension of particular truths, and his analysis is helpful in reminding us that it is not only in the areas of religion-theology-faith that we find ideological stubbornness, dogmatic assertion or unexamined prejudices.

Newman's *Idea of a University* continues to attract attention in discussions of the nature of the university, a medieval Christian institution in its origins but clearly one that has gone through significant changes, particularly in recent centuries. It is one of the fields on which contemporary 'culture wars' are often most hotly engaged. For Newman – and this will be scandalous to some – philosophy and theology are essential if the goal of a university is to be pursued, at least as that goal was understood when the institution was first conceived. All serious reflection in any area of science, whether the natural or the human sciences, along with all serious reflection on art or music or literature, leads inevitably to questions that are properly philosophical. If we want to bring together the distinct undertakings of different disciplines then some principle or methodology that unites the various undertakings will be necessary, and this once again guides us towards philosophy. The service theology offers to the university is, says Newman, to steady the various disciplines in their proper work. Without it, one or other of those disciplines will inevitably begin to claim its place and present itself as in effect a 'theology': the queen of the sciences, whether it be physics, or biology, or sociology, or psychology, or even philosophy. Theology well done knows that it must be forever humble before its subject matter even while rejoicing in the multiplicity of creation and in the capacity of human reason to understand and engage with creation in all its different facets.

Another thing gained from the presence of theology on the university campus is the reminder that human beings, desiring knowledge and understanding, also desire – and need – wisdom, a knowledge and understanding that remain fully and properly human, answering to the needs of the human world considered holistically. Aquinas speaks of theology as 'science', by the criteria of science he finds in Aristotle's writings, but he also speaks of it as 'wisdom', a knowledge in which truth and goodness, fact and value, head and heart, are integrated and never separated.

CULTURE AND COUNTER-CULTURE?

The Vatican Apostolic Library is just one institution of the Catholic Church dedicated to the needs of study and research. One can list also the various commissions and academies established by the

Church, not only in areas such as theology and biblical studies, but in properly scientific areas, in music, archaeology and art, along with its involvement in communications, astronomy, social and economic questions, and so on.

If today some Catholic voices speak of being counter-cultural this is not, one hopes, in order to disown the centuries-long Christian humanism that has been the mainline tradition of the Church since it ceased to be a persecuted sect. The Church continues to have a prophetic responsibility, to call everybody to the wisdom of the cross. We have noted already that tensions and conflicts at certain points are inevitable. Just as each individual is engaged in a spiritual struggle, more or less strong, to make all things subject to Christ in their personal life, so at the level of communities and societies there is a comparable struggle. The Church will articulate its vision of what is true and what is good for human beings, but that vision will not necessarily neatly or completely coincide with that of others.

If we think of Catholicism as 'Christian humanism with a prophetic edge', the edge will cut at different points at different times. At one time the world was exercised by questions in Christology, at another time by questions of grace and freedom, then by arguments over Eucharistic theology, and, later, wars raged linked with questions about the authority of the Bishop of Rome. Moral questions seem to be the point of greatest conflict at the present time, particularly in relation to how the human being is understood in his and her physical reality, the meaning of the human body, of sexual orientation and practice, and related issues. It is important to note that it is not the Church alone that decides what the hot button issues are to be, but the encounter between the Church and the dominant culture in which it finds itself. Today, a statement from the Church about some question in sexual morality is likely to get far more attention, and provoke far stronger reactions, than a statement about Christology or grace, or even about other moral issues such as the impact of market capitalism on the poor, for example, the ecological concerns of *Laudato sí*, the plight of migrants, or nuclear disarmament.

161

As in those earlier moments of tension and conflict, there is a need for the best possible engagement with current questions, which includes a serious intellectual engagement, working with others, across the 'universe of knowledge', to seek the truth, to appreciate what is good and to promote what is judged best for human flourishing. While the Church as a whole has stayed within the mainline movement of culture, at least until now, the relationship of the Church and the State in its various forms has always been one of the main points of tension and conflict. Just as the doctrinal areas that excite interest and argument have changed, so the points of conflict between Church and State have not always been the same. There is much to be learned from earlier experiences while at the same time recognizing that each generation has to do its own thinking and find its own solution to whatever problems are current.

The Old Testament scholar Walter Brueggemann has given a lot of attention to the experience of exile, which was central to the experience of the Jewish people and which informed some of the most powerful and creative prophetic texts in the Bible.[2] In his analysis of how exiles ought to respond to their situation, Brueggemann advises them, among other things, not to turn inwards. It is a temptation, he says, but it is a way of giving up, withdrawing from engagement with the surrounding culture and its challenges. A moment of looking inward is necessary, he continues, there is need for self-examination and *ressourcement*, but we must also learn the language of the dominant power(s) without forgetting our own mother tongue.[3] Brueggemann is writing out of the recent experience of American Protestantism, but it is also how we might describe the intellectual challenge facing Catholicism today, not least in some of its traditional heartlands: how to learn the language of the culture that has become dominant and still speak our own mother tongue (the language of scripture, theology and Catholic spirituality).

If we are living in an 'in-between' time where an old form is gone and a new one is not yet here, what flavour ought that situation give to Catholic preaching and teaching? Learning from the great prophets of the Exile, and what the people made of everything they went through in Babylon, such preaching would encourage people to let go in order to see God anew, to move from the experience of God's seeming absence towards an as yet untasted experience of God's newness.[4] This is what the great prophets of Israel achieved, figures like Jeremiah, the Second Isaiah and Ezekiel. Great imagination and creativity will be called for in engaging intellectually with where the world is, Brueggemann adds. In the plaintive words of Psalm 137(136), how are we to speak our old language, sing the Lord's song, in a land that is alien to us? That land is not alien to God who is Creator and Lord of all: this insight is one of the great achievements of Hebrew prophecy at the time of the exile. But there is a need in those who believe in God to find new stories, new ways of framing our lives, to see how the song we want to sing is to be sung in a new environment. *The Passion according to John*, for example, has been set to music by, among others, Heinrich Schütz (1585–1672), Johann Sebastian Bach (1685–1750) and James Macmillan, the same text responding to enquiring minds and searching hearts in quite different centuries and cultures.[5]

The new commandment is an old commandment, we read in the First Letter of John (1 Jn 2.7), a commandment of holiness and neighbourliness, ancient virtues that are always radically new.[6] The capacity to live by this commandment is a gift of the Holy Spirit. The challenge for us is to live by the Spirit's gift rather than rely on purely human initiatives. An exclusive focus on self and its desires is the tendency of sin in us at all times and it easily supplants our trust in God even in our religious aspirations. There should then be a new freedom for preaching and witnessing, for singing our song. We will experience once again the joy and well-being that come from knowing the Lord and that cannot come from any of the alien gods to whom we might be tempted to give our homage: those gods have no power to give either the joy or the well-being that we seek and need.[7]

Such a preaching, such a presence and action of the Church, will also be counter-cultural (how can it not be if we continue to read – even sing – the Gospel of John with its critique of 'the world'?), and it will be alternative and subversive (how can it not be since we look forward to a new heaven and a new earth where righteousness will be at home?). So how do we keep this prophetic edge without becoming sectarian, without withdrawing into our own sub-culture, into our own inward-looking life?[8]

The Lord, the God of Israel, is the God of all: this is what the exiles learn more clearly than ever before. God has no favourites and anyone, in whatever nation, who does what is right is acceptable to God: this is a point on which Peter (Acts 10.34), Paul (Rom. 2.11-13; Eph. 6.9; Col. 3.25) and James (Jas 2.1, 9; 3.17) are in agreement. This apostolic unanimity about the universality – the catholicity – of the Church's mission, present from the beginning, remains essential to what is being received anew from Christ. There is only one God, living and true, the Lord of Israel and the Father of Jesus, who is the God of all people, beyond the boundaries of the chosen people and the Church, and often coming to us from beyond those boundaries, as we see already in the Old Testament. Cyrus, King of Persia, for example, intervenes to restore the temple in Jerusalem and is even called 'messiah' (Isa. 45.1). The Lord spoke and acted on behalf of his people through foreigners like Ruth, Job, Balaam, Rahab and others, for all human beings are creatures of the one Creator and all human beings are destined to live as children of the one Father. Abraham is called to be a blessing for all the nations of the earth, and Jesus, when he is lifted up, draws all people to himself (Gen. 12.3 and Jn 12.32).

So Catholic Christianity is at one and the same time a humanism – *nihil humanum alienum a se putans*, considering nothing human to be foreign to it – and a counter-cultural element in human society, listening as it does for a voice that comes from beyond, a beauty ever ancient and ever new, as Saint Augustine puts it, which is at once affirming of all that is good and true and beautiful in creation and at the same time radical in calling human beings to live the ancient commandment of holiness and neighbourliness.

THE ZEAL OF SAINT PAUL

Saul, who became Paul, encapsulates in his personal journey the two aspects of culture and counter-culture to which this reflection on the intellectual element of Catholic Christianity has led us. We have seen the brilliance of the rhetoric in which he disclaims any rhetorical ability. We know that he spent some years after his conversion in his home city of Tarsus, one of the important intellectual centres of the Hellenistic world. For Aquinas, Saint Paul is simply 'the apostle', from whom he receives many important insights, not least the text in Romans 1.20 that served Aquinas as the biblical point of departure for a natural theology: 'Ever since the creation of the world God's invisible nature, namely, his eternal power and deity, has been clearly perceived in the things that have been made.' It is not original with Paul, since earlier Jewish writings like the Book of Wisdom, as well as the main philosophical traditions, taught that studying the world would lead people to a knowledge of God, at least to a knowledge of God's existence and of some of his attributes.

As Saul, his zeal for the honour of God took its lead from the actions of Phinehas, which, according to Chapter 25 of the Book of Numbers, ended a plague afflicting the people of Israel, something Phinehas achieved by killing a mixed-race couple, an Israelite man and a Midianite woman. It was assumed that the plague was a punishment from God for the Hebrews mixing with foreigners, not just by marrying them but by participating in their worship of a false god (see Psalm 106(105).30). Phinehas was regarded as a heroic defender of the holiness of God and Saul of Tarsus wished to follow him in that service and with comparable zeal. Hence his persecution of the first Christian community who dared to insult the holiness of God by claiming that God had acted through a cursed thing, namely a man hung on a tree (Deut. 21.23; Gal. 3.13-14).

As Paul, following an encounter with Jesus on the road to Damascus, he was obliged to think things out again from the beginning. It was not something achieved in the three days he spent waiting to be baptized: it took some years before Saul was fully transformed into Paul, acting and speaking with the same energy and zeal as before, but now placing those gifts at the service of preaching the gospel rather than preaching against it. Zeal means passion, or in Latin *studium*, that to which we give our energy and our love, what it is we study. From his Damascus experience onwards, Paul's study was simply Christ.

One of the things that seems to be in the background in Paul's accounts of his struggle is the story of Jacob wrestling with the angel (Gen. 32.24-32). Where Jacob's experience is presented as a night-long wrestling with a mysterious 'other', Paul's experience is drawn out over many years during which he is obliged to engage, again and again, with opponents and critics, with successes and failures. The spiritual combat he undertakes is played out not just in moments of meditation or prayer alone with God, but through the relationships he has with the first apostles, with his companions on his journeys and with the members of the communities he established. It is all very concrete and ordinary, even banal, this struggle centred on human relationships marked by rivalries, jealousies, quarrels, misunderstandings and betrayals. It can seem as if there is nothing noble in it, no stirring arguments about theology, but simply petty, ordinary, flesh and blood weaknesses. I would love to come and be with you, he says to the Corinthians, but my fear is that we would both be disappointed, even hurt (2 Cor. 1.23–2.4). You find my letters impressive but my physical presence weak and my speech inadequate (2 Cor. 10.1, 10). Besides, Paul will find himself once again subject to attacks from two sides: from those who think he should be staying closer to the requirements of the Jewish law and from those who think he is not spiritual enough, not mystical enough for them.

So, this inadequate apostle must defend his authority and vocation over and over again. He is not an academic theologian, clearly, but he is a fully engaged intellectual theologian, responding to the questions and problems presented to him in such a way that we can talk about a 'Pauline theology', a thought-out presentation of the gospel developed in the answers he gave to their questions and problems. Above all it was the church in Corinth that challenged Paul, provoking in him external conflict and internal fear (2 Cor. 7.5), weaknesses from within and challenges from without, differences of class and gender, questions of wealth and poverty, disturbing the unity of the community. And Corinth itself is the world, we can say, a great metropolitan city, full of everything, a permissive society, a crossroads, a melting pot, pluralist and multi-cultural. The infant Church has to find its way in this big place, surrounded by huge numbers of people not Christian, interested in all kinds of other things. They were just a small group of believers, numerically weak but also morally and spiritually weak – and yet Christianity ever since owes so much to that group of people struggling in their weaknesses.

This is the paradox that Paul himself is trying to bring out in his letters to them. Not that he stands over them – he says this himself – as if he is not also limited by the same weaknesses and fears. There is at least this consolation for us: to see that this is how it was, that the Christian gospel has always been about the transformation of human beings, flesh and blood, earthen vessels, existing not four feet off the ground but immersed in the world, society and culture in which they live out their lives. The Word has become flesh – our flesh and blood – which means that the grace of Christ operates not at a height above us but in us and through us, within our weaknesses, limitations, our failures, coming even to heal us of our sins and to make our wounds glorious.

We are indebted to these weak Christians of Corinth also for this: that they brought these letters out of Paul, and we see his genius, the gift of God to him, in how he responds to them. Where other people might have been tempted to regard their preoccupations as petty, arguments and disagreements unworthy of the gifts they were receiving, small things not at all at the heart of what Christianity is about – instead of responding with criticism and impatience, telling them to concentrate on more important things, Paul takes each of their difficulties as an opportunity to reflect on the great central teachings of the faith. If there are questions about money, he speaks to them about grace.

If there are questions about authority, he speaks to them about the Spirit and the service of Christ. If there are questions about law, he speaks to them about freedom. If there are questions about freedom from law, he speaks to them about their obligations to each other. If there are questions about wealth and poverty, he speaks to them about Christ emptying himself and becoming poor so that we might be rich. If there are questions about sexual behaviour, he speaks to them about the meaning of the body, that we are temples of the Holy Spirit and therefore places in which God is present. If there is rivalry about the distribution of talents and responsibilities, he speaks to them about the gifts that are better than any others, faith, hope and love, and the greatest of these is love, the gift that makes them like Christ, the gift that enables them to live by the great commandment. Even while being these weak, conflicted and troubled people, we are already ambassadors for Christ, Paul says. We have been reconciled and are now entrusted with bringing to others the news of their reconciliation (2 Cor. 5.18-21).

Paul sometimes uses battle imagery, and we can talk about his spiritual and intellectual engagements as a kind of 'spiritual warfare' (Rom. 8.35ff.; Eph. 6.12-17). In the text that gives its title to this chapter he speaks of defeating arguments, bringing down strongholds and taking every thought captive for Christ (2 Cor. 10.5). If Jacob's wrestling is in the background when Paul describes his own struggles, it is helpful to remember that Jacob emerged from that struggle victorious and defeated at the same time. A number of biblical texts catch this paradox. The Book of Wisdom tells us that Jacob/Israel was given the victory so that he might learn that godliness is more powerful than anything (Wis. 10.12). The prophet Hosea says that he strove and prevailed but also that he wept and sought God's favour (Hos. 12.4). We can therefore say that Jacob is victorious because he survives the encounter, but he is wounded and limping at the end of it and has learned something essential. We can even ask whether it is the same man who sees the new day dawning. Jacob is no more and is replaced by Israel, a new name that, in Hebrew culture, means a new reality. We can therefore describe it, not as a fight to the death, but as a fight to the birth of a new person. Saul's experience was similar. He had three days of blindness before undergoing baptism, which he himself later described as a way of dying with Jesus. In his case, Saul is replaced by Paul, who does not hesitate to describe the transforming experience as 'a new creation' (2 Cor. 5.17; Gal. 6.15).

The Catholic faith is therefore about knowledge and about wisdom. It is not anti-intellectual for it seeks to incorporate in its vision of the world and of human life the best that science, philosophy and reason can determine. It is not counter-cultural except where it meets principles or practices that it finds to be unworthy of the dignity and destiny of the human person. If we take Saint Paul as the archetypal intellectual of the Christian faith then he is that because he was ready to receive every question, ready to engage with every difficulty, ready to bring to bear on all concerns the light he saw shining from the cross of Christ.

9

THE LIFE OF A COMMUNITY

Saint Peter was our guide in Chapter 7, on the institutional-historical element of Catholicism, and Saint Paul took his place in Chapter 8, where we considered the intellectual-doctrinal element. For this chapter we look for the guidance of another apostle, this time Saint John, usually identified also as the beloved disciple whom we meet a number of times in the Gospel of John. He leads us in thinking about the mystical-active element in the Church's life, its maturity as a human community reaching the fullness of its characteristic life, which is life according to Jesus's new commandment of love.

We begin by noting the importance of the Greek term *koinonia*, in Latin *communio*, which is found some twenty times in the New Testament and which has taken on great importance in certain parts of the Church as a term particularly well suited for defining the reality of the Church's life. According to Gustave Thils (1909–2000) '*communio* ecclesiology' refers to

> an ecclesiology which defines the Church as an organic whole composed of spiritual bonds (faith, hope and charity) and of visible structural forms (the profession of faith, the sacramental economy, the pastoral ministry), and which culminates in the eucharistic mystery, the source and expression of the unity of the Church, or rather of the one Church. This ecclesiology obviously makes use of the essence of the constitutive elements of the Church – the Holy Spirit, theological activity, its ministerial structure, the papacy – but each of these 'elements'

is considered in so far as it promotes, conditions, realizes or brings about the 'communion' which is the Church.[1]

It will be clear that the approach taken here is along these lines, and the present chapter will focus on that culmination in the Eucharistic mystery that is 'the source and expression of the one Church', or, in the words of *Lumen gentium*, the 'source and summit of the Christian life' (*LG* 11).

In fact, the best-known use of the term 'communion' within Catholicism and in Christianity more generally is in relation to the Eucharist, which is often also called simply Holy Communion. Another popular way of translating the term *koinonia*, however, is with the English word 'fellowship'. It is with this meaning, and alongside a reference to the Eucharist, that we find it used in Acts 2.42, its first occurrence in the New Testament as the texts are now arranged. This verse gives us a snapshot of the life of the first Christians in Jerusalem, even before they had been so named: 'they held steadfastly to the apostles' teaching and fellowship, to the breaking of the bread and to the prayers'. Fellowship is not simply identified with the breaking of the bread, for it means also being in relationship with the apostles, sharing their company and their life, receiving the teaching of Jesus from them, the leaders of this new community as it comes to birth. The apostles hand on what they learned in their experience of fellowship with Jesus, they pray according to the Jewish hours and practices of prayer, and they celebrate the Eucharist: all of this makes up the 'fellowship' that is the *raison d'être* of the new community.

It depends on how one chooses to translate it, but the term *koinonia* may also be taken to mean fellowship in some of its uses by Saint Paul – for example in 1 Corinthians 1.9; 2 Corinthians 6.14; 13.13 – as well as in the First Letter of John where we find it four times in the opening chapter: 'That which we have seen and heard we proclaim also to you, so that you may have fellowship with us; and our fellowship is with the Father and with his Son Jesus Christ' (1.3); 'If we say we have fellowship with him while we walk in darkness, we lie and do not live according to the truth; but if we walk in the light, as he is in the light, we have fellowship with one another, and the blood of Jesus his Son cleanses us from all sin' (1.6-7). If fellowship means simply being in a positive relationship with others, and sharing life with them, what we also see from these references is that fellowship in the human community, when people are living it sincerely, means also fellowship with Christ and with the Father in the Holy Spirit.

Other uses of *koinonia* seem to require translations such as 'partnership' or 'sharing'. These also describe being in a positive relationship with others, but perhaps with a specific focus on collaboration, joining with others in a common project. This seems to be the sense required in Philippians 1.5 and 3.10 as well as in Philemon 6. It comes through most strongly in Galatians 2.9, where Paul and Barnabas, having spoken with the apostles in Jerusalem about their work of preaching and church-building, are given 'the right hand of fellowship' by James, Peter (Cephas) and John, as they agree to share the work of preaching the gospel and caring for the poor.

'Don't forget the collection' is a comment often thrown around, usually humorously, where a Catholic priest is engaged in organizing some religious event. It may come as a surprise to know that the term *koinonia* in the New Testament sometimes has this very meaning, a contribution to a collection of money. To be in partnership with others, to share life with them, if it is serious fellowship and friendship, will also mean sharing material goods with them when necessity requires it. Paul uses the term in this way when he speaks to the Romans about the collection that he is organizing to meet the needs of the Christian community in Jerusalem (Rom. 15.26). He devotes a lot of space to that collection in 2 Corinthians as he encourages them also to be generous in their contribution to it (2 Cor. 9.13, but see all of chapters 8 and 9 of that letter).

Finally, *koinonia* is one of the Greek terms used for any kind of participation or taking part in something. Sometimes it is concrete and ordinary, like taking part in the collection for the poor at Jerusalem (2 Cor. 8.4), but in other places it has a more profound significance. Thus, in Philippians 2.1 it means participating in the Holy Spirit, which may be its meaning also in the Trinitarian blessing of 2 Corinthians 13.13, although there it is often translated with 'fellowship'. The most important use of the term in the sense of 'participation' is in 1 Corinthians, where Paul is speaking about the Eucharist and reminding them that the bread broken at the Eucharist is a participation in the body of Christ and that the cup of blessing that is blessed at the Eucharist is a participation in the blood of Christ (1 Cor. 10.16). Sometimes, therefore, the term is translated in that text as communion in the body of Christ and communion in his blood.

THE EUCHARIST AND THE CHURCH

The oldest New Testament witness to the words of Jesus at the Last Supper is found not in any of the Gospels but in Paul's First Letter to the Corinthians. He makes it clear that he is passing on a tradition that he had received, saying even that he had received it 'from the Lord'. We can easily imagine that this was something from Jesus that was held on to very strenuously and passed on with great care to the first generations of believers as they were being instructed in the faith. What Paul says he received from the Lord and passed on to his converts at Corinth was this:

> that the Lord Jesus on the night when he was betrayed took a loaf of bread, and when he had given thanks, he broke it, and said, 'This is my body that is for you. Do this in remembrance of me.' In the same way he took the cup also, after supper, saying, 'This cup is the new covenant in my blood. Do this, as often as you drink it, in remembrance of me.' For as often as you eat this bread and drink the cup, you proclaim the Lord's death until he comes. (1 Cor. 11.23-26)

Much could be said about the background to this moment at the Last Supper, just as much could be said about what has been stimulated by it across the two thousand years of Christianity.

It took place on the evening before the death of Jesus and is intimately linked with his death, as Paul immediately points out. There is background in the Passover meal, which preceded the liberation of the Hebrews from slavery in Egypt, a meal ceremoniously re-enacted by Jews to this day (Exod. 12–13; Josh. 5). The Last Supper took place in the context of just such a meal. There is important background also in the feeding of the people with manna as they wandered in the desert (Exod. 16.3-35; Num. 11.7-9; Deut. 8.3; Ps 78(79).24-25; Wis. 16.20). We are particularly indebted to John's Gospel for Jesus's teaching about this. The whole of John 6 is given to a miracle of feeding, followed by a discourse by Jesus on how he is 'the bread of life' and 'the living bread'. 'Your fathers ate manna in the desert,' he says, 'but my Father will give you the true bread', which not only nourishes a physical life but also establishes and nourishes eternal life in you (Jn 6.49-50).

The distinction between 'the bread of life' (Jn 6.35, 48) and 'the living bread' (Jn 6.51) is of great significance. The first evokes those traditions in Jewish Wisdom literature that speak of Wisdom as a lady who has prepared a banquet of fine food and wine and who goes through the city calling people to come and participate in the meal she has prepared (Prov. 9.1-6; Song 5.1ff.; Sir. 15.3; 24; Ps 23(22)). It means feasting on the Word or the Wisdom of God, learning from God and being nourished by him, living according to God's laws and precepts which were given to the people precisely so that they might flourish through their relationship with God. This is what it means to receive 'the bread of life': to know God, to take his word and his law into ourselves, and so to live by God's wisdom, often personified in the Old Testament as 'Lady Wisdom'. As she taught her disciples, Jesus speaks of doing the will of the Father and of gathering those who come to believe in him. This is the Father's will which he has come to do, to draw into unity all those who learn from him, come to believe in him, and so do the works of God. That was their question at the beginning of this discourse: 'What must we do, to be doing the works of God?' (Jn 6.28). Jesus's answer is

175

that they must come to him and believe in him because he is the bread of life (Jn 6.35).

Jesus changes the phrase in a way that might at first seem trivial, but something new and radical appears with this change: not only is he the bread of life, he is also the living bread. 'The living bread which I am', he says, 'is my flesh for the life of the world' (Jn 6.51). He takes a step beyond anything envisaged up to then. He is saying not only that they must eat his teaching – 'swallow the scroll': Ezekiel 3.1 – but that they must eat him! Not surprisingly there is a strong and immediate reaction to this. It is bad enough that he is claiming to have come down from heaven as bread from the Father, but now he is asking that they eat him! In his response to their reaction, he intensifies the scandal: this living bread that is his flesh is to be masticated, chewed and digested. Not only are they to eat his flesh but they are also to drink his blood! Although the Gospel of John is often referred to as the most spiritual of the Gospels, here and in other places it is actually the most physical and intimate of the Gospels. 'My flesh is food indeed', Jesus continues,

> and my blood is drink indeed. He who eats my flesh and drinks my blood abides in me, and I in him. As the living Father sent me, and I live because of the Father, so he who eats me will live because of me. This is the bread which came down from heaven, not such as the fathers ate and died; he who eats this bread will live for ever. (Jn 6.55-58)

For some it is too much and they give up going around with him. Their communion with him is broken precisely in the moment in which he speaks about this radically new kind of communion that he wants to make possible for them. In this first Eucharistic controversy, we can perhaps see already an intimation of the many moments of controversy that have marked Christian history in relation to how the Eucharist is to be understood and celebrated.

How the other evangelists and Paul speak of the Eucharist is, however, completely in line with what we find in John's Gospel.

We have seen that Paul describes the bread of the Eucharist as a communion in the body of Christ and the cup of blessing as a communion in the blood of Christ. To profane the Eucharist is to profane the body and blood of the Lord, he says, and woe to anyone, therefore, who eats and drinks 'without discerning the body' (1 Cor. 11.27, 29). 'The body' clearly refers to the reality carried under the forms of bread and wine as well as to the body of believers participating in that meal. The issue that led him to talk about it here is the problem of factionalism and discrimination when the Christians come together for the Eucharist. They are failing to understand the meaning of the Eucharist, that its whole purpose is the unity of the Church – it was for this that Jesus laid down his life and shed his blood – and so they are profaning the body in two senses: the community that is damaged by the divisions among them, and the body and blood of Christ in the bread and cup that are thereby profaned.

Luke's account of the Last Supper is close to what we find in 1 Corinthians 11. That a covenant was sealed in the blood of a sacrificed victim explains Jesus's words over the cup as Paul and Luke record them: 'this is the new covenant in my blood' (Lk. 22.20). The note of sacrifice is already present in what he says over the bread – 'my body given for you' – but is so much clearer in what he says over the cup because the reference is clearly to the blood that seals a covenant. This is spoken of in the Book of Exodus, as a sprinkling of the altar and of the people with the blood of sacrificed animals, thereby sealing the covenant between God and the people. This act is followed immediately by seventy of the elders of Israel eating and drinking in the presence of God (Exod. 24.3-11). The reference to the blood of the covenant is repeated by Mark (Mk 14.24) as well as by Matthew, who tells us yet one more thing, that Jesus spoke of the blood of the covenant being 'poured out for many for the forgiveness of sins' (Mt. 26.28). Although in speaking of the new covenant the prophet Jeremiah did not refer to sacrificial blood, he did however add these words from the Lord: 'I will forgive their iniquity and I will remember their sin no more' (Jer. 31.34).

There are other Old Testament meals that are important for understanding the Christian Eucharist. There is, for example, the meal that Abraham and Sarah prepared for their heavenly visitors (Gen. 18.1-8). That is just one of a number of meals that seal or celebrate a covenant, whether with God (Noah: Gen. 8.20-22; 9.8-17; Moses: Exod. 24.3-11), with angels (Lot: Gen. 19.1-3) or between human beings (Isaac and Abimelech: Gen. 26.26-33; Jacob and Laban: Gen. 31.43-54). There is also the great celebratory meal that is foretold for the last days when the Lord will establish his kingdom in a definitive and enduring way. That will be a banquet of fine food and wine to which all the nations of the earth will be given access (Isa. 25.6-9; 55.1-5).

All of these Old Testament meals inform the New Testament's understanding of the Eucharist. As we have seen, the Last Supper took place within a Passover meal and there are other references to Jesus as himself the Passover victim, the lamb that is sacrificed: John 1.29; 19.34-37 and 1 Corinthians 5.7. We have noted the link between the Eucharist and the covenant meals of the Old Testament as well as its links with the meal prepared for her disciples by Lady Wisdom. People stuck in a wilderness are miraculously fed by Jesus, a miracle recorded in all four Gospels, recalling and re-enacting the feeding of the people with manna during their years in the wilderness.[2] But it also has a new Christian resonance, as Jesus takes, blesses, breaks and gives the bread, four actions that still provide the basic structure of the Eucharistic liturgy.

The meal of the last days, spoken of in the Book of Isaiah, becomes even more central in the New Testament, for the 'hour' of Jesus is the beginning of the last days.[3] And it becomes a wedding banquet, the marriage supper of the Lamb of God, a final covenant meal in which the union of the Lamb and his bride is celebrated.[4] Jesus is spoken of as the bridegroom, the Church as the bride – this is a theme already sounded in the Gospels ('how can they fast when the bridegroom is with them?') and developed particularly in Ephesians 5 and in the closing chapters of the Book of Revelation.

This development also throws into sharper relief one particular meal at which Jesus was present: the wedding feast of Cana (Jn 2.1-11). It can be understood as Wisdom's meal and also as the meal of the last days, for the Wisdom of God himself is present, and the best of wine is offered generously, the good wine kept to the end. It is also closely linked with the death of Jesus as John speaks of it in Chapter 19. There Jesus again calls his mother 'woman' as he had done at Cana. There he speaks of his thirst where he had acted before to satisfy the thirst of others. We know that Calvary is his 'hour', which had not yet come at Cana. And as Cana was the first sign through which he revealed his glory, the cross is the final sign through which he reveals his glory more clearly and more powerfully than ever. To provide the wine for the wedding feast was the bridegroom's responsibility and so at Cana Jesus is invited by his mother to reveal himself as Israel's bridegroom. He says to her that the time has not yet come for that. At Calvary, however, the time had come, the hour when he was to pass from this world to the Father, the hour in which the new covenant would be sealed.

Finally, there are meals at which Jesus is present and that seem to have no precedent in the Bible. Eating with tax-collectors and sinners is one of the things he did that caused great scandal.[5] But it was the heart of his teaching: that he had come for the sick and for sinners, to be with them and to lead them into the communion of love that is the life of his kingdom. After his resurrection the disciples encountered him in various situations, sometimes in the context of a meal.[6] It is one of these encounters that introduces the phrase 'the breaking of the bread' as an early Christian designation of the Eucharist, an action in which the Risen Lord is paradoxically present even in his absence (Lk. 24.30-31, 35). Luke 24 tells of Jesus accompanying two downhearted disciples on the road to Emmaus, showing them the meaning of scripture in reference to himself, and then revealing himself to them as he breaks bread, in the very moment in which he disappears from their sight. Luke 24 bears comparison with John 6, for in both we find the pattern that still structures the Catholic celebration of the Eucharist: a Liturgy of the Word, in which the people are fed with the bread of life through the proclamation of the Word of God, and a Liturgy of the Eucharist, in which the people are fed with the living bread, the Body and Blood of Christ, present under the appearances of bread and wine.

COMMUNION FRAGMENTED

The Church's life consists therefore in receiving the teaching of the apostles, being in fellowship with them, participating in the prayers and breaking the bread. This is how people receive and live the life of the disciples of Jesus. As the source and summit of the Christian life, the Eucharist is the beginning and the end, the point of departure and the point of arrival. It is from the Eucharist that people receive the teaching and the life of Christ, and they return to it to celebrate what that teaching and life have made possible through them in the work of building Christ's kingdom in the world. The greatest sadness in Christian history, therefore, has been the loss of communion, when the fellowship is broken, and those who had been brothers and sisters, sharing all these things together, or who ought to be brothers and sisters sharing all these things together, can no longer do that.

There is already great variety and diversity within the Catholic Church: we have spoken of it here at length. The 'Catholic instinct' is, above all, to maintain unity, to go on living in the communion that is the purpose of the Church's existence. All belong to the one people of God, a royal, prophetic and priestly people. The articulated body of ordained and lay members; of bishops, priests and deacons; of religious both male and female, monks, nuns, friars and missionaries; of various states of life, married and single; of engagement in works of charity, apostolic involvements, and different kinds of service and witness; of degrees of holiness in response to the call that each one has received – all of that makes up the one body of the Church.

Catholicism is not simply a 'Roman' or 'Latin' community, although sometimes, even to some of its own members, it can seem as if it is. There are also many Greek Catholics, living by their own laws and celebrating their own liturgies, following their own customs and practices, in full communion with the Bishop of Rome. Communion means sharing the same faith, participating in the fellowship of the Church's life, and accepting the same governmental structure for the community. This the 'Eastern Catholic Churches' do. They are seen, at least from the West, as a bridge to the Orthodox Churches of the East, sharing with them a common liturgy as well as some elements of practice and government – a married clergy for example – and in particular the principle of patriarchal government, whose observance Vatican II described as 'a prerequisite for any restoration of union' with the Eastern Orthodox Churches. For such a restoration of union there are possibilities in the notion of the Church as *communio*, a theme that is dear to Eastern Orthodox theology and from which Western theologians have learned much in recent decades.[7] It would mean thinking through more precisely the relationship between particular churches and the universal Church: how is this relationship to be understood and how is it to be lived in practice?

Vatican II, in recognizing that from the very beginning there were rifts in the Church that in subsequent centuries became more serious, also acknowledged that often enough both sides were to blame for the events that broke the communion of the Catholic Church. Great strides were taken in the last century to try to heal the fragmentation that happened in Christianity, particularly during the second millennium of its existence. The Great Schism of 1054 and the Protestant Reformation of the sixteenth century are the deepest wounds that the communion of Christians has suffered. The ecumenical movement – the movement of restoring unity among Christians – was initiated in the Protestant communities but included the Orthodox Churches and members of the Roman Catholic Church from very near the beginning. That beginning can be dated to the turn of the twentieth century when Protestant denominations began to meet to discuss matters of 'Faith and Order' and 'Life and Work'. Much progress was made among those denominations and with the Anglican communion, for example. That communion traditionally regarded itself as a bridge between Catholics and Protestants and has been acknowledged as such by the Roman Church, for which it occupies a special place as having maintained some Catholic traditions and institutions.

There was great enthusiasm about this question at the time of Vatican II. Pope John XXIII had inaugurated what many regarded as a new springtime for the Church in which the question of Christian unity was at the top of the agenda. In his first encyclical, *Ad Petri Cathedram* (1959), John spoke about unity, citing Newman to the effect that controversies within the Church do not necessarily disrupt the Church's unity. John spoke of 'unity in essentials, freedom in uncertainties, in all things charity' (n. 50). Encouraging people to pray for unity, he described his own contribution as 'a father's call to unity'. As a papal diplomat he had served in Bulgaria and Turkey and so had first-hand knowledge of the divisions among Christians and even between people of different faiths. Later, as papal nuncio in France, he would have been well aware of the pioneering work of Yves Congar, who gave himself to working for Christian unity from the beginning of his priestly life. Ten years into that work, Congar published *Divided Christendom* (1939), in which he argued that what gives urgency to this work are statements from Jesus himself, in which he prays for unity among his disciples and among those who would come to believe in him through their preaching (Jn 17.11, 20-23). If the Church is to be the representative community for humanity, the light to the nations, the sacrament or sign of unity for humanity, then its lack of unity is a scandal that seriously wounds its credibility. At least the impulse towards unity must remain, and a realization that it would be wrong to rest from such efforts until unity is achieved.

In the years that followed Vatican II a series of dialogues was initiated between the Catholic Church and various other Christian communities. The work of the World Council of Churches was strengthened and there were many concrete changes in the ways in which Christians of different denominations related to each other. If we check it against Acts 2.42 we can say that the ecumenical movement enabled Christians at least to join together for 'the prayers' and to strengthen their fellowship in common works of charity and in the promotion of justice, even if they still disagreed in interpreting the teaching of the apostles, and about whether or not their communion had reached the point where they could honestly break the bread of the Eucharist together. There have been some significant advances in regard to the interpretation of the teaching of the apostles, notably in statements agreed with the Anglican communion on a range of issues as well as an agreed statement with the Lutherans on the question of 'justification', on how the grace of Christ saves and heals human beings.

It has not been a totally smooth journey since then. For example, the ordination of women is a major question that divides many of the Protestant communities from the Catholic and Orthodox churches. Traditional points of difference remain, concerning the authority of the Pope, for example, the place of Mary in the work of redemption, and how the change of bread and wine into the body and blood of Christ is to be understood. A document from the Congregation for the Doctrine of the Faith in 2000 caused much offence to other Christians and was regarded as a further setback to ecumenical conversations. Called *Dominus Iesus*, it introduced itself as being about the Catholic Church's relations with 'world religions' but then slipped into talking about other Christians. To add what some felt was injury to insult, it said that Christian 'ecclesial communities', a phrase used often in the years after Vatican II, could not be considered 'churches' in the proper sense.

The World Council of Churches has an agreed basis on which membership is granted to communities that wish to be members. This basis is found also in Vatican II's *Decree on Ecumenism*, which refers to 'those who invoke the Triune God and confess Jesus as Lord and Saviour' (n. 1). They are 'Christians who openly confess Jesus Christ as God and Lord, the only Mediator ... for the glory of the one God, the Father, the Son, and the Holy Spirit' (n. 20). It affirms that all who have been baptized in the name of the Blessed Trinity are already in communion with each other and therefore also with the Catholic Church. Not all 'others' will want to accept this, and for the Catholic Church itself baptism is only a beginning and the communion in many cases remains incomplete (*Decree on Ecumenism* n. 3 and n. 22).

In many ways *Dominus Iesus* simply repeated what was said in *Lumen gentium* and in the *Decree on Ecumenism*, except that in the 1960s it was a question of other Christians being told that their glass was not empty – which was good news after centuries of often bitter controversy – whereas in 2000 they were being told that their glass was not full.

This is recalled here simply to remember the sadness there is in Christianity concerning the fragmentation of the communion to which all aspire, to remember the desire for communion that motivated people so strongly in the last century, and to recall also the obstacles and challenges that remain to making progress in these matters. Pope Pius XII is said to have described Karl Barth, a great Protestant theologian, as the most important Christian theologian since Thomas Aquinas. Let us leave this particular point with a short reflection from Barth:

> The quest for the unity of the Church must not be a quest for Church-unity in itself; for as such it is idle and empty. The quest for the unity of the Church must in fact be identical with the quest for Jesus Christ as the concrete Head and Lord of the Church: the blessing of unity cannot be separated from Him who blesses ... and only in faith in Him can it become a reality among us. 'Homesickness for the *una sancta*' is genuine and legitimate only in so far as it is disquietude at the fact that we have lost and forgotten Christ and with Him have lost the unity of the Church.[8]

MARY: MOTHER, VIRGIN, EKKLESIA

It might seem provocative to follow a consideration of fragmented communion among Christians with a consideration of Mary, the mother of Jesus, whose role in her son's work became such a controverted question, especially after the sixteenth century. There is much about her, however, in the New Testament and in the traditions of the undivided Church, and a justified desire to avoid distorting her role and relationship with Jesus should not push us to ignoring what is actually there.

She is our mother and our sister, linked also with imagery in which the Church is represented as virgin and bride. We saw that metaphors and images from human relationships and family life are used in the Bible to speak about the people of God and about the Church. From the beginning feminine imagery has been used to refer to the Church. The Greek term itself, *ekklesia*, is feminine and this aspect is made explicit in imagery that is not only feminine but is further qualified as virginal, spousal or nuptial, and maternal.

The love poetry of the Old Testament, gathered in the Song of Songs, was already read by Jewish teachers as symbolic of the relationship between God and the people. This allegorical or symbolic interpretation was proposed by rabbis, long before Christian mystical interpretations appeared on the scene. Most of the Old Testament references to a 'bride' are in the Song of Songs. In the Book of Wisdom, another work attributed to Solomon, wisdom itself is referred to as the bride of Solomon, his preferred spouse (Wis. 8.2). We have noted that the wisdom of God is often represented as a feminine figure, Sophia, sometimes even personified. She is a figure of great importance for the New Testament, for understanding the Word of God as presented in the prologue of John's Gospel, for understanding the Eucharist – as we have seen: Wisdom prepares a banquet for her clients – and therefore also for understanding the Church.

The eschatological marriage feast spoken of in the Book of Revelation – the great event that brings the whole Bible to its conclusion – is anticipated in the prophets. Isaiah has the people of Israel rejoicing in the Lord, who dresses them with the garments of salvation and the robe of righteousness, as the bridegroom prepares his bride and himself for their wedding day (Isa. 61.10). The wedding feast is the most joyful of celebrations and it is frequently the way in which the communion of God and the people is described – as the bridegroom rejoices over the bride, so shall your God rejoice over you (Isa. 62.5). The rejoicing of bride and groom confirms that all is well: if weddings are being celebrated, life is continuing as normal. When such celebrations cease, or are not possible – as the time of Covid-19 lockdowns taught us very clearly – it is a sign of serious trouble, an indication that the whole people is in mourning.

The communion of God and the people, now understood as a love story of bridegroom and bride, is referred to by others of the prophets. They refer in particular to the idyllic time of first love, the honeymoon, when Israel as a young bride, in the time of the wilderness wandering, responded to God in holiness and integrity (Jer. 2.2; Hos. 2.14-23). The romantic idealization of that period is not so extraordinary when we think of how people recall the early days of being in love.

The people's infidelity to the covenant is therefore adultery: they have given themselves to other lovers, they have worshipped other gods, they have turned away from the One who alone deserves all their devotion and worship. This is most dramatically presented in Ezekiel 16, where the anger and sadness of the betrayed husband does not spare the blushes of the one who has betrayed him. And this leads us into the references to weddings, brides, bridegrooms and wedding feasts that we find in the teaching of Jesus and in the writings of the apostles.

Jesus refers to himself as the bridegroom (Mt. 9.15; Mk 2.19-20; Lk. 5.34-35). In the Gospel of John, it is the Baptist who bears witness to Jesus as not only the Lamb of God, the light, the one who ranks before him, the Son of God, but also as the bridegroom. 'It is he', John the Baptist says, 'who has the bride, and I am a friend of the bridegroom, hearing his voice and so my joy is full' (Jn 3.25-30). A parable of Jesus talks of virgins (translated sometimes as 'maidens') waiting to greet a bridegroom, virgins who are wise or foolish depending on their readiness for his arrival (Mt. 25.1-13). The parable is clearly to be taken as a reference to the coming of the Son of Man, the bridegroom being Jesus himself, the one who is to return. The focus of the parable as it was told by Jesus seems to have been this: to be alert and attentive, watching and ready. The focus is not in the first place on Jesus as the bridegroom, but the implication is clearly there in view of his earlier description of himself as 'the bridegroom'.

Although Paul is familiar with this imagery, he makes only one explicit reference to the Church as a bride, which, however, evokes many of these earlier sources: 'I feel a divine jealousy for you,' he says to the Corinthians, 'for I betrothed you to Christ to present you as a pure bride to her one husband' (2 Cor. 11.2). Implicit in other texts of Paul is the same imagery, particularly Ephesians 5 where the 'great mystery' he speaks about, represented by the union of husband and wife, is the union of Christ and the Church (Eph. 5.21-33).

It is in the Book of Revelation that the New Testament use of this imagery reaches its climax. 'The marriage of the Lamb has come', the voice of a great multitude proclaims, 'and his bride has made herself ready' (Rev. 19.7). She is clothed with fine linen – linen is a priestly cloth in the Bible, associated with the purity needed to offer sacrifice worthily – but now this clothing of the bride is the righteous deeds of the saints (Rev.19.8). And a beatitude is added: 'Blessed are those who are invited to the marriage supper of the Lamb' (Rev. 19.9). We have seen that this is the fulfilment of a line of thought originating in the Old Testament that establishes one essential level of meaning in the Eucharist: the Eucharist anticipates, in the sacramental life of the Church, the marriage supper of the Lamb so that we already share in the wedding supper, which is the life of the kingdom of heaven.

So, at the end of the Church's pilgrimage is the celebration of a wedding, the wedding feast of the Lamb and of his bride the Church. Here the metaphors get mixed, for she is both spouse and mother,

THE SPIRIT OF CATHOLICISM

a mixing that is mediated by Jerusalem. For the bride of the Lamb is also Jerusalem (Rev. 21.2, 9), coming down out of heaven like a bride adorned for her husband. The city is at once a bride and 'our mother' (Gal. 4.26). This sends us back to the great vision of Revelation 12, of heaven opened and the ark of the covenant visible within it, and of a woman clothed with the sun, with the moon under her feet and on her head a crown of twelve stars. She is *Ekklesia*, the Church, and she is Mary, because she is the mother of the Messiah as well as mother of the messianic people (Rev. 11.19–12.6, 13-17).

The woman of Revelation 12 is the Christian *Selene*. As *Ekklesia*, the Church, she is the mother of all who come to life in Christ, and she is destined to be pursued by the powers of evil until the end. The drama of sin and redemption that began in Genesis 2–3 continues in climactic form as Christ's work takes hold in creation. The darkness tries to extinguish the light, to drag those enlightened by it back into nothingness, but the darkness has not and cannot overcome the light of the Word become flesh (Jn 1.5).

The woman of Revelation 12 is also Mary, the mother of Jesus, established by God as a sign, and more than a sign, of God's grace at work in the salvation and sanctification of humanity. We can rightly call Mary a 'sacrament' as well, because she is not only a sign but also a channel of that grace. She is 'mother of the church', entrusted with the care of the disciples by her son as he died (Jn 19.26-27).

In Catholic tradition Mary is only understood from her relationship with Christ and with the Church: without those two relationships we would not recognize her. As the human being whose vocational name is 'full of grace' she is, in the words of Karl Rahner, simply the most beautiful part of the Church's theology of grace. As such she epitomizes the life of the Church. All grace is a gift to an individual person for his or her proper vocation and personal sanctification in a unique relationship with God. But all grace is also a gift to the community and a call to an individual for a particular mission in the service of the community.

The particular vocation and relationship of Mary is to be the mother of Jesus and so *theotokos*, the God-bearer, the mother of God. She is the first believer in her son and the first to carry the good news of his coming to another person. She is an exemplary figure as well as a particular graced subject in her own right. She is one individual Christian but, in the exemplarity given to her as part of her personal grace, she is *ekklesia*, the woman clothed with the sun, standing on the Moon and with twelve stars round her head.

We are clearly in symbolic territory once again, typical of what we can call the Catholic imagination. A capacity for symbolic and analogical thinking is essential if we are to do justice to this world, and we saw in earlier chapters of this book that the term 'sacrament' invites us into such a way of thinking, a particular kind of *poiesis*, 'poetry', that is creative not only with words but with things, persons, events and institutions. We must, however, be careful not to obliterate the 'Mary of history', subsuming her totally into this mystical figure. Just as the Church is an embodied community in history, so Mary is a woman whose human strength and resilience carried her through exceptional experiences, the unusual birth of her child, the anxiety of losing him when he was twelve years old, the challenges of his public ministry, and the piercing grief of seeing him die a terrible death as a young adult.

If Christ is the sacrament of God, and the Church is the sacrament of Christ, then Mary is the sacrament of the Church. Who can doubt that a renewed Mariology – right thinking and speaking about Mary – will be essential for a renewal of Catholicism? Even those who prefer to remain outside recognize that such thinking and speaking are integral to the spirit of Catholicism. Recognizing her place in the working out of redemption, and devotion to her on the basis of that recognition, have been part of the Catholic story from the centuries of the undivided Church down to our own day. A renewed Mariology will be one nourished also by Eastern Christian thinking about Mary and devotion to her, and by Eastern Christianity's thoughts about the feminine in the transformation of individual lives and of human life shared in community.

Controversy about it has often made it difficult to have a clear view of Mary's place in the story of Christ's redemptive work, of the biblical background to her vocation, and of her relationship with her son and with the community of his disciples. If the admixture of ideas and practices drawn from other sources served to distort those things, so too did the reaction to that eclecticism. The earliest surviving prayer to our Lady dates from the third century. When in many other ways the Christian communities have been divided and separated from each other, this prayer continues to unite East and West, ancient, medieval and modern: 'We fly to your protection, O Holy Mother of God. Do not despise our prayers in our necessity but ever deliver us from all dangers, O glorious and blessed Virgin.' Mary, the mother of Jesus, can be described as a sacrament of the Church. She is its first member, the first to be born into the body of her son.

The first of the signs worked by Jesus, according to the Gospel of John, is the turning of water into wine at the wedding feast of Cana. We have already considered its importance in thinking about the Eucharist; now we focus on what it teaches us about Mary and about the Church. Here there is a rich density of meaning as the 'woman', Mary, asks him to anticipate his 'hour', which he does in a figurative way by satisfying the thirst of the people, and satisfying it abundantly with the finest wine. These points all return when the hour of Jesus has truly come and he is dying of thirst on the cross. Seeing his mother standing there, he addresses her as 'woman' as he had done at Cana, and says 'Behold your son' (Jn 19.26). Although this comment is usually taken as twinned with what follows, Jesus saying to the beloved disciple, 'Behold your mother' (Jn 19.27), could it be that he is actually referring to himself when he says, 'Woman, behold your son'? The thought was sown in my mind by Herbert McCabe, in a retreat conference many years ago, and I discovered later that, as with so many of his thoughts, he found the suggestion in Aquinas. It is as if Jesus, who addressed Mary as woman at Cana, is now saying to this same woman, 'Here I am, did you realize what you were asking when you asked me to anticipate this hour?' Then, in dying, he gave up his spirit, the spirit already symbolized in the abundance and quality of the wine produced for the wedding feast, the Spirit of God breathed out through the thirst of Jesus on the cross.

Just before that he had said to the beloved disciple, '"This is your mother", and from that hour the disciple took her to his own home' (Jn 19.27). Is it simply a dying man making arrangements for the care of his mother? Hardly, when it is the Gospel of John we are dealing with, and so it has been understood as Jesus confirming Mary as not only mother of the Messiah but as mother of the messianic people, Mother of the Church.

The early teachers and preachers did not shy away from the implications of what they believed about the relationship between Mary and Jesus. If she had given birth to him in the physical creation, he had given birth to her in the new creation. Her faith and love, her union with her son in his life, suffering and death, are paradigmatic therefore, particular to her and her unique relationship with God, but also having a universal significance, epitomizing something that is true of all who believe in Christ, making visible what is contained in the call to follow him.

Mary and the Church, bride and mother, is also the virgin daughter of Israel, one who has kept herself for the Lord. The virgin is first given a symbolic meaning by the prophet Isaiah, whose reference to 'the virgin daughter of Zion, the daughter of Jerusalem', is quoted at 2 Kings 19.21. It is a way of referring to the people, or to the nation as a whole, who, at least for the moment, can feel safe from the threat of the Assyrians (Isa. 37.22). Not too much can be made of this, however, since the cities of Sidon and Babylon, the countries of Israel, Judah and Egypt, all receive from Isaiah and Jeremiah the same description of 'virgin daughter' (Isa. 23.12; 47.1; Jer. 14.17; 18.13; 31.4, 21; 46.11; Lam. 1.15; 2.13). It seems to be a way of saying that a city has not been invaded by attacking armies and will be kept safe from them, in the same way as the city of Derry, in Ireland, is described as 'the maiden city' for having survived intact in the face of a long siege. Perhaps it is a way of describing also the vulnerability of a city, nation or community, which is therefore promised the Lord's protection. The practice of referring to a city or nation as 'virgin daughter' receives a new variation in Saint John calling the Christian community, to whom he addresses his second letter, 'the elect lady' (2 Jn 1.1).

Catholic theology today never speaks of Mary without speaking also of Christ and of the Church, since her particular grace and calling are only understood with reference to Christ and to the Church. She is mother to both. From early on she is honoured also as ever-virgin, referring to her availability to God, her exclusive devotion to her mission, and the miraculous way in which God worked through her without doing any violence to her. It seems strange to think of Mary also as the bride, since the bridegroom is her son! But, within the poetry of the Bible and of the Catholic tradition, Mary represents the Church as the archetypal disciple and is also therefore the one whose communion with him has a unique intimacy and depth.

The Spirit and the bride together say 'come': this is the note on which the Bible ends. The Church is longing for her wedding day and asks the bridegroom to come (Rev. 22.17). The Lord answers, through the one who received those extraordinary visions, 'Surely I am coming soon' (Rev. 22.20).

CONCLUSION

The mystical-active element of religion brings it to its maturity, building on the institutional-historical and the intellectual-doctrinal. We have asked the apostles Peter, Paul and John to symbolize these elements and to guide our reflections on them. It was right to consider the Eucharist in this chapter, as the source and summit of the communion that is the characteristic life of the Church, and to do so by paying close attention to what we learn from the Gospel of Saint John. It was right also to consider the fragmentation of that communion, which remains such a deep wound for Christianity. And it seemed right to speak in this context also of Mary. To associate the mother with nourishment is one of the deepest instincts in human nature. Jesus himself brings John and Mary together, entrusting them to each other's care, and designating Mary as mother of the beloved disciple. We have seen how the figure of Mary already has archetypal and representative significance within the New Testament. It is the mother who watches over the children and rejoices in their flourishing.

The Eucharist is the fullness of the Church's life *ad intra* as it reflects on its own definition and nature. But it is also the source of the Church's life *ad extra*, its mission outwards and its relations with other Christians, already considered here, with other believers, and with the world as a whole. The final movement of this work, therefore, will consider the elements that constitute the life of the Catholic Church *ad extra*, not just as gifts of God to the Church for itself but as gifts of God to the Church for the world.

PART FOUR

WITH THE SON: CHRIST, THE HEAD OF HUMANITY

One of the first saints to be canonized by Pope Francis was the Jesuit, Peter Faber, a man to whom he has deep devotion. It was a canonization that seemed to come from Francis's personal initiative. In the interview Francis gave in 2013, Michel de Certeau is reported as saying that Faber was a man in whom interior experience, dogmatic expression and structural reform were inseparable.[1] In those three things we recognize immediately the mystical-active, the intellectual-doctrinal and the institutional-historical, the themes we considered in the previous three chapters, von Hügel's description of the mature religious person.

Many people see a similar maturity in Pope Francis himself that has found expression in his preaching, in his actions and also in his encyclical letters. In *Fratelli tutti* (2020), his encyclical letter on fraternity, he speaks of the nature and destiny that are common to all human beings. *Evangelii gaudium* (2013), the first encyclical properly his own, dealt with evangelization, the Church's service of the world, in which Francis said that all baptized men and women are, under the inspiration of the Holy Spirit, 'missionary disciples'. *Laudato sí* (2015) focused on creation, the common home of humanity, to be appreciated and cared for by us as a gift of the Creator. These three encyclicals can serve, therefore, as further reading for the remaining chapters of this book, which will consider, first, Christ in his role as head of humanity and so the first among brothers and sisters, then the Holy Spirit as the energy of the Church's mission, and finally the Father as the source of this created world and the glorious destination towards which the Son and the Spirit, sent by the Father, are leading and guiding humanity.

CHRIST AS HEAD OF THE CHURCH

A joke often told tells of a newly arrived person being shown around heaven by a welcoming angel. They come upon a wall, from the far side of which can be heard the sounds of happy people. 'What's the meaning of this wall?' the newly arrived person asks. 'Oh,' replies the angel, 'the Catholics/Jews/Muslims/Protestants [choose according to one's preference] are on the far side of that wall: they think they are the only ones up here.'

The word 'catholic' means universal, and its use in relation to the Catholic Church underlines the universal character of its mission. That mission is not a self-appointed one but originates with Christ, who was sent by the Father to reveal God's love for the world and to open the way for humanity to healing, forgiveness and eternal life (Jn 3.16). 'When I am lifted up from the earth,' Jesus says, 'I will draw all people to myself' (Jn 12.32). 'God wants everyone to be saved', we read in 1 Timothy 2.4, 'and to come to knowledge of the truth.' Once again something the Church claims for itself – its catholicity or universality – it can only do on the basis of its relationship with Christ, from the fact that it is his body.

We have seen that Thomas Aquinas, in interpreting the texts in the Letter to the Romans and in the First Letter to the Corinthians that speak of the Church as the body of Christ, presses the metaphor of the body very far. Here we want to say something about texts in Ephesians and Colossians that use a different phrase, speaking instead of Christ as the head of the Church. In his commentaries on these texts, Aquinas again takes very seriously the references to the physiology of the organic animal body. In fact, his commentaries illuminate for us the extent to which Paul himself had done the same.

For Aquinas, the entire corpus of Paul's letters is about the Church as the body of Christ and particularly about the unity that Christ effects in that body. In the prologue to his commentary on the Letter to the Romans, which is actually a prologue to the entire set of commentaries he made on Paul's letters, Aquinas explains how the letters of Paul, taken together, present a full teaching about the grace of Christ. Nine of the letters are addressed to the Church of the Gentiles, he says, four are addressed to 'prelates and princes' of the Church, and one, the Letter to the Hebrews, is addressed to the people of Israel. This 'full teaching about the grace of Christ' is in three parts, he goes on. Hebrews speaks specifically of the grace of Christ as head of the Church. The four letters to prelates and princes (1 Timothy, 2 Timothy, Titus, Philemon) speak of that grace as it is given to 'more important' members of the Church. The grace of Christ in the whole mystical body is considered in the nine letters addressed to the Gentiles. Romans deals with this grace in itself, 1 Corinthians deals with the grace of Christ as it is in the sacraments, 2 Corinthians is concerned with the dignity of those who administer the sacraments, and Galatians is directed against those who wanted to keep the old sacraments alongside the new. Finally, there is a consideration of the grace of Christ as it effects the unity of the Church. Thus, Ephesians deals with the establishment of the Church's unity, Philippians with its strengthening and progress, Colossians with defending that unity against errors, 1 Thessalonians with defending it in the time of present persecutions, and 2 Thessalonians with defending it in the time of future persecutions, especially those associated with the time of Antichrist. The letters to the 'more important' members of the Church are likewise concerned with the Church's unity, 1 Timothy dealing with the institution, teaching and government of ecclesiastical unity, 2 Timothy dealing with strength against persecutors who would threaten the Church's unity, and Titus dealing with defence against heretics who would do the same. The letter to Philemon teaches temporal or secular rulers about their Christian responsibilities.

Thus, for Aquinas, Paul presents a comprehensive ecclesiology in his letters, whose main concern is the Church as the body of Christ, with an emphasis on the unity of that community, its unity being the principal effect of Christ's grace in the life of the Church. It may be described as a *koinonia* ecclesiology, therefore, an ecclesiology of communion, where the structures of the body are at the service of its life. In his best-known systematic work, the *Summa theologiae*, we find what some regard as the heart of Aquinas's ecclesiology, a consideration of the 'capital grace' of Christ, meaning his grace as head of the Church and even as head of all creation (*ST* III 7–8).

The idea of the 'capital grace' of Christ is clearly based on texts of the New Testament that refer to him as the head, either of the Church or of all things. Ephesians 1.22-23, for example, speaks of him as having all things placed under his feet, as being therefore the head of the Church, which is his body, and 'the fullness of him who fills all in all'. In his commentary on this text, Aquinas is keen to stress that it is in his humanity that Jesus Christ is placed over all things, and this is remarkable news. As the eternal Son of God, all things are already subject to Christ as their Creator. The meaning of all things being placed under his feet – taking the phrase as a metaphor, Aquinas adds, and not just figuratively – is that Christ in his humanity, represented by his feet, is made head of all creation. It means Christ is the head not just of human beings but of all things, including the invisible created powers of the universe (Col. 2.10).

Aquinas turns to the physiology implied in the metaphor. The head has a triple relationship with the body, he says, pre-eminence because of its position, diffusion of power because all sensation derives from the head to the members, and conformity of nature between the head and that of which it is the head. The first two, pre-eminence and diffusion of power, apply to Christ's relationship with the angelic world as well as to his relationship with the human world. But the third, conformity of nature, applies only to his relationship with the human world with which he shares the same nature. If the Church is Christ's body, then it stands in this

200

triple relationship to him as its head. In support of this, Aquinas cites 1 Corinthians 12.12-13 which, as we saw already, is a text in which the whole body is identified as Christ and not just the head.

Aquinas takes the final phrase in Ephesians 1.22-23 – 'the fullness of him who fills all in all' – to mean that the Church is the fullness of Christ and it is Christ who fills all in all. Whatever is accomplished through the members of the Church is contained within the power of Christ – all spiritual senses and gifts, everything in the life of the Church – it all flows from him in whom it is all superabundantly present, flowing from him to his members to be fulfilled by them. The phrase 'all in all' thus means that whatever gift is found in a member of the Church – wisdom, justice, love and so on – is derived from Christ's wisdom, Christ's justice, Christ's love, and so on.

Another very physical text is to be found in Ephesians 4.16: Christ is the head 'from whom the whole body, joined and knit together by every joint with which it is supplied ... makes bodily growth and upbuilds itself in love'. In his commentary on this Aquinas cites two of his favourite scripture texts that speak of God's grace working through human actions. One is Isaiah 26.12, 'You have wrought for us all our works'. The other is 1 Corinthians 12.6, 'It is the same God who works everything in everyone'. If Aquinas speaks of the particular grace of Christ, he is also clear that the particular grace of any creature is always 'Christological', related to the particular grace of Christ as the head of all things.

The great Christological hymn in Colossians 1 already refers to Christ as 'the head of the body which is the church' (Col. 1.18). This is because 'he is the beginning, the firstborn from the dead'. Here Aquinas presents the privileges of the head in slightly different terms. Clearly thinking of the brain, he says that it is superior in dignity to all other members of the body as a source and ruler within the body, because the fullness of the senses is in the head, and because there is a flow of 'sense and movement' from it to all the other members of the body.

Once again applying the metaphor fairly literally, he says that this dignity of the head is transferred in all three ways to Christ in his role as head of the Church. He has the dignity of being the Church's source and ruler, in him is the fullness of grace or in other words the fullness of the life of the Church, and from him the whole life of the Church is influenced, taking 'influence' in its strongest possible sense to mean informed, shaped and sustained. He is the beginning, Colossians says, and so he is the head of the Church also in its historical pilgrimage. He is the Alpha. But as 'the firstborn from the dead' he is also the head of the Church in its eschatological fulfilment, its fulfilment at the end of time, in glory. So, he is also Omega. He contains the fullness, the *pleroma*, and because Aquinas's version lacked 'of God' he takes this once again as referring to the fullness of grace. Christ's influence permeates the life of the Church as the influence of the head (brain) permeates the life of the animal body. This influence of Christ shows itself in the first place, according to this Colossians text, through his reconciling to himself all things, God and humanity, heaven and earth, Jew and Gentile, a harmony he established through the blood of his cross. It brings us back to the primacy of unity in thinking about the Church and to the fact that it is from Christ as its Head that the Church gets its unity. The whole purpose of the Church is to be the reality of communion between those who have come to faith in Christ and in whom the life of charity is flowing.

These points are developed throughout Paul's letters, Aquinas says, and are particularly clear in the final reference to Christ as head of the Church, which is in the Letter to the Colossians. This text is very similar to Ephesians 4.16, equally physical in its description of the organic body, which owes everything to the head, 'from whom the whole body, nourished and knit together through its joints and ligaments, grows with a growth that is from God' (Col. 2.19). Once again Christ is to be understood as the head because of the function that the head (brain) has in the human body. The entire well-being of the body depends on it, both in its articulation and coherence, in what makes it to be an organism and not just a collection of parts, and in its growth. These are the two goods of the natural body that in the spiritual or mystical body are supplied by Christ: its union or the joining together of its members, and its growth. Besides the articulation of parts connected by physical juxtaposition there is the internal connection of ligaments and nerves, and so Colossians 2.19 refers to visible joints and invisible ligaments. In the Church, Aquinas says, its members are therefore joined ('jointed') by faith and understanding, a union that is completed by the ligaments of charity and the sacraments, charity knitting it together and the sacraments nourishing it and causing its growth.

CHRIST AS HEAD OF HUMANITY

Aquinas gives a systematic presentation and development of these ideas in *Summa theologiae* III 7–8. He begins by distinguishing three kinds of grace in Jesus Christ. There is the 'grace of union', which refers to the fact that the created human nature of Christ is united personally to the Son of God (*ST* III 2). This way of expressing the mystery of who Christ is developed in the early centuries of the Church's life, using philosophical categories, particularly those of 'nature' and 'person', to articulate what is found in the scriptures. A second kind of grace is Christ's grace as an individual human being with a unique mission (*ST* III 7) and the third kind is the grace Christ has insofar as he is head of the Church (*ST* III 8). In fact, as he develops his argument, Aquinas eventually identifies these last two, saying that the personal grace of Christ is his grace as head of the Church, since that is his personal mission.

The soul of Jesus, Aquinas says, is not intrinsically divine, but like other human beings it must be made divine by the kind of participation that comes with grace (*ST* III 7, 1). In his case this participation is perfect, which means he has a fullness of grace and lived a life of perfect virtue (III 7, 2). Aquinas is clear, however, that while Christ had perfect charity, because of the grace of union already mentioned, he did not have the theological virtues of faith and hope in exactly the same way in which other human beings have these virtues (*ST* III 3–4). By contrast, he enjoyed the gifts of the Holy Spirit in an outstanding way, being perfectly docile to the Spirit's movement (*ST* III 7, 5). We can even say that he experienced fear of God, when understood properly as a deep reverence for God (*ST* III 7, 6). He had the charismatic gifts of grace ordered to the preaching of the gospel because he is the first and original teacher of spiritual doctrine and faith (*ST* III 7, 7), and in this later work Aquinas does not hesitate to see Jesus as also having the charism of prophecy, capable of a knowledge that transcended the situation he shared with all other human beings (*ST* III 7, 8).

Already Aquinas begins to speak of Jesus as a 'universal principle' in the realm of grace and graces. Because of his intimacy with God, all God's gifts to humanity and to the world necessarily pass through him (*ST* III 7, 9–11). This then leads him to consider explicitly the grace of Christ as head of the Church. Taking up from what he found in Paul's letters, he says that the head of something is its beginning, its perfection and its power (*ST* III 8). Spiritually, all three are found in Christ: as the firstborn among many brothers and sisters he is the highest and the first (Rom. 8.29), he has the fullness of all graces (Jn 1.14), and he causes grace to flow into all the members of the Church (Jn 1.16).

There is an interesting objection in the first article of *ST* III 8 that raises the question of the heart: would that not be a better metaphor for Christ's position and relationship with other human beings? Because the influence of the heart on the body is hidden, Aquinas says, it is a better symbol for the Holy Spirit, who invisibly gives life and unity to the Church. Christ is compared to the head by reason of his visibility, seen as he was as a human being among human beings (*ST* III 8, 1 ad 3). Aquinas believes it is important, therefore, not to misunderstand the term 'spiritual' as applied to the headship of Christ. The

204

entire humanity of Christ, body and soul, acts upon human beings, primarily on their souls but also on their bodies (*ST* III 8, 2). It is yet one more way in which we see the centrality of the body, of sacramentality, in the Catholic understanding of Christ and the Church.

Christ is therefore the head of all men and women, past, present and future, but their relationship with him can vary considerably (*ST* III 8, 3). There are three ways of being a member of the Church, Aquinas says: by faith, by charity, and by being in the glory of heaven. Christ is head in the first place of those united to him in glory, second of those united to him by charity, third of those actually united to him by faith, fourth of those potentially united to him and who will someday actually be so united, fifth of those potentially united to him with a potentiality that will never be actuated and who, when they die, will cease to be members of Christ. We will return to this last point in the next section, for it raises a number of crucial questions.

Taking his cue from references in Saint Paul to Christ as head of creation and not just of humanity (Col. 1.15-20; 2.10; Eph. 1.20-23), Aquinas then goes beyond Paul and argues that the angels too should be included as members of the Church. This is because he believed that humans and angels together constitute a single body with a common purpose, namely the glory of enjoying God (*ST* III 8, 4). At this point he also begins to identify the personal grace of Christ and his grace as head of the Church. What is his own grace except the grace from whose fullness we have, all of us, received (Jn 1.16)? He is the 'head' in the realm of grace – the first, the perfect, the most powerful. Just as we cannot understand what the Church is without reference to Christ, then, neither can we understand the grace of Christ without reference to the Church (*ST* III 8, 5; 7, 9–10).

Can Christ share his 'headship' with anybody else? As regards the intrinsic functions of the head, these cannot be shared with any other member of the body. But the head is also related externally to the body of which it is the head, Aquinas says. It directs and controls not only internal operations of the body but its external activities as well (*ST* III 8, 6). While he can share this aspect of his headship with others, it can never be in precisely the same way. He is the head of all who pertain to the Church at any time, in any place and under any condition. Others can only share at certain times or certain places or under certain conditions. Thus, the prophets of the Old Testament and bishops of the New Testament participate in some limited way in Christ's headship, and even the Pope, whom Aquinas describes here as '*caput totius Ecclesiae*', the head of the whole Church, is that only for the duration of his pontificate. After the resignation of Benedict XVI and the election of Francis, people sometimes spoke about there being 'two Popes' and there was even a popular film with this title. But it is incorrect: there can only be one Pope – part of the point of a head is that there be just one – and so Benedict is more properly referred to as Pope Emeritus or former Pope. Such participations in the headship of Christ, Aquinas concludes, are concerned only with the Church in its condition as a pilgrim in history. In any case, it is perfectly clear that Christ alone is head by his own power and authority, all others having whatever share in it they do have simply as delegates of Christ (2 Cor. 2.10; 5.10).

SALVATION OUTSIDE THE CHURCH?

Thomas Aquinas belongs to the school of Augustine at least in this: that he thinks we know that there are people in hell. This has never been taught by the Church, although many people's experience of Catholic and Christian teaching 'on the ground' will have left them in no doubt that there are people in hell. The Church did condemn a heresy that claimed to know the opposite: that hell will in the end be empty, and many people will interpret Jesus's comments about Judas – 'better for that man if he had never been born' (Mt. 26.24) – to mean that we know of at least one occupant of that dreadful place. But we do not have the opposite of canonizations, solemn declarations that somebody is in hell. All judgement belongs to God in this regard. We cannot claim to know the outcome of God's judgement beforehand or the final condition of anybody's soul. To live by the great commandment of loving our neighbour as ourselves seems impossible if we do not hope for the salvation of our neighbour. For how can we honestly love another person and at the same time contemplate their eternal damnation?

However, there is also in the tradition the phrase *extra ecclesiam nulla salus*, 'outside the Church there is no salvation'. We can quickly think of texts in the New Testament that are very clear on the point and that have given rise to this phrase. There are at least categories of people who will be lost: whether in the end those categories have any membership is another question. Thus, in Mark 3.28-29 we hear Jesus saying that 'people will be forgiven for their sins and whatever blasphemies they utter; but whoever blasphemes against the Holy Spirit can never have forgiveness, but is guilty of an eternal sin'. Later he tells us that 'the one who believes and is baptized will be saved; but the one who does not believe will be condemned' (Mk 16.16). We find similar statements in the Gospel of John ('Truly, truly, I say to you, unless one is born of water and the Spirit, he cannot enter the kingdom of God' – Jn 3.5), in the Acts of the Apostles ('There is salvation in no one else, for there is no other name under heaven given among men by which we must be saved' – Acts 4.12) and in the Letter to the Hebrews ('If we sin deliberately after receiving the knowledge of the truth, there no longer remains a sacrifice for sins, but a fearful prospect of judgement, and a fury of fire that will consume the adversaries' – Heb. 10.26-27; see also 6.4-6). The judgement scene of Matthew 25 is another text that seems to make it very clear that there will, at the end, be sheep and goats, the saved and the lost.

It is the same Cyprian of Carthage to whom we owe the finest theological definition of the Church – a people brought into unity from the unity of the Father, the Son and the Holy Spirit – who also gives us the first version of 'outside the Church there is no salvation'. *Salus extra ecclesiam non est*, Cyprian says, there is no salvation outside of the Church.[2] The phrase is echoed by Fulgentius of Ruspe (462–527), who says: 'it is certain that all who die outside the Church will go into the eternal fire which is prepared for the devil and his angels'.[3]

It might seem that the views of these theologians are easily enough interpreted: we simply broaden our understanding of the ways in which people can be within the Church, in other words within the reach of God's saving grace. To help us do this we have the support of an explicit condemnation by the Church of the view that 'no grace is given outside the Church', *extra ecclesiam nulla conceditur gratia*. This was in 1713, in a bull issued by Pope Clement XI in which he condemned the Jansenistic errors of a theologian called Paschasius Quesnel (1634–1719). So, to be clear, the belief that no grace is given outside the Church is a view condemned by the Church itself. In his encyclical letter on the Church, Pope Pius XII wrote:

> These, too, who do not belong to the visible structure of the Catholic Church ... we invite them all, each and every one, to yield their free consent to the inner stirrings of God's grace and strive to extricate themselves from a state in which they cannot be secure of their own eternal salvation; for, though they may be related to the mystical body of the Redeemer by some unconscious yearning and desire yet they are deprived of those many great heavenly gifts and aids which can be enjoyed only in the Catholic Church.[4]

He is not saying that everybody who does not belong to the visible structure is therefore lost, nor is he saying that everybody who does belong to it has complete assurance about their personal salvation. It is clear that people who do not belong to the visible structure can nevertheless be related to it by a yearning or desire that might even be unconscious. A few years later the Holy Office, as the Congregation for the Doctrine of the Faith was then called, in response to the extreme view that anybody who was not baptized into the Catholic Church could not be saved, sent a letter to Cardinal Cushing, Archbishop of Boston, where this extreme view was being promoted, in which it stated: 'that one may obtain eternal salvation, it is not always required that he be incorporated into the Church actually as a member, but it is necessary that at least he be united to her by desire and longing'.[5] The letter refers back not only to the encyclical of Pius XII from six years earlier but also to the teaching of the Council of Trent and confirms that the desire and longing mentioned need not be explicit. God accepts also an implicit desire, the letter says, 'so called because it is included in that good disposition of soul whereby a person wishes his will to be conformed to the will of God'.

Clearly these questions are crucial, not just because they involve the claims of a religious institution in relation to all of humanity, but because they touch on the deepest concerns of the human being: the questions of truth, right living, integrity and a person's standing 'before God'. *Lumen gentium* returned to these questions, and it is important to note two texts from that dogmatic constitution:

> Basing itself on scripture and tradition [the holy Council] teaches that the Church, a pilgrim now on earth, is necessary for salvation: the one Christ is mediator and the way of salvation; he is present to us in his body which is the Church. He himself explicitly asserted the necessity of faith and baptism (cf. Mk 16.16; Jn 3.5), and thereby affirmed at the same time the necessity of the Church which men enter through baptism as through a door. Hence, they could not be saved who, knowing that the Catholic Church was founded as necessary by God through Christ, would refuse either to enter it, or to remain in it. (*LG* 14)

We have seen that there are many texts in the New Testament, besides the ones referenced in *LG* 14, that teach the necessity of faith and baptism for salvation. At the same time there are texts, also already noted, that tell us of God's will that all be saved and tell us also of the universal significance of the death of Jesus. To know this necessity and yet refuse it or reject it is the perversion that we call sin. But obviously it implies that not everybody will necessarily come to see that necessity. There is a further comment on this that is more explicit:

> Those also can attain to everlasting salvation who through no fault of their own do not know the Gospel of Christ or His church, yet sincerely seek God and, moved by grace, strive by their deeds to do His will as it is known to them through the dictates of conscience. Nor does divine Providence deny the help necessary for salvation to those who, without blame on their part, have not yet arrived at an explicit knowledge of God but who strive to live a good life thanks to his grace. (*LG* 16)

A final magisterial document can be cited to bring this section to a conclusion. This is from Pope John Paul II, who in his encyclical letter *Redemptoris missio*, on the mission of the Redeemer and of the Church, says the following:

> The universality of salvation means that it is granted not only to those who explicitly believe in Christ and have entered the Church. Since salvation is offered to all, it must be made concretely available to all. But it is clear that today, as in the past, many people do not have an opportunity to come to know or accept the Gospel revelation or to enter the Church. The social and cultural conditions in which they live do not permit this, and frequently they have been brought up in other religious traditions. For such people salvation in Christ is accessible by virtue of a grace which, while having a mysterious relationship to the Church, does not make them formally part of the Church but enlightens them in a way which is accommodated to their spiritual and material situation. The grace comes from Christ; it is the result of his Sacrifice and is communicated by the Holy Spirit. It enables each person to attain salvation through his or her free co-operation.[6]

THE CIRCLES OF THE CHURCH'S PRAYER

Catholic Christianity believes itself to have received a universal mission, and so it must think about its relationship to all people and their relationship with it. It means thinking not just of those who belong visibly and explicitly to its fold, as we have just seen. Nor does it mean thinking just of other Christians, with whom it believes itself to be already in a real if incomplete communion by baptism and by a shared faith in the Trinitarian God and in the salvation that comes through Christ. The Church is obliged to relate itself to all men and women since its faith holds that there is only one God who is creator of all, and one Saviour in whose name alone the human race will be healed of its wounds having already been promoted to a wonderful dignity and called to an eternal destiny.

An interesting way to see the circles of humanity within which the Church positions itself is to see for whom it prays in the Good Friday liturgy. In the solemn prayers that make up a substantial part of that liturgy we see how the care of the Church expands and reaches out in a way to include all men and women.

The first four prayers are for the Church itself, for the Pope, for all 'orders and degrees' of the faithful, and for catechumens, those who in any particular year are preparing for baptism at Easter. There is no explicit reference to the 'Catholic Church' in these prayers, although communion with the Pope implies that those for whom they are offered are Christians in full communion with the Bishop of Rome. There are references to 'the holy church of God' which is spread throughout all the world (catholic in that sense), to the 'holy People of God' governed by the Pope, to 'the Christian people governed by God their maker', and to the whole body of the Church that is sanctified and governed by the Spirit of God. In other texts that consider the 'circles of humanity', the Church thinks first of those who are furthest from its life and faith and it moves inwards from there, ending with those who are in full communion. Here it moves in the opposite direction, beginning with prayers for those who are members of the Catholic Church in its various rites and moving outwards to include others and eventually all people.

The remaining six prayers reach out from there to include, in the first place, other Christians. They are recognized as belonging to 'the flock of the Son' and as already consecrated by the one baptism. The prayer is for the unity of all Christians, that they may be joined together by integrity of faith and united in the bond of charity. As they live the truth, the prayer concludes, may God gather them together and keep them in his one church.

The next group to be acknowledged and prayed for is the Jewish people, 'to whom God spoke first'. The prayer is that they might advance in love of God's name and in faithfulness to his covenant. This was, in the past, one of the most controversial moments in the Catholic liturgies, with a derogatory reference to the Jewish people that contributed significantly to anti-Jewish thinking along the many centuries of the Church's history. It is one of the essential gains of the renewed liturgy of the last century that this derogatory reference has been removed. The prayer is now expressed in terms that seek to honour central elements of the Jewish faith – the love of God's name, and fidelity to the covenant – and prays that the people God first made his own may attain the fullness of redemption.

It is to be noted also that Judaism is not here treated as 'another religion', for the inescapable dependence of Christianity on its Jewish origins is recognized and accepted. God first spoke to the Jewish people, established his covenant initially with them, and drew them in the first place into the love of his name. Nor are the Jewish people counted among those who do not believe in Christ (the next prayer), because it is from them that we have learned about the Messiah; it is from them, as Jesus himself says, that salvation comes (Jn 4.22), and it is to that people that Jesus Christ forever belongs.

The next group prayed for is people who do not believe in Christ, implying people of religious faiths other than the Christian or Jewish ones. The prayer is not a simply 'may they be converted to Christianity', but rather 'may they enter on the way of salvation' and, by walking before God with sincere hearts, may they find the truth. This is another area of reflection and action that has received much attention in recent decades. It has become ever more urgent in a world that is in many ways increasingly united while in other ways it remains afflicted by deep divisions, rivalries and mistrust.

Also contained in this prayer is an acknowledgement that Christians are not always helpful in showing to others the beauty of their faith. By being constant in mutual love, it says, and by striving to understand more fully the mystery of God's life, may believers in Christ be more perfect witnesses to God's love in the world. It makes clear that holiness, and the witness of a good life that it brings about, is the most powerful tool in the missionary equipment of the Church as it seeks to show to the world what faith in Christ brings about in human lives.

There are yet three more prayers on Good Friday, three other groups of people that the Church has in its 'thoughts and prayers' at the holiest time of the Christian year, as humanity stands before the cross of Jesus. The first of these are people who do not believe in God. Perhaps such people would prefer not to be prayed for, if they regard prayers as at best an illusory activity, at worst a form of mental illness! But people normally appreciate good wishes even when the way in which those wishes are expressed seems to them to be gauche, childish or misled.

The prayer of the Church is that people who do not believe in God might follow what is right in sincerity of heart and so find the way to God himself. Saint John of the Cross has helped numerous people trying to find their way through the darkness that inevitably disrupts the spiritual journey, even the journey of those whose faith is strong (perhaps more so the journey of those whose faith is strong, as we see in the experiences of saints such as Thérèse of Lisieux and Teresa of Calcutta). *En una noche oscura*, begins the most famous of John of the Cross's poems, 'On a dark night': moving by the light of faith, the one seeking truth and love is led to find the One being sought.

This Good Friday prayer for those who do not believe in God applies the same conviction. 'Follow what is right in sincerity of heart', it says. What else can anybody do except follow whatever light of truth they have? The conviction of Christians is that any truth, no matter where it is found, no matter by whom it is enunciated, no matter what it is about, is a spark of the Eternal Logos, a glimpse of the Eternal Wisdom. The idea comes from Justin Martyr, the second-century philosopher whose quest, in sincerity of heart, led him finally to faith in Christ and even to dying as a martyr rather than deny that faith. Augustine of Hippo, some centuries later, developed an argument for the existence of God starting from the existence of truth, any truth, the simplest truth, the only truth perhaps to which one can commit oneself in a dark night – it does not matter, for truth points us to Truth, which is what people mean when they speak of God.

The Good Friday liturgy does not enter into arguments for the existence of God, although the event it commemorates raises that question more powerfully than any other moment in the Christian year. It commemorates the death of one believed by the centurion who saw him die to be the Son of God (Mk 15.39), a faith shared subsequently by millions. It is the death of a man accepted by most people as at least one of the best human beings who ever lived. All must be struck by the apparent abandonment of that good man, in the moment of his greatest need, by the one he called 'Father'. The prayer does not enter into 'theodicy', God and the mystery of evil. Instead, it continues in this way, echoing Augustine and Justin, John of the Cross and Paul too in his speech to the philosophers of Athens (Acts 17) – God created all people to seek him by desiring him and to come to rest by finding him; may all people recognize the signs of God's fatherly love as well as the good works done by those who believe in God. May they then come to faith in God, 'father of our human race'. And may they do that, the prayer adds, 'despite every harmful obstacle', accepting that people's reasons for not believing in God are sometimes compounded, and perhaps sometimes provoked in the first place, by either the scandalous witness of believers, or the inadequacy of their understanding and presentation of the mystery of God.

The final two prayers concern not two further circles of humanity but people from all the groups already prayed for – Catholics, other Christians, Jews, people of other religions, unbelievers. For it is from all of these groups that those in public office are drawn and the penultimate prayer is for them. It is a prayer for peace, freedom, prosperity and security, that God might direct those in authority so that these things will be assured for the people for whom they have direct responsibility, and for the whole world.

The final prayer is also for people drawn from all the circles already mentioned. It is a prayer asking God to cleanse the world of errors, banish disease, drive out hunger, unlock prisons, loosen fetters, keep travellers safe, bring pilgrims home, give health to the sick and salvation to the dying. It is a prayer for all human beings who find themselves in circumstances that cause anxiety or suffering. It is a prayer for all of humanity without exception, since every man and every woman and every child will be in one or other of these circumstances sooner or later.

This final prayer outlines a full programme for social and political action, for human development and progress. It may seem strange that in the immediate presence of the cross of Jesus – what comes next in the Good Friday liturgy is the veneration of that cross – we think of our most basic needs and of our most common difficulties. But they are never far from us and we are never far from thinking about them. It is as if we are thanking God for the sacrifice we commemorate on Good Friday, by which the world is saved, but at the same time are saying, 'so let's now see this great mercy have its effect in the concrete and ordinary preoccupations to which we will be returning as soon as this liturgy is over'. It is an instinctively Catholic thing thus to pray for all people, all the more striking in the liturgical setting in which it is done on Good Friday.

THE CIRCLES OF THE CHURCH'S CARE

There are a number of other places in which the circles of humanity to which Catholicism believes itself obliged to relate are considered. One is *Ecclesiam suam*, the first encyclical letter of Pope Paul VI, which he issued in 1964, just a year before the promulgation of *Lumen gentium*. Although overshadowed by *LG* it is a text that still repays attention, not just for getting a sense of the preoccupations of the moment in which Paul VI began his pontificate, but for what it has to say particularly about dialogue. It was one of the 'buzzwords' of 1960s theology, taken up in a serious way by the new Pope, who offers what seems to be the only sustained theological reflection on the concept of dialogue in any conciliar or papal document. We shall look at it more closely in the next chapter.

Regarding the circles of humanity, the Pope presents them in the opposite direction to that taken by the Good Friday prayers. Thus, he speaks first of the Church's dialogue with unbelievers, next of its dialogue with believers in God, then its dialogue with other believers in Christ, and finally he speaks of dialogue within the Church.[7]

Lumen gentium does follow the direction taken by the Good Friday prayers, speaking first of the Roman Catholic Church and then of Eastern Catholic Churches in full communion with the Bishop of Rome.[8] Next come the Eastern Orthodox Churches, the Christian communities closest in doctrine and practice to Catholicism.[9] There is a shared history of a thousand years and a shared library of theological and spiritual works. Many great saints, martyrs and theologians continue to be honoured by both 'lungs' of the Christian world, and certainly the Catholic side of the relationship is greatly helped by the spiritual riches of the Eastern traditions. There were a number of occasions during the second millennium when efforts were made to heal the great schism between East and West. Great steps forward in this direction were taken in the 1960s, facilitated by the work of Vatican II and by the building of a fraternal relationship between

216

Paul VI and the Ecumenical Patriarch Athenagoras. The mutual excommunications were revoked, many fraternal meetings took place and joint commissions to explore theological differences were established.

This ecumenical opening on the part of the Roman Church is seen also in its relationship with the next two circles: that of the Anglican Communion and that of the Protestant Churches (*LG* 15; *Decree on Ecumenism* 19–23). In each case observers were invited from these communities to attend sessions of the Council, and dialogue about doctrine and practice was initiated with many different groups.

The circles continue from there to consider first Judaism, then Islam, and finally other world religions, especially Hinduism and Buddhism. Once again unbelievers are addressed and their concerns acknowledged (*LG* 16). Vatican II devoted two further documents to thinking about the Catholic Church's relationship with other religions, a *Declaration on Non-Christian Religions* and a *Decree on Religious Freedom*.

Although in recent decades it is dialogue between Christianity and Islam that has taken central stage, at the time of Vatican II – just twenty years after the Shoah – it was the relationship with Judaism that took priority. Recognizing humanity as one community from one stock and with a common destiny, Vatican II reproved any discrimination or harassment of people on the basis of race, colour, condition in life or religion (*On Non-Christian Religions*, 5). It acknowledged the spiritual ties than link Christians, the people of the New Covenant, with the stock of Abraham, the Jewish people. The Church's faith and calling begin with Abraham and Moses and the revelation God gave to his chosen people is received by the Church by way of that people. The Church draws nourishment from that good olive tree onto which the wild olive branches of the Gentiles have been grafted. The image is from Saint Paul, in Romans 11.17-24, and those three chapters of Romans, 9–11, are basic for the Church's understanding of its relationship with Judaism. God does not take back the gifts he bestowed or the choice he made, the Council says, quoting Saint Paul once again (Rom. 11.28-29). It gave special attention to stressing that neither all Jews indiscriminately at the time, nor Jews today, can be charged with the crimes committed during the passion of Jesus. It deplored all hatreds, persecutions, displays of anti-Semitism levelled at any time or from any source against the Jews (*On Non-Christian Religions*, 4). Great strides have been made in dialogue and in fraternal relationship between the Catholic Church and Judaism in the intervening years, the most recent substantial document from the Church being one that considers *The Jewish People and their Sacred Scriptures in the Christian Bible*.[10]

Muslims are held in high regard, Vatican II says, because they worship God as one, living and subsistent, merciful and almighty, Creator of heaven and earth, who has spoken to human beings. They strive to submit themselves without reserve to God as Abraham did, they worship Jesus as a prophet, and they honour and invoke Mary, his virgin mother. They await the day of judgement and the reward of God following the resurrection of the dead, they esteem upright living and worship God by prayer, alms-deeds and fasting. There is a long history of quarrels and dissensions between Christians and Muslims, but now, along with remembering the past, the dialogue strives to achieve understanding for the benefit of all, and to preserve peace, liberty, social justice and moral values. While the latter concerns have become more urgent in the intervening decades, the work of Pope Francis and the Grand Imam of al-Azhar in initiating a joint reflection on the theme of fraternity is a very significant positive development in this relationship.[11]

Believers in other religions are respected for their awareness of a hidden power, supreme being, or Father, an awareness that enables them to live with a deep religious sense and, in some civilizations and cultures, to develop well-defined concepts and precise language regarding religion. Hinduism is mentioned for its sense of divine mystery, myth, philosophy, ascetical practices, meditation and recourse to God, and so too is Buddhism, for its stress on the essential inadequacy of this changing world and its teaching of a way of life that aims at liberation and illumination either through human effort or with divine help (*On Non-Christian Religions* 2).

The Church expresses respect for other religions also, saying that it rejects nothing of what is true and holy in them because that reflects a ray of the truth that is for the enlightenment of all people. At the same time the Church continues to proclaim Christ as 'the way, the truth and the life' (Jn 14.6), believing as it does that all truth, goodness and beauty find their source, their proper development and their fulfilment in him. Dialogue and proclamation remain the two main instruments with which the Church carries on its mission in the world, alongside the witness of good people.

RECONCILIATION OF JEWS AND GENTILES, GOD AND HUMANITY

In two Dominican churches in Rome we find representations of the reconciliation of Jews and Gentiles, their coming together to form one body, centred on Christ, the Messiah of Israel and the Head of the Church. The basilica of Santa Sabina dates from the fifth century and has a mosaic dating from its foundation in which the Jews and the Gentiles are represented by female figures, standing on either side of the monumental inscription that tells of the building of the Church. The present church of San Clemente dates from the twelfth century and has a mosaic dating from its foundation in which the Jews and the Gentiles are represented by lines of sheep, one coming out of Jerusalem and the other out of Bethlehem, to join the Lamb of God who stands in the centre. It is striking that a theme that is of such urgency in the early years of the Church's life, as we see from the Acts of the Apostles and the letters of Saint Paul, should have retained its representational power, for here it is still in the fifth century and again in the twelfth century. It is because the reconciliation of Jews and Gentiles is, for Christianity, paradigmatic of all reconciliations, between all classes and groups of people but also, more fundamentally, between humanity as a whole and God.

We spoke earlier of the Church as the sacrament of the unity of humanity, a community that is meant to be a sign and fulfilment of the fraternity, solidarity and communion for which humanity is made and which all human beings somehow desire. We saw that for Aquinas the principal effect of the grace of Christ in the Church is its unity. This is based on many texts from the New Testament: Christ as the head of the Church, the fullness of God dwells in him, God was in Christ reconciling all things to himself, making peace by the blood of his cross (Col. 1.19-20; Eph. 2.13-18; Col. 1.22; 3.15; Heb. 10.10; 1 Pet. 2.24). These references are, in the first place, to the physical body of Jesus, suffering and dying on the cross, and to his blood poured out for the healing and redemption of humanity. But because of the strong association between the physical body of Christ and the Church as the body of Christ in another sense, it is impossible, when reading these texts, not to think of both meanings. Thus, we are reconciled to God in one body through the cross (Eph. 2.16) and Jews and Gentiles are now members of the same body (Eph. 3.6). It is even clearer in Colossians 1.22, which says that the reconciliation is 'in his body of flesh by his death', and yet almost immediately the second meaning comes in as Paul speaks of completing in his own flesh what is lacking in Christ's afflictions for the sake of his body, now understood as the Church (Col. 1.24). Not surprisingly we hear both meanings in a text such as Colossians 3.15, 'the peace of Christ to which you were called in the one body', to which is added a third, Eucharistic, meaning in a text like 1 Corinthians 11.29, 'in eating which we are to discern the body'. So, there is the actual physical body of Jesus, there is his body the Church, there is the Eucharistic body. And a fourth meaning can be added, for there is also the resurrected body, which gets particular attention in 1 Corinthians 15.

In his commentary on texts of Saint Paul that speak of reconciliation between Jews and Gentiles, Aquinas is keen to speak always of reconciliation between God and humanity.

The cause of enmity between people is sin and its remedy is mutual love. But neither part of that, either the analysis or the solution, can be understood without reference to God, for sin is a theological concept and mutual love is only possible as a gift from the Holy Spirit. Not to love my brothers and sisters is not to love God; to be fully and truly reconciled with my brothers and sisters happens only within the deeper reconciliation between God and humanity, the forgiveness of sins and our participation in the fruit of the sacrifice that takes sin away (Rom. 5.10; 2 Cor. 5.19; Gal. 1.4; Eph. 2.14-18; Col. 1.19-20; Heb. 9.28).

This takes effect through the Spirit that was given up by Jesus on the cross and breathed on his disciples after his resurrection (Jn 19.30; 20.22). Having considered the life of the Church with the Son, and the common human nature that is healed through that life, we turn next to consider the life of the Church in the Holy Spirit, and the personal gifts the Spirit bestows on each one who is sent to bear witness, to build up the communion and to love not just in words and in speech but in deeds and in truth (1 Jn 3.18).

II

In the Spirit: The Love of Christ Urges Us On

'He just keeps saying to her, and over and over again, the word "love".' This was in a letter from a friend, telling me about her brother and how besotted he was with his infant daughter. 'Of course,' my friend went on, 'the little one has no idea what her father is saying to her, but what the word means is being built up between them as he goes on saying it and she goes on looking at him.'

One of the most beautiful phrases in Thomas Aquinas's extensive writings is the phrase *'verbum spirans amorem'*, a word breathing love. We find it near the beginning of his *Summa theologiae*, in question 43 of the first part, a question that considers the missions of the Persons of the Trinity. The Son and the Spirit are sent from the Father: this is what the New Testament teaches. The Son is also called the Word, because he is the communication of God's wisdom and intentions. Aquinas explains that this Word is not just a word with intellectual content and rational meaning. It is also, and always, a word breathing love. Just as my friend's brother was creating love between himself and his daughter through the word he was speaking to her, God establishes Love between himself and his people through the word he speaks to us. If Word is a name for the Son, Love is a name for the Holy Spirit.

The Son and the Spirit, Word and Love, cannot be separated in God or in God's actions towards the world. God speaks the Word whose meaning is Love. He is addressing us and perhaps like my friend's little niece we are not quite sure what exactly is being said to us. But the meaning of what is said – Love – is being built up between us as God goes on speaking his Word and we continue looking towards God as he utters it.

Just as there is no human word without the warm breath that sustains the articulation of the word, so there is no Word of God without the warm Breath that is the Holy Spirit and that sustains the articulation of that Word. We cannot separate the work of the Son and the work of the Spirit. We saw that Aquinas considered the heart a better metaphor for the Holy Spirit than the head, which is more appropriate to Christ, he says. One is invisible, the other visible; one is internal, the other external. We might even say one is feminine, generating internally, and the other is masculine, generating externally. Whatever images and metaphors we use, the important thing is that we speak of both whenever we speak of one. Jesus breathed forth his spirit, the Gospel of John tells us, and it has the double meaning: he died, and in that moment he breathed forth the Spirit (Jn 19.30). It is made explicit in the following chapter when he appeared to his disciples, breathed on them, and said 'Receive the Holy Spirit ... as the Father has sent me, even so I send you' (Jn 20.21-22). 'The Lord is the Spirit', Paul says in 2 Corinthians 3.17. 'God's love has been poured into our hearts through the Holy Spirit who has been given to us' (Rom. 5.5), and it is this same love, the love of Christ, that 'urges us on' (2 Cor. 5.14).

From the Word breathing Love comes not just understanding, therefore, but also energy and vitality. To receive the gift of God – and 'Gift' is another name for the Holy Spirit – means not just to be loved but to become a lover. Because the Word that is spoken to us is a Word that breathes Love, we have not really received it until we begin to love. So the Church, the body of Christ in the world, is only truly hearing and receiving the Word when it becomes a force for love in the world. That love expresses itself in the Church's mission to the world and its service of the world, a mission and service it believes Christ entrusted to it when he breathed on his disciples and sent them, just as the Father had sent him, on the same mission, to continue the same service.

So in this chapter we will speak about the Church *ad extra*, the Church in its relations with those widening circles of humanity for which it prays. It is the Spirit that urges us to pray and it is the same Spirit that urges us to act. We have seen already the different groups of people to whom the Church believes it must relate. Here we will think about the different ways in which the Church acts in the world, the different matters with which it is concerned, and the different 'faces' it presents in different contexts, for it is at once a religious community, a moral voice, a political actor, a very particular NGO (non-governmental organization), and so on.

MISSION AND SERVICE

The Church seeks to fulfil the mission received from Christ by proclaiming the good news of what he has done for humanity, in other words by preaching the gospel and seeking to 'evangelize'. That last word can sound a bit threatening – as if someone is coming after me with the intention of doing something to me, putting me under some kind of pressure to change my life, to change my ideas, to align myself with what that person believes to be true and right. It is as if the only way of 'evangelizing' is the way in which we sometimes experience it at the hands of very earnest people, sincerely convinced of the truth they want to share with us but with a determination that sometimes prevents them genuinely listening to the one they are seeking to 'evangelize'. So we end up feeling it is something they need to do more for themselves than for us.

Break open the word 'evangelize', however, and it means to 'gospel' somebody, to share good news with another person. The motivation of the one sharing the news needs to be thought about, just as the content of the news and the method of its sharing need to be considered. The best place to look to see how it ought to be done is to look back at Jesus and to see what kind of teacher he was, what kind of evangelizer. How did he go about things?

How did he relate with people in order to help them understand what he was teaching? We will see below how he entered into dialogue with people, but it was not all straightforward even for him. People misunderstood very often, including his closest disciples. Things needed to be explained more than once, their minds needed to be broadened and deepened, people continued to get the wrong end of the stick. Some of his teachings were so challenging, strange and threatening that many who had initially been attracted to him gave up and went away. Others became convinced that he needed to be silenced.

The preaching of the apostles as recorded in the Acts of the Apostles is another rich source of information about the first proclamation of the gospel. We see Peter, Paul and others speaking with Jewish congregations and with non-Jewish congregations, with religious people and with those not particularly religious, with civil leaders and with philosophers – all kinds of encounters that usually ended with some people coming to believe in Christ and others deciding against it. Sometimes the apostles were arrested or driven out of town, sometimes they were celebrated and even regarded as 'gods'. Their preaching, we are told, was helped by signs and wonders that accompanied it, but as things developed it became clear that the most powerful sign of the truth of what they were saying would be the witness of their lives and the lives of those who came to believe through their preaching.

The later years of John Paul II's papacy saw him speaking often about the need for a 'new evangelization', a fresh presentation of the gospel that would be new in its methods, energy and expression. The end of the twentieth century was not the first time that the Church needed this kind of renewal. We see it in the eighteenth century, for example, with the foundation of preaching orders such as the Redemptorists and the Passionists. We see it in the sixteenth century with the foundation of the Jesuits. We see it in the thirteenth century with the establishment of the mendicant orders, the Franciscans and Dominicans, whose particular task was to be bands of preachers, witnessing not just by their words but by the simplicity and joy of their lifestyle. It is, it seems, a perennial need in the Church.

Pope Francis has not spoken as often about 'new evangelization' but rather of 'missionary discipleship'. It is a phrase he brought with him from South America, a theme of the great meeting of Latin American and Caribbean bishops at Aparecida, in Brazil in 2007. He has shared it with the whole Church, particularly through his encyclical *Evangelii gaudium*, the *Joy of the Gospel* (2013). Christ shares with every member of the Church his prophetic, priestly and royal functions. It means that every baptized and confirmed Christian is to be not just a disciple but a missionary disciple, one who speaks and acts and witnesses on behalf of the good news about Jesus Christ. Thomas Aquinas, in his account of the sacrament of confirmation, says that it is the sacrament of Christian adulthood, which means receiving the grace not only to participate personally in the life of the Church (to be loved) but to speak up and witness to what one believes and treasures (to be a lover).

It is, however, more through its actions than through its words that the Church proclaims the good news effectively and shows to the world the joy of the gospel. The many works of service that Church communities offer in all parts of the world are ways in which those communities speak the Word that breathes Love. In the documents of the Church that consider its mission in the world, the importance of the witness of people's lives is stressed again and again. In a famous letter on evangelization in 1975, Pope Paul VI commented that modern people listen more willingly to witnesses than to teachers, and if they do listen to teachers, it is because they are witnesses. 'It is primarily by her conduct and by her life that the Church will evangelize the world,' he says, 'by her living witness of fidelity to the Lord Jesus – the witness of poverty and detachment, of freedom in the face of the powers of this world, in short, the witness of holiness.'[1] The opposite is also true, of course, that the greatest obstacle to evangelization will be the counter-witness of scandal and betrayal, division and compromise, the ways in which the Church's members fall short of the life and mission they have received.

A THEOLOGY OF DIALOGUE

For the same Pope, Paul VI, the most important instrument of the Church's engagement with the world is dialogue, and he presented a theological reflection on this theme in his first encyclical, *Ecclesiam suam*. We understand God to be in dialogue with the world through his people, Pope Paul says, and how God has approached us in Jesus provides the pattern for how we ought to approach other human beings. This is not just a strategic observation, a comment about methodology. Being part of the Church means accepting a call to bear witness to Jesus Christ and to live by his Spirit, to abide in God as God abides in us (Jn 14.23); it means we have even come to share in the divine nature (2 Pet. 1.4). The point has been made already: if we have truly received the gift of God, we are not just people loved by God but people whom God is making to be lovers and so speakers and witnesses of the Word breathing Love. Our way of being in dialogue with others, therefore, will be a continuation of the way in which God is in dialogue with us: this is the deeper meaning intended.

The history of the various inter-Church and inter-religious dialogues initiated from the mid-1960s and carried on even today would require a long detour from the road on which we are travelling. Suffice it to say that the Church has continued to contribute to these dialogues, not without hiccups and bumps along the road. These dialogues have also been extended to include groups not initially envisaged, such as some of the smaller Protestant denominations, as well as engaging with more recent phenomena such as charismatic renewal, popular and contemporary religiosity, new forms of spirituality, and so on. We noted already that as regards other religions the dialogue with Judaism was an urgent priority in the 1960s, while dialogue with Islam became more urgent in the following decades.

It might be suggested that this concern with dialogue was simply a 'sign of the times' in the heady days of the 1960s, something seen as obligatory with the need to heal the wounds of terrible wars and to build peace and security in a world threatened by nuclear annihilation. Every council of the Church takes place within a particular social and political context and, not surprisingly, takes on something of the flavour of its time. But Pope Paul VI's theological reflection on dialogue has a more permanent value because it identifies as an essential aspect of its own nature this need of the Church to be in relationship with the Church's 'others'. If mission traditionally consisted in the proclamation of the gospel, passing on to others the invitation to believe in Christ, it seems clear that it must also mean dialogue with those others, learning about their beliefs and practices as well as understanding their questions and their needs.

For Pope Paul VI the approach of God to humanity in the Incarnation of the Son is a model for Christian approaches to the world.[2] This is simply taking seriously the missionary mandate recorded in Saint John's Gospel, that his disciples are sent by Jesus 'just as' Jesus was sent by the Father. It is not only the simple fact of being sent that is passed on to them, but also the goal of the sending, its motivation and its form. The features of this dialogue between God and humanity are first that *the initiative is from God*. The First Letter of John speaks of this: 'in this is love, not that we loved God but that he loved us and sent his Son to be the expiation for our sins' (1 Jn 4.10). A little later he adds, 'we love because God first loved us' (4.19). If the Church is to 'imitate God', as Paul tells the disciples they must do (Eph. 5.1), then the Church must not wait for others to seek dialogue but must reach out, take the initiative, and offer such dialogue to them.

In human affairs, there is often suspicion and mistrust, even, and perhaps especially, when one is being invited to enter into dialogue. So the motivation for the Church reaching out to others has to be carefully considered. How 'unconditional' can any human being's engagement in dialogue be? If we are sharing about deeply held convictions regarding what is true, how seriously can we say that we are 'open' to dialoguing about them? Are we ready to change or is it only the other person who must consider that?

(Note that the point applies not just to religious convictions but to deeply held opinions in other areas of life as well.)

In God's dialogue with humanity *the motivation is simply God's goodness and love*. The famous text of John 3.16-17, which some regard as the heart of the Gospel, summarizes this: 'God so loved the world that he gave his only Son ... not to condemn the world but that the world might be saved through him.' If the Church's motivation for dialogue is to be sincere love, then this cannot be done without a radical self-awareness and a sustained discipline on the part of those charged with such dialogue.

Another temptation in entering into dialogue is to see it in political terms, in terms of compromise perhaps, but also in terms of its practical usefulness. Looking once again to God's conversation with humanity, we see that *it perseveres* through many changes on the part of God's dialogue partners. Pope Paul refers to Luke 5.31, a saying of Jesus repeated elsewhere, that he has come not for the healthy but for the sick. This is not to be taken to mean that the Church regards itself as healthy and others as sick: the point is that the dialogue should have no terms or conditions attached to it, that its interest is the well-being of the other with whom the dialogue is undertaken and not something done by the Church for its own advantage. It was while we were sinners, Paul says, that Christ died for us (Rom. 5.8), contributing that most remarkable act of love to the ongoing conversation between God and humanity. 'As I have loved you, so you must love one another' is the new commandment of Jesus (Jn 15.12). The entire parallel between God's way of dialogue and that of the Church is contained in those four little words, 'as I ... so you'.

A dialogue that takes place on the basis of love for another person and concern for that person's well-being *must remain free*. If there is any coercion, manipulation or intimidation then the freedom of the other person is taken away and the dialogue loses its meaning. Once again we can look to the history of God's dealings with the people. His whole purpose is to establish a people capable of responding to him in love. Far from being a threat to human freedom, it is God's grace that establishes human beings in their full freedom. It is one of the most important points to communicate today, when people are sometimes encouraged to think that there is more freedom in atheism than in faith. 'For freedom Christ has set you free', Paul says to the Galatians, 'stand fast therefore, and do not submit again to a yoke of slavery' (Gal. 5.1). 'To continue in my word', Jesus says, 'is to know the truth, and the truth will make you free' (Jn 8.31-32). We see it concretely in Jesus's personal interactions with others. 'What do you want me to do for you?' he asks of a blind man, not presuming on the answer but leaving the man free to speak (Mk 10.51). 'Do you want to be healed?' he asks a man who has been ill for thirty-eight years, again not presuming on the answer but leaving the man free to speak (Jn 5.6).

Paul VI makes two final points in presenting his 'theology of dialogue'. The first is that the dialogue of salvation *is for all human beings*. This is clear from the very first moment of the relationship between God and humanity, when God called Abraham to be the father of a great nation and a blessing for all the nations of the world (Gen. 12.2-3). The Church's dialogue, therefore, must seek to include all human beings and even if, for various reasons, some parts of this dialogue get stuck, or never really get going, the Church's 'catholic' character will not allow it to rest. Even if the dialogue with this or that particular circle of humanity stalls, and even if it stalls for a long time, sooner or later the nature of the Church itself will move it to fresh efforts. It will move it at least to this extent, that it will not forget any section of humanity but will continue to pray God's blessing and the healing power of God's love for all men and women.

The final point of Pope Paul's reflection is that the dialogue of salvation *is progressive*. Once again the source of this insight is the history of salvation as recorded in the Bible. Again and again the dialogue between God and the people needed attention. Again and again the people wandered away from the requirements and promises of the covenant. Again and again God seemed absent and unconcerned about their situation. But again and again God called them back and invited them to renew the covenant once more. There is a lot for the Church to learn here also. Who knows what the pace of human and historical development will be? We have become so accustomed to things happening immediately, to instantaneous communication, that perhaps we are in danger of losing the capacities needed for moral and spiritual growth, for real knowledge and understanding. The disciplines required for such growth – not least the virtue of patience – are the same as those required for maintaining any dialogue that would have the features outlined above. All that can be done is to persevere, to be ready always to begin anew, to continue to seek the virtues that make genuine dialogue possible. Note that all this, although developed in regard to the Church's dialogue *ad extra*, with those outside, applies also to dialogue *ad intra*, to the conversations that are needed within the community and communion of the Church itself.

ONE CHURCH, DIFFERENT FACES

Catholicism relates to many different circles of humanity through proclamation and witness, through dialogue and service, but it relates as different things to different sections of humanity. The Catholic Church is a religious and spiritual community that relates to others as such and is related to by others as such. It is also a social and political reality whose interventions and contributions to social and political life are more or less welcome depending on the views and interests of the different groups of people affected by those interventions and contributions. The Church is also a moral authority for many people within and without, and although this authority has been damaged on many occasions over the years, over the centuries indeed, the Church continues to be a moral voice in the world. How things are received depends also on the receiver, and so the Church's teachings about moral and social questions are received differently depending on the interests and concerns of the receiver. For some, what is most important is the Church's defence of human life from the moment of conception to its natural end in death. For others what stands out is the Church's promotion of human dignity and its defence of human rights such as religious freedom. For still others it might be the Church's teaching about creation and ecology, or its teaching about capital punishment, about just war, and so on.

Where its moral authority becomes confused with political influence the Church has often given in to the satisfactions of such an arrangement, but when it comes to an end, as inevitably it must sooner or later, much work can be needed if the Church is to recover. Experiences of the Catholic Church in the twentieth century and on into the twenty-first, in places like Quebec, Ireland and Flanders, are lessons in the dangers and temptations that always accompany political influence and power. There is a wonderful paradox in the fact that it was precisely at the time the Church lost its temporal power in Italy that it gained a new authority through the tradition of social teaching that began with Leo XIII's encyclical letter *Rerum novarum* in 1891. This positioned the Church for over a century as a distinctive voice on social, economic and political questions, one that could never be simply identified with 'left-wing' or 'right-wing' political positions, even when forces from those corners put pressure on the Church to side with one or the other. It does not mean that individual members of the Church did not have political convictions and preferences, some of them admirable and others not so, and belonging not just to one of the usual political wings. The official teaching of the Church itself always remained independent and focused on values that it believes come from its own mission and service of the world: the dignity of the human person, the social nature of human beings, human rights and freedom, solidarity/ fraternity/social charity, the common good, development, subsidiarity, participation ... There are many agencies of the Church that continue to promote and develop these principles and there are many parishes, religious communities, charitable organizations and other groups that seek to apply them 'on the ground' in a range of concrete situations.

So the Church has a number of 'faces' and people relate to it according to the face that stands out for them. For some it is the institutional-historical face of the Church that is most prominent, its character as a religious institution proclaiming its message and witnessing to that message in how it lives, in its pastoral care of its members and in its liturgical life. For others it might be the intellectual-doctrinal face of the Church that predominates, its teachings about God and human dignity, and its contribution at the level of culture and education. For still others it might be the Church as a social and political reality, seen for example in its social teaching and its work of dialogue, its involvement as an NGO, in effect, in so many development projects, in healthcare and social welfare, as also in its advocacy on behalf of people who are without power. It exercises an influence also through the extensive network of diplomats who serve the Catholic Church in many countries and provide a valued service of the human community. That the Holy See has such a network of diplomatic missions is an accident of history and not part of the essential structure of the Church, but one that nevertheless does much good. It is yet another level of complexity in what is often referred to simply as 'the Vatican'.

Finally, we can recall the three hierarchies discussed earlier: that of pastors, that of teachers, and that of saints. In discussing them we spoke of a teaching authority that accompanies each one, a *magisterium* appropriate to its character and its place in the structure of the Church. Depending on how these hierarchies have been encountered and experienced, and on which of them has been most important for particular individuals, the Church once again is a reality of many faces.

All of this as it originates and is undertaken by the Church is regarded as the work of the Holy Spirit, the Love the Church breathes in the Word it preaches. 'There are varieties of gifts but the same Spirit', to quote 1 Corinthians 12 yet one more time, 'there are varieties of service, but the same Lord, and there are varieties of working, but it is the same God who inspires them all in every one' (1 Cor. 12.4-6). We have seen how that text has been applied to the internal life of the Church as the body of Christ. Here we simply note that it applies also to the external life of the

Church, its mission and service of the world, which is even more variegated than its internal life but still held together in unity by the Holy Spirit.

SOME UNUSUAL METAPHORS

The Word is *Logos* and *logos* means definition and order. The Spirit is Breath or Wind and blows where it wills (Jn 3.8). So the wisdom of the Word is accompanied by the creativity of the Spirit, by a certain unpredictability and even wildness. Hence some unusual metaphors generated by the Spirit on the pages of the Bible, a number of which repay our attention at this point. They are all found in Paul's Second Letter to the Corinthians, where he is speaking of the community's outreach, its radiance or impact beyond itself.

Having just mentioned the diplomatic service of the Holy See we can begin with Paul's description of himself and his fellow preachers as *ambassadors*. It is another way of speaking about the mission. An ambassador is one who is sent from one place to another in order to represent the one who has sent him before the ones to whom he is sent. Paul's idea is that he has been sent by God to the Corinthians to make representations to them on God's behalf. 'God makes his appeal through us', he says, and the ambassador immediately turns into a beggar pleading with them to 'be reconciled to God' (2 Cor. 5.20). What has promoted him to this status of ambassador is the new reality that comes with Christian faith and it applies to all who are 'in Christ', not just to Paul and the other apostles. This 'new creation', as he calls it, means yet again that we are not only the recipients of grace but the recipients of a call implicit in that grace to bring to others what we are ourselves receiving. Here the grace is reconciliation: God was in Christ reconciling the world to himself, we believe that we have ourselves been included in this reconciliation (Paul can speak with more authority than most of us about this), and part of the deal is that we are now entrusted with the 'ministry of reconciliation': we are to be not just reconciled but reconcilers (2 Cor. 5.17-20).

A stranger metaphor is found earlier in the same letter: we are the *aroma of Christ*, Paul tells them (2 Cor. 2.15). Early in his papacy Pope Francis said he wanted the priests of the Church to have the smell of the sheep about them. He meant they should be as closely involved in the lives of the people as the shepherd is with the sheep, to the point of smelling of the sheep. They should be getting their hands dirty is probably another way of saying the same thing, not living at a distance from the people to whom they are sent, but sharing their lives.

Smell is probably the last of the senses we would think of using as a metaphor for spiritual realities. It seems to be the most crudely physical of the senses. Seeing and hearing are fine, touching and tasting as well, but smell can seem like a sense too far. We are told that it is the sense that is left quite underdeveloped in most human beings, and perhaps therefore most of us are only aware of smells when they are extreme. In fact, smell has a place in the Church's tradition precisely in speaking about the Holy Spirit. Like the wind, smell is invisible, it gets everywhere, it moves around without any control, it persists. We are told that the anointing of the newly baptized Christians produced a rich smell in the Easter liturgies of the early Church. We are to imagine people being anointed with aromatic oils as they emerge from the baptismal font. It was not just a token dab on the forehead but an anointing all over. Now imagine a good number of people so anointed and the aroma that would spread from them around the Church. Combine it with incense and the smell of wax burning in the candles, add flowers and food and wine, and you have an experience that is olfactorily very rich! The oil of chrism in particular is taken to represent the Holy Spirit in a sacramental way, as a reality that functions also as a symbol in which the Holy Spirit is present and working.[3]

Paul may be thinking of this link already: the practice of anointing the sick with oil was well established and the story of Jesus having his feet anointed is recorded in all four Gospels. The name 'Christ' means the anointed one, the Messiah, and those who came to believe in him were also counted among the 'anointed'. A

Christian, a 'christened' one, ought therefore to have a particular smell about them. It is the fragrance of the knowledge of Christ (2 Cor. 2.14), the smell of the Holy Spirit.

Paul continues with an even stranger thought, saying that different people will experience this aroma in radically different ways. Those who are on the road of faith will experience it as a pleasant smell, a smell of life, but for those who are not on the road to faith it will be an unpleasant smell, a smell of death. You have a choice between life and death, the people of Israel were told in the Book of Deuteronomy (Deut. 30.15), and here Paul seems to be saying the same thing using his metaphor of the aroma of Christ. Depending on people's disposition it will be experienced as a very welcome perfume or as a very unwelcome stench.

There is yet another image Paul uses in 2 Corinthians, again with reference to the influence of the Christian community beyond itself. You are *a letter of recommendation*, he says, from Christ, written by us, not in ink on paper, but with the Holy Spirit on your hearts (2 Cor. 3.1-3). The immediate context is Paul's defence of his own preaching ministry. With what letters of recommendation did I arrive in Corinth, he asks them. You yourselves are my letter of recommendation for all the world to read, is his reply. It is something we mentioned above: that as the Church developed it quickly became clear that the most convincing sign of the message being preached was the life of the communities that gathered around that message.

This letter of recommendation is delivered by us, Paul says; I am the postman and you are the letter. It means the Christian reality is to be read off the community, it is to be known by seeing that community, how it lives and how its members are serving each other and the world. Simply by being Christians, believers in Christ and followers of him, we ought to be communicating something to the world, as if we were a letter sent by Christ to the world. He said it himself in these words: 'by this everyone will know that you are my disciples, if you love one another' (Jn 13.35).

BEING MADE TO ACT FREELY

In speaking of Christians as a letter written by him with the Holy Spirit on their hearts, Paul evokes the text of Jeremiah 31.31-34, which speaks of a new covenant written not on tablets of stone but directly onto human hearts. Later, Christian thinkers spoke of this as the 'new law', beginning from many things Jesus says in the Sermon on the Mount (Mt. 5–7). This new law moves people to act from within rather than obliging them from without, it is motivated by love of the good rather than fear of punishment, and it consists primarily (so Thomas Aquinas puts it) in the grace of the Holy Spirit itself and only secondarily in laws that can be written down on paper or chiselled into stone.

The Holy Spirit, Aquinas says, 'makes us act freely', and that sounds like a proper paradox, if not sheer contradiction. If I am made to act by another agent, how can it be free? Paul uses an expression that is not quite as strong but that points us in the same direction. The love of Christ 'urges us on', he says (2 Cor. 5.14), and he uses a Greek term that has also been translated as constrains us, controls us, rules us, compels us, possesses us. Such an influence of the Holy Spirit, God's Love, on human hearts seems to leave little room for human freedom. The very idea of being commanded to love raises the same difficulty. If it is to be truly love, then it must be free. If it is done in obedience to a command, or out of a sense of obligation or duty, how can it be free? How could it be love in any meaningful sense of the word? Aquinas sees the difficulty even while using the phrase 'the Holy Spirit makes us act freely'. The point for him is that a person acts with freedom only when they choose what is good simply and solely out of love for that good and not because they have been told to do it, or because they fear the consequences if they do not, or for any other reason. He even says this about obeying God – to do what is good out of obedience to God is good, obviously, but we are still not acting with the kind of freedom we could have, he says. It is only the grace of the Holy Spirit that gives us that freedom, healing the wounds of our nature, giving us clear minds and purified desires, fixing our will simply on what is good, enabling us to be lovers of the good.

God's love is not a rival power to human freedom, a more powerful agent in the same network of agents. God's love is the power that sets us free and makes it possible for us, perhaps for the first time, to choose what is good with full freedom. Paul is never far away: 'For freedom Christ has set us free', he says to the Galatians (Gal. 5.1), and that wonderful final movement in Romans 1–8 begins with him reminding his readers that 'the law of the Spirit of life in Christ Jesus has set us free from the law of sin and death' (Rom. 8.2). To live under this new law is to be radically free, enjoying those fruits of the Spirit that Paul lists in Galatians 5.22-23: love, joy, peace, patience, kindness, goodness, faithfulness, gentleness, self-control – against such, he concludes, there is no law.

The question of motivation is at the heart of Christian life and mission in the world. While we can, with Pope Paul VI, say that God's initiative in his dialogue with his people comes purely and simply from his love for that people, human motivation is rarely if ever pure and uncontaminated by self-interest. The influence of the Holy Spirit in the body of Christ is to move people towards that kind of love, to make it possible for human beings to love God and to love one another with God's own love. This is what the love of Christ (*agape*, charity) means, and it is 'the way that is better than any other' (1 Cor. 12.31). It is not something we can generate within ourselves through earnest wilfulness or persistent thinking. It is always the gift of love, of the Holy Spirit who is called both Gift and Love, and our participation in it is always a response to a prior initiative. In contributing to the ongoing mission and service of Christ for the world the Church is therefore joined with a mission and service that originate in God's initiative from the beginning.

WE SEEK BECAUSE HE FIRST SOUGHT US

It was a privilege and a pleasure on one occasion to be in the presence of the Dalai Lama and to hear him speak about Buddhist meditation. There were two Christian contributions that day, about forms of meditation in Catholic religious orders. The Dalai Lama said that he could agree with everything the Christian speakers said, making just one change, and that was to replace the term 'God' with the phrase 'ultimate reality'. Human beings seek ultimate reality: about this there was agreement. A question came from the audience, however, and it has remained with me ever since as the key moment in that conversation. 'Accepting that we seek ultimate reality,' the questioner said to the Dalai Lama, 'would you say that ultimate reality seeks us?' He thought for a while and then he said, 'No, I would not say that ultimate reality seeks us.'

Buddhism, according to Henri de Lubac, is the supreme achievement of human spirituality if we leave aside the incarnation of the Word, if we leave aside the belief that in Jesus Christ the Word of God, the Word that breathes Love, became flesh and dwelt among us. In other words, if we leave aside the belief that ultimate reality seeks us. But that is the heart of the Christian faith: 'We love because God first loved us' (1 Jn 4.19). We seek because we have been sought. We love because we have been loved. How do we know this? We know it because we believe that the one Jesus calls his 'Father' sent the Son to heal our common nature and the Spirit to strengthen us as individual persons. That is also how we know that God is love, a statement that we could not intend in any literal sense apart from this revelation. We might already see that God could be benign, kind, condescending, compassionate and merciful to creatures. But to speak of the nature of God as love, and to speak of human persons made able to participate in that divine nature: all of this is only possible through the work of the Son and the work of the Spirit. It is Father, Son and Spirit together who make God to be love. It is Father, Son and Spirit together who have sought out humanity, the Father embracing us through the Son and the Spirit, and inviting us into the mystery of their life of love.

The Church's life *ad extra*, its mission and service of the world, is founded on this mission and service of humanity that originate in God's own missionary nature. In the previous chapter we considered how the Church's life is always a life with the Son, head of the Church and head of humanity. In this chapter we have considered how it is always a life in the Holy Spirit, the Love breathed by the Word, animating and motivating the Church in its internal and external life. It remains for us to consider how the life of the Church is a life directed towards the Father, the one to whom both Jesus and the Spirit point us, the source of all things and, as we believe, the one who in seeking us draws us to seek him.

To the Father: From Glory to Glory

THE PRAYER OF THE CHURCH

'Show us the Father', the apostle Philip says to Jesus, 'and we shall be satisfied' (Jn 14.8). 'He who has seen me, has seen the Father', replies Jesus (Jn 14.9). Saint Paul tell us that 'when we cry "Abba, Father", it is the Spirit himself bearing witness with our spirit that we are children of God' (Rom. 8.15-16). He repeats the point in his Letter to the Galatians: 'God has sent the Spirit of his Son into our hearts, crying "Abba, Father"' (4.6).

The Son and the Spirit are sent by the Father but the Father is not Himself sent. So how are we to know the Father, except through the Son who has made Him known (Jn 1.18) and the Spirit who pours His love into our hearts (Rom. 5.5)? The Son and the Spirit are like the arms within which God embraces the world while the Father in Himself remains mysterious to us, in what we see in Jesus Christ and in what we receive through the Holy Spirit. We use the name 'Father' because it is the one Jesus used when he speaks about the One who had sent him and to whom he was returning.

All works of God are works of the entire Trinity of Persons, but traditionally creation is appropriated to the Father who is the source and the origin of all things just as He is the end and the destination of all things. In a book about Saint Joseph, the Brazilian theologian Leonardo Boff writes as follows:

We need the presence of the three divine Persons among us, Father, Son, and Holy Spirit. The Father must be joined with the Son and the Holy Spirit. Otherwise, we are left as if floating in air, without a sense of origin and of the end of all mystery of revelation and of God's communication in history, which are represented in the Person of the Father.[1]

This book has been about the Church and ends with a reflection on God the Father. As a people animated and guided by the Holy Spirit, the Church is the body of Christ and the sacrament of the unity of humankind. It is also, 'already and not yet', the kingdom that is coming, the 'new heavens and new earth where righteousness dwells' (2 Pet. 3.13). The prayer of the Church, therefore, which has its essential form in the great Eucharistic Prayer, is made to the Father, through the Son, in the Holy Spirit. That prayer includes the words of institution from the Last Supper as well as the prayer of *epiclesis*, calling on the Holy Spirit to transform the bread and wine into the body and blood of Christ and to make us one body and one spirit in Christ. And it concludes with the Trinitarian doxology, or hymn of praise, 'through him (Christ), with him, and in him, O God, almighty Father, in the unity of the Holy Spirit, all glory and honour is yours, for ever and ever'.

PRAYER AND HOPE

Prayer is the fundamental action of a person or community that hopes in God. A poem by George Herbert entitled 'Prayer' consists simply of a litany of beautiful phrases, one of which is 'heart in pilgrimage'. The Church is a pilgrim in time, living in a present moment, always remembering and celebrating its origins while living towards a future culmination of which it has received the promise and the pledge.

We saw that some of the biblical images for the Church are taken from the world of construction: it is a building, a city, a pillar and buttress, a temple. But other images are less fixed, less established and more fluid: the Church is itself a way, a road, a dispersion made up of exiles, a new Exodus. On the one hand it is already the sabbath rest while on the other it is the age that is yet to come. 'We have here no abiding city, but seek one that is to come' (Heb. 13.14). If prayer is the characteristic act of the virtue of hope, hope itself is what keeps the pilgrim travelling. It is about living in time: on the basis of what we have come to know about God and his actions in the past, hope gives confidence for the future, and frees us to live joyfully in the present.

Pope Benedict XVI issued a series of encyclical letters on the theological virtues of faith, hope and love. His encyclical on hope was published in 2007 and was entitled *Spe salvi*, 'saved in hope', a phrase we find in Romans 8.24. He began his letter by distinguishing the attitude of hope from related concepts that might seem to be practically equivalent: progress, evolution and history itself. Although we can talk about progress and evolution in relation to the Church, and the Church is obviously a community in history, the attitude of hope is not simply identical with any of these. The shocks of the twentieth century undermined the confidence in the inevitability of progress with which the century began. So 'progress' is not enough. The concept of evolution is now central in many fields of thought, but, when applied to human relationships and institutions, it seems to leave no room for freedom, understanding the development of those relationships and institutions as the product of forces and laws over which human beings themselves have little or no influence. So 'evolution' is not enough. The 'end of history' was famously proclaimed in 1989, with the fall of the Berlin Wall. It seemed that the great ideological stand-off between communism and capitalism had been resolved in favour of the latter and the threat of 'mutually assured destruction' through nuclear annihilation was lifted. Subsequent events, however, such as the attacks on the United States in September 2001, the deepening consensus about climate change and the precarious health of the planet, the persistence of wars and the challenges of migration in many parts of the world, a worldwide pandemic wreaking havoc – all of these things serve to make it clear that history is in fact continuing. While it does leave room for human freedom, of itself history does not necessarily support hope for the future.

Hope is distinct, then, from progress, evolution and history. What makes it distinct is that it regards the human being as essentially a pilgrim or wayfarer, on a journey towards a destination that is good, and supported in the course of that journey by one who is also the journey's destination. Any hope has this double object, the good for which we hope and the one to whom we look for help if we are to attain that good. When it is theological hope, this double object becomes one: the good we seek is God and the one to whom we look for the help we need is also God.

Hope can be quickly dismissed. For the French poet Charles Péguy (1873–1914) hope is a little girl and little girls can be easily overlooked. This little girl, however, is not offering us 'pie in the sky when we die' but the strength to face and accept the difficulties that attend the journey toward the realization of our hope. It is the virtue that surprises God, Péguy says: faith and love are exactly what God would expect from us, but hope is unexpected and it brings creativity and spontaneity, a certain kind of freedom and joy in responding to God's gifts.[2] Thomas Aquinas frequently speaks of the human being as a *viator*, a pilgrim or wayfarer. For him also hope is a youthful virtue, a confidence that there is plenty of time and space ahead of us, there is potential yet to be realized, goals still to be achieved. We can say it is indeed the secret of eternal youth!

Another author who has written powerfully about hope is the German Catholic philosopher Josef Pieper (1904–97), for whom our condition as pilgrims is not just historical but metaphysical. At the deepest core of the human being is this condition of being a *viator*, a pilgrim, because we are creatures coming from nothing and moving towards participation in a life that is eternal. That sets up an extraordinary orientation within us, giving us some purchase on a future yet to be fully revealed, while contextualizing all our present moments, which fall between where we are coming from and where we are going.

CHURCH IN PILGRIMAGE

Vatican II's consideration of the Church included a chapter on the 'pilgrim Church' (*LG* 48-51). The theme emerges inevitably in any consideration of the Church as the people of God, since the entire story of that people is a kind of pilgrimage. There are many episodes in the Bible that tell us of journeys the people were obliged to make and that took on great significance for them. We read of their escape from Egypt, for example, and their wandering in the wilderness for forty years. They crossed the Jordan into the promised land but later were taken away in captivity to Babylon. The journey that marked their return to the promised land was a kind of new exodus, the opportunity for a fresh beginning. In the New Testament there are the journeys of Jesus and his disciples, culminating in the travels of Saint Paul that brought the good news to the whole inhabited world, even to Rome at a time when reaching Rome meant reaching everywhere. These geographical journeys of the Hebrew people and of the Church were always underpinned by what we can call the theological journey, their being towards God, their status as a pilgrim people.

In his book *Cadences of Home: Preaching among Exiles*, spoken about already in Chapter 8, Walter Brueggemann identifies a number of 'ecclesial conditions' that marked the pilgrimage of God's people in time.[3] He focuses particularly on the Babylonian Exile, but this was just one of a number of conditions in which the people found themselves along the course of their history. Brueggemann identifies four such conditions that become paradigmatic not only for the people of Israel but also for the Church.

There is the time of wandering in the wilderness when the people are being liberated from oppression and slavery, and are being led towards freedom in a promised land. It is the time of the community being formed, the time of God's promise, when they had left Egypt, assured that the Lord was travelling with them.

Next comes the time of settlement, when the people have arrived in the land. It is the time of the community becoming comfortable and secure, enjoying the blessings of the covenant. This condition reaches its high point in the reign of King David and his family. They are successful politically, militarily and economically, possessing the wealth of the promised land. But they begin to become corrupt, to make compromises in their religious practice and to turn away from fidelity to the covenant. This is the time of God's demand, but their responsiveness to that demand waxed and waned. The Books of Judges and Kings reveal the rhythm that marked their lives in this condition. They wandered from their relationship with the Lord and then returned to it. They sinned and then were reconciled. They worshipped other gods and sacrificed to them, but then God renewed the covenant with them and they could begin again.

Third, there is the time of exile, when the people lost all the physical, social, political and economic supports that sustained their trust and confidence in God. It was all taken away, the land and the city, the temple and the monarchy, the priesthood and the sacrifices, and even the glory of the Lord departed from them. It is the time of God's absence and the people become strangers in a strange land. After the Exodus from Egypt this is the other defining moment in Israel's history, the time of the community in exile. They had learned how to be a community being formed and they had learned how to be a community settled in the land. But how were they to be in exile when they had lost not only structures and institutions but, as it seemed, the very presence of God with them? What were they to do and how were they to live? How could they go on hoping in the time of God's absence? The prophets of this era helped them to find a way forward through a radically renewed understanding of God and his relationship through them with the world.

The fourth paradigmatic condition is the time of homecoming, the time after exile. The community, wounded by its experience of loss, was to be healed through the restoration of at least some of what it had enjoyed before. But they quickly realized that it could never be the same again, and once more it is the prophets who helped them to see this. What was required was not simply a restoration or a reconstruction but a new reality, a new basis for their identity. There is no re-establishment because there is no going back, and they must continue on the journey towards God as God continues the journey with them. Brueggemann describes this as the time of God's newness. In the post-exilic period in Israel a new future needed to be imagined, a new destiny that continued to include the land and the city but now transfigured and placed in a new register that is called 'eschatological', looking beyond the ordinary limits of time and space. Thus, we find in this period the first biblical texts to speak clearly of resurrection (the Book of Daniel, the Books of the Maccabees), as well as a clearer than ever presentation of the universal reach of Israel's vocation, looking to a future gathering of all the nations in Jerusalem (Isa. 56–66).

Each of these conditions – wandering, settlement, exile, homecoming – presented the people with different challenges. The prophets helped them to see that responding to the challenges required in the first place a theological reading of the historical moment in which they found themselves: is it a time of God's presence or a time of God's demand? Is it a time of God's absence or a time of God's newness? Note also that in the conditions of exile and homecoming the people seemed to develop a stronger sense of God as their parent, either as a father (Isa. 63.16; 64.8; Jer. 3.19; 31.9; Mal. 1.6; 2.10) or as a mother (Isa. 42.14; 49.15-16 ; 66.13).

Clearly our reason for reviewing these 'ecclesial conditions' is to see how they might help us in thinking about the situation of the Catholic Church today. We could try to identify the Church's present condition globally, but it might be more helpful to recognize that different parts of the Church are living different ecclesial conditions contemporaneously. Some local churches, particularly in Africa and Asia, are communities in formation. Some are settled in the place in which they find themselves. Some are in exile, having lost the things that once assured them of God's presence, and still needing time to lament that loss. Some might already be 'homecoming', waiting for a new moment of inspiration and energy, praying for a fresh impulse of the Holy

Spirit to strengthen their life in Christ. Perhaps there are still other conditions to be identified and other theological readings of what a particular church community is experiencing.

Different moments in the history of God's people, and different texts of the Bible, speak more directly to different parts of the Church depending on the condition in which they find themselves. Seriously oppressed communities, for example, who feel powerless and are being persecuted, will understand the Book of Revelation, finding light and meaning in it. This text is often practically unintelligible to other Christian communities, particularly those that have become settled politically, economically and socially. Communities seeking to build more just societies will look to the Exodus from Egypt, a paradigmatic moment for theologies of liberation, especially in Latin America and South Africa, where communities struggling to emerge from situations of oppression found hope in recalling the experience of the Hebrew slaves led out of captivity by Moses. The collapsed churches in places like Quebec, Ireland, Flanders and Spain, where there was a practical identification of the Catholic community with civil and even political power, are probably the places for which the texts of the exile will at present mean most. Brueggemann himself regards contemporary American Protestantism as being in this condition. It seems clear that Catholic communities such as those just mentioned are facing challenges similar to those faced by the people of Israel in exile: how to understand where they find themselves and what to do in response. They have lost that purchase on the society to which they had become accustomed – through education and healthcare, through influence in culture and society, even in law and politics, they were comfortable, settled in their own land and secure in their understanding of how things ought to be. There are challenges specific to each of these conditions. And it may be that the condition varies not only between countries, local churches or dioceses, but even between local communities and within local communities. Individual believers may be living a spiritual condition of the Church that differs from that of other believers, who are yet their contemporaries and neighbours.

HISTORY AND PROVIDENCE

The first Christian preaching speaks much of the history of Israel and of its fulfilment in what had just happened in the life, death and resurrection of Jesus. As they had learned from that earlier history, what happened through human freedom and agency was always contained and underpinned by what God was doing in order to work out His own purpose. 'The one you crucified and killed', says Peter, 'was delivered up according to the definite plan and foreknowledge of God' (Acts 2.23). It was those who killed him, says Paul, 'who fulfilled all that was written of him' (Acts 13.29). All is held within God's providence, within the 'will of the Father'.[4] Human beings make their decisions and execute their judgements and in doing so they are, says Aquinas, 'participants in providence'.[5] The apostolic preaching invites people to accept that what God has done in Jesus is a new point of reference to which can be referred any and all of the conditions in which the people of God find themselves at any moment in history.

For Christian believers, a theological understanding of the condition in which they find themselves will recognize these two levels. There is what is happening in the course of human history and there is the purpose of God being worked out through the course of that history. The first is variable and unpredictable, whereas the second is sure and dependable. Catholic Christianity continues to read the Old Testament and to understand its own experiences in the light of those texts. One of the earliest heresies proposed that the Hebrew texts were no longer needed, but this was immediately rejected by the Church. Like Judaism, Christianity is a faith centred on what God has done within human history. All those conditions through which the people of Israel learned important things about themselves and about God are also conditions in which the Church will find itself from time to time, in order to relearn important things about itself and about God. But for the Church there is also, and above all, the work of Christ as the key to human history, illuminating the

251

earlier history of God's people as well as shining on all present and future historical circumstances.

Because it believes that Jesus is the Messiah, Christianity adds a new condition to those identified in the Old Testament, a condition that it calls 'realized eschatology'. Where the Jewish believer looks forward to the coming of Messiah, the Christian looks forward to the return of Jesus, who has already come and will come again to bring us to the Father. This adds another aspect to the eschatology we find in the Old Testament, namely that its promises have already been fulfilled in what has happened in Jesus Christ and that this fulfilment will itself be completed in his return. 'We are already the children of God,' says the First Letter of John, 'but what we are to be in the future has not yet been revealed' (3.1-3). Those simple words 'already ... not yet' sum up what is meant by 'realized eschatology'. They give expression once again to the fundamental condition of the human being as a pilgrim who, while still on the way, already experiences what belongs to the destination that has not yet been reached. We are, says Saint Paul, 'saved in hope' (Rom. 8.24).

REMEMBERING THE FUTURE

It is interesting that Brueggemann, a Protestant scholar of no mean authority, speaks of the liturgical and sacramental life that emerges when the people find themselves in the condition of exile.[6] What are people to do in the time of God's absence but remember and celebrate the past while looking forward in hope to the future? It is another aspect that Catholic Christianity sees in its sacramental celebrations, where the life of human beings, extended in time between past, present and future, is brought into a particular focus. Saint Paul's account of the Eucharist concludes with him saying to the Corinthians that 'as often as you eat this bread and drink the chalice, you proclaim the Lord's death until he comes' (1 Cor. 11.26). An action done in the present remembers the past and anticipates the future. Christ has died, Christ is risen, Christ will come again. In an antiphon that he composed for the liturgical celebration of Corpus Christi, the feast of the body and blood of Christ, Thomas Aquinas gives us another version of this: 'O sacred banquet, in which Christ is received, the memory of his passion is renewed, the soul is filled with grace, and a pledge of future glory is given to us.' Past and future are present in this present action.

The pilgrim people take time, therefore, to celebrate what they have received, what they are receiving and what they will receive. And it is all happening in a present moment, past and future effective in what is being done here and now. The special meaning of remembrance, *anamnesis*, in Jewish thought is well known. At the Passover meal the one presiding reminds those present that they are the people coming out of Egypt and that the great act of God was not just for their ancestors but is for them also. As they recall what God did then, they now receive the same grace and blessing. For Christians, celebrating the memorial of the Lord's supper means not only remembering the past – doing this as a memorial of Jesus, as he instructed them – but remembering also the future, making present already what is not yet, the marriage feast of the Lamb already underway sacramentally.

We spoke at length in the opening chapters of this book about the particular meaning of sacramentality for Catholicism. The sacrament is a sign or symbol that not only points elsewhere but makes effectively present that to which it points. This applies to the dimension of time as much as it does to that of space. The sacrament is a sign or symbol that not only points towards a future reality but also makes effectively present now that to which it points. 'What you have come to is Mount Zion', says the Letter to the Hebrews referring to the Eucharist, 'the city of the living God, the heavenly Jerusalem, the assembly of the firstborn' (Heb. 12.22-23). We are already in the presence of the Father, as his beloved sons and daughters, when we celebrate the Eucharist, the central prayer of the Church that we offer to the Father, through the Son, in the Holy Spirit.

TRACKS OF BEAUTY

Normally pilgrims pass through the towns and countryside they visit without leaving many, if any, traces of their passing. They travel light and they do not stay around for very long, anxious to keep moving because the goal of their journey beckons. In its deepest reality the Church is oriented towards the kingdom that is coming, holding by its hope to that future reality, professing in its creed that it looks forward to the resurrection of the dead and the life of the world to come. However, that orientation has never prevented the Church from engaging with the world in all the times and places to which its journey takes it: we saw this in the previous chapter.

The 'Church in pilgrimage' has also left many signs of its presence, not least many objects of great beauty that continue to speak long afterwards of the faith, hope and love of those who have passed that way. Manuscripts like the Book of Kells and the Lindisfarne Gospels, buildings like the cathedral at Chartres and Saint Peter's in Rome, works of art such as the medieval mosaic of the Tree of Life at San Clemente, the *Pietà* of Michelangelo and the *Descent from the Cross* of Rogier van der Weyden, music such as the Masses of Bruckner and the Holy Week responsories of Victoria … in modern times the basilica of La Sagrada Familia in Barcelona, the music of James Macmillan, the short stories of Flannery O'Connor: there is a Catholic aesthetic that shows that these pilgrims have not been indifferent to beauty. The Australian poet Les Murray (1938–2019) dedicated all his books 'to the glory of God'. Works such as those mentioned, along with countless others, have a beauty here and now precisely because they were conceived by eyes and hearts looking also there and then, towards the destination of this pilgrimage. The radiance of that hope is also inscribed in these works of art.

If Catholicism teaches what it believes to be true and what it regards as good, it has also left much evidence of what it admires as beautiful. Just as faith is not 'reason's opposite' in coming to understand what is true and appreciate what is honourable and just, neither is faith 'beauty's opposite', for it values and admires 'whatever is lovely, whatever is gracious, any excellence, anything worthy of praise' (Phil. 4.8). There have been moments of hesitation about the seductiveness of beautiful things, fears that they might distract and turn the believer aside from the road on which they are travelling. There have been moments of 'iconoclasm', when the beautiful objects have been rejected, thrown out and destroyed for fear of such distraction or even idolatry. These purifications have sometimes themselves produced beautiful things of their own – the simplicity of the Gaelic psalm-singing in a Highland kirk or the clean lines of Shaker furniture. It is as if beauty must break through, even where believers have come to fear the exuberance of the Baroque or the majesty of the Gothic. Such experiences of conflict about the beautiful are yet one more sign of the in-between character of the Christian life, the *status viatoris* of the human being, already and not yet, our condition as pilgrims.

FROM GLORY TO GLORY

To the glory of God – it is the pilgrim's destination, to see, hear, taste, touch, perhaps even smell something of this reality. The beauty of the liturgical and sacramental celebrations of the Church seeks to express already our appreciation of what we hope for, recognizing that because God is love, Father, Son and Holy Spirit, then God is not only true and good but is also beautiful.

'Far be it from me to glory except in the cross of our Lord Jesus Christ', says Paul in Galatians 6.14, by which he means that all other grounds for taking pride in what God has done for us are replaced by this one reality, the cross of Christ. 'We have seen his glory, as the only Son from the Father', we read in the prologue of John's Gospel (Jn 1.14), and it is clear from what John says later that the moment in which this glory was definitively revealed was Calvary. Once again, we face a paradox: the one who had 'no form or majesty that we should look at him, nothing in his appearance that we should desire him' (Isa. 53.2), is the same one who reveals the glory 'which no eyes have seen, which no ears have heard, and which is beyond our imagination, the things God has prepared for those who love him' (1 Cor. 2.9).

We have already seen 1 John 3.1-3, one of the great eschatological texts in the New Testament: we are 'already' the children of God, but what we are to be has 'not yet' been revealed. When it is revealed, that text continues, 'we shall be like him, for we shall see him as he is'. This idea that we become what we see is found also in the letters of Saint Paul. 'When we see face to face,' he says, 'and no longer dimly as in a mirror, then we shall understand fully, even as we have been fully understood' (1 Cor. 13.12). In another text he speaks of us beholding or reflecting the glory of God and being changed into his likeness from one degree of glory to another (2 Cor. 3.18). Are we beholding the glory or are we reflecting the glory? The Greek term, it seems, can mean either or both of these. As we behold it, we reflect it. Once again, we are told that we become what we see. And what we see, says Paul, is the glory of God in the face of Christ (2 Cor. 4.6). By looking at Christ, and seeing the glory of God in his face, we become what we look at and are changed into his likeness from one degree of glory to another.

Such texts provide the basis for a specifically Christian understanding of contemplation. Like all human beings we desire to know what is true and good. And like all human beings we desire to experience what is beautiful. The Christian person meditates by contemplating the face of Jesus Christ and will thereby radiate the glory of God: this is the teaching of John and of Paul. In looking towards Christ they will take on something of his beauty, a beauty that is love, first and last, for the glory of God is the love God is.

The paradox of the beautiful crucified One, and the conflicts about the use of icons and images along the course of Christian history, point to this truth: that the One we are seeking, the One Jesus calls the Father, 'cannot be represented by the art and imagination of human beings' (Acts 17.29). The image of the Father in creation is the Son, who restores that likeness in us also, but the glory of the Father is revealed most powerfully in the moment of the Son's death. The disciples at Emmaus recognized Jesus as he disappeared, in the breaking of the bread, and so too the love of God is seen in the moment in which (it seems) it is extinguished in this world, in the breaking of the body of Christ.

Theological language also serves its purpose best in the moment in which it breaks down. Just as God is not like representations in gold or silver or stone (Acts 17.29), neither can God be captured in concepts, images or experiences. The peculiar character of theological language is yet one more way in which we experience the tension of living between an already and a not yet. That language is at the same time cataphatic, affirming things of God, and apophatic, negating things of God, sometimes the very same things being negated as have just been affirmed.

All efforts to speak about God in theology, of God in preaching, or to God in prayer, break down. Out of this crucible emerges what is called mystical theology, another term for contemplation, a particular way of glimpsing the invisible and seeing the mystery in the moment in which language fails. For Catholic Christianity the central icon of such contemplation is the Crucifix, which can seem shocking, weird and even scandalous. But so it is, for this is the moment within human history in which God opened his heart to reveal that the divine life truly is Love, a Trinity of the Son who commends his Spirit into the Father's hands. This is the beauty seen in the cross of Christ, the glory of the divine life thereby revealed.

The Church is a pilgrim in history, living from the past but living also from the future, believing that it beholds and reflects already the glory of a kingdom that is coming. It believes itself to be the sacrament of that kingdom, a sign or symbol that not only points towards the reality to come but, at least in mystery, is already the presence of that reality. Its characteristic life consists of hope as well as faith and these two are true when love is real and active, not just words or mere talk (1 Jn 3.18).

We leave the final words to a woman who lived this life of the Church in a heroic way. She is one of the witnesses to hope summoned by Pope Benedict XVI in his encyclical letter on that virtue. Saint Josephine Bakhita (c.1869–1947) was a Sudanese slave and later a religious sister. From the beatings she received as a slave she carried many scars on her body. When she learned about Jesus, she found a Master different to all other masters she had known. She came to know one whose body was also scarred and whose love for her had carved her in the palms of his hands. Not only that, but he was waiting for her at the Father's right hand. This opened her heart and mind to the great hope that she expressed in this way: 'I am definitively loved and whatever happens to me – I am awaited by this Love. And so, my life is good' (*Spe salvi* n. 3). If the Catholic Church only succeeds in continuing to show people the truth of those words, then it offers the world an inestimable gift.

NOTES

INTRODUCTION

1 Guardini, R. (1952), *The Faith and Modern Man*, London: Burns & Oates, p. vii, first published in German as *Glaubenserkenntnis*, Werkbund Verlag, Würzburg.
2 Clément, O. (2000), *On Human Being: A Spiritual Anthropology*, New York: New City Press, p. 93, first published in French in 1986 as *Questions sur l'homme*, Editions Anne Sigier: Sainte-Foy.
3 Chesterton, G. K. (1943), *St. Thomas Aquinas*, London: Hodder & Stoughton, p. 21.
4 Op. cit., p. 30.
5 O'Connor tells the story of how she came to say this in a letter of 16 December 1955: see O'Connor, F. (1979), *The Habit of Being*, Letters of Flannery O'Connor, edited and with an introduction by Sally Fitzgerald, New York: Farrar, Strauss and Giroux, pp. 123–7; the quotation itself is on p. 125.
6 For biblical references and citations, I have generally used either the Revised Standard Version 2nd Edition (1971) [= RSV] or the New Revised Standard Version Catholic Edition (2007), San Francisco: HarperCollins Publishers [= NRSVCE].
7 *The Foundations* 5, 15, in Teresa of Avila (1985), *The Collected Works of St. Teresa of Avila*, Volume Three, translated by Kieran Kavanaugh, O.C.D. and Otilio Rodriguez, O.C.D., Washington, DC: Institute of Carmelite Studies Publications, p. 122.
8 *De Oratione Dominica* 23 (Migne, *Patrologia Latina* 4:553).
9 Healy, N. (2000), *Church, World and the Christian Life: Practical-Prophetic Ecclesiology*, Cambridge: Cambridge University Press.

CHAPTER 1: A PEOPLE OF GOD?

1 The interview, with Antonio Spadaro, S.J., was simultaneously published in all the major languages. The English-language version was published in

America 209.8 (30 September 2013) and can also be found on the Vatican website, among Pope Francis's speeches for September 2013.

2   The Second Vatican Council took place between 1962 and 1965 and is referred to here as 'Vatican II'. There will be many references to the documents it produced, in particular to its Dogmatic Constitution on the Church, which, from the first words of the text in Latin, is called *Lumen gentium*, 'Light of the Nations'. This will be abbreviated to *LG*.

3   Dulles, A. (1991), *Models of the Church*, New York: Image Classics.

4   Preston, G. (1997), *Faces of the Church: Meditations on a Mystery and its Images*, Edinburgh: T&T Clark.

CHAPTER 2: CHRIST, IMAGE AND SACRAMENT OF GOD

1   See Schillebeeckx, E. (1963), *Christ the Sacrament of the Encounter with God*, London: Sheed and Ward.

2   *A Catechism of Catholic Doctrine* (1951), Dublin: M. H. Gill and Son Ltd, p. 77, n. 332.

3   McCabe, H. (1985), *The Teaching of the Catholic Church: A New Catechism of Christian Doctrine*, London: Catholic Truth Society, p. 15, n. 68.

4   *Sermon* 74.2 (Migne, *Patrologia Latina* 54:398).

CHAPTER 3: THE CHURCH, SACRAMENT OF CHRIST

1   *De Oratione Dominica* XXIII, quoted in *LG* 4. See p. 16 above.

2   McCabe, op. cit., p. 15, n. 68.

3   See Paul Murray, O.P., 'Ratzinger's Moon', *Spirituality* Volume 12 (2006), 78–9.

4   This is clear in how the *Catechism of the Catholic Church* considers the works of the Holy Spirit: nn. 683–747. It is clear also in the renewal of baptismal promises at the Easter Vigil.

CHAPTER 4: EMBODIMENT MEANS LIFE AND STRUCTURE

1   Bedouelle, G. (1995), *Saint Dominic: The Grace of the Word*, translated by Sister Mary Thomas Noble, O.P., San Francisco: Ignatius Press, Chapter 6, first published in French in 1982 as *Dominique, ou la grâce de la parole*, Fayard-Mame.

2   The Greek word *pneuma* means 'breath' or 'spirit', hence the rather unwieldy term 'pneumatological' to refer to any consideration made from the perspective of the Holy Spirit.

3 See, e.g., Eucharistic Prayer III in the Roman Missal: 'by the same Spirit graciously make holy these gifts ... that they may become the Body and Blood of your Son'; 'grant that we, who are nourished by the Body and Blood of your Son and filled with his Holy Spirit, may become one body, one spirit in Christ'.

CHAPTER 5: FORMS OF CORRUPTION IN THIS BODY

1 On this see Ian Ker (1990), *Newman On Being a Christian*, Notre Dame, IN: University of Notre Dame Press.

2 Congar, Y. (2011), *True and False Reform in the Church*, Collegeville, MN: The Liturgical Press. The work was first published in French in 1950 and the 2011 English translation is of the 1967 French edition.

3 Op. cit., p. 52.

4 Op. cit., pp. 129–30.

5 See p. 7 above.

6 De Lubac, H. (1956), *The Splendour of the Church*, London: Sheed and Ward, first published in 1952 in French as *Méditation sur l'église*, Paris: Editions Aubier Montaigne.

7 See p. 17 above, with note 9 on p. 259.

8 This letter in English was also called *The Church in the Modern World* and so needs to be distinguished from *Gaudium et spes*, Vatican II's Pastoral Constitution on the Church in the Modern World, which is usually given the same name in English. Paul VI's encyclical was quickly eclipsed by the publication of Vatican II's document just a year later.

9 Healy, op. cit., p. 145.

10 Healy, op. cit., p. 24.

11 Julian of Norwich, *Revelations of Divine Love*, Chapter 27.

12 See, for example, Balthasar, Hans Urs von (1975), 'Why do I still remain in the Church?', in *Elucidations*, London: SPCK, pp. 208–16 and Murray (2006), Chapter 3, note 3 above, p. 46, referring to an article by Joseph Ratzinger with the same title.

CHAPTER 6: CHRIST'S THREEFOLD MISSION AND THE CHURCH'S THREEFOLD NATURE

1 Newman, J. H. (1869), *Sermons Bearing on Subjects of the Day*, London, pp. 52–62. The sermon is entitled 'The Three Offices of Christ'.

2 Loc. cit.

3 Newman, J. H. (1970), *The Philosophical Notebook of John Henry Newman*, edited by E. Sillem, revised by A. J. Boekraad, vol. 2, *The Text*, Louvain, p. 167.

4 Newman, J. H. (1877), *The Via Media of the Anglican Church*, 3rd edition, London, xl.

5 Lash, N. (1988), *Easter in Ordinary: Reflections on Human Experience and the Knowledge of God*, London: SCM Press Ltd, Chapter 10. I am indebted to Lash for the references in Newman's writings: op. cit., pp. 136–8, nn. 12–16, 18–19.

6 See Levering, M. (2002), *Christ's Fulfilment of Torah and Temple: Salvation According to Thomas Aquinas*, University of Notre Dame Press; Congar, Y. (1983), 'Sur la trilogie: Prophète-Roi-Prêtre', *Revue des sciences philosophiques et théologiques* 67, 97–115, especially 101–2 for texts of Aquinas, and Wainwright, G. (1997), *For Our Salvation: Two Approaches to the Work of Christ*, Grand Rapids, MI: Eerdmans Publishing Co.

7 Calvin, J., *Institute of the Christian Religion*, Book II, Chapter XV.

8 See his *Letters to a Niece* (1995), p. vi and letter of 21 April 1920, pp. 92–5.

9 Op. cit., letter of 22 February 1921, pp. 119–25.

10 Op. cit., letter of 11 April 1922, p. 165.

11 Von Hügel's most important published works are *The Mystical Element of Religion as studied in Catherine of Genoa and her Friends* (1908), *Essays and Addresses on the Philosophy of Religion* (2 volumes, 1921 and 1926), *Eternal Life: A Study of its Implications and Applications* (1912), *Letters to a Niece* (1955, republished by Fount Classics, HarperCollins Publishers, London, 1995), and *The Reality of God* (1931), this last being the incomplete manuscript of his Gifford Lectures for 1924–5, which he was too ill to deliver.

12 Knox, R. (1949), *Enthusiasm: A Chapter in the History of Religion*, Oxford: Clarendon Press; See von Hügel, F. (1908), *The Mystical Element*, pp. 3–82, for what is summarized on pp. 119–21 here.

13 See von Hügel, F. (1908), *The Mystical Element*, pp. 70–7 for this and the other citations given in this paragraph.

CHAPTER 7: AUTHORITY, SERVICE AND LEADERSHIP

1 *Summa theologiae* will be referred to as '*ST*', followed by an indication of the question and article referred to.

2 See, for example, the Congregation for the Doctrine of the Faith's *Instruction on the Ecclesial Vocation of the Theologian* (1990), and the International Theological Commission's *Theology Today: Perspectives, Principles and Criteria* (2012). Also relevant is the Pontifical Biblical Commission's *Unity and Diversity in the Church* (1988).

3   Citations of documents of Vatican II are taken from *Vatican Council II: The Conciliar and Post Conciliar Documents*, ed. Austin Flannery OP (1975) Dublin: Dominican Publications.

4   Balthasar, op. cit., pp. 209–12.

CHAPTER 8: TAKE ALL THOUGHT CAPTIVE

1   Cahill, T. (1996), *How the Irish Saved Civilization*, New York: Anchor.

2   See in particular Brueggemann, W. (1997), *Cadences of Home: Preaching Among Exiles*, Louisville, KY: Westminster John Knox Press.

3   Op. cit., pp. 10–11, 23, 53.

4   Op. cit., pp. 115–18.

5   I am indebted to Thomas McCarthy, O.P., for this example.

6   Brueggemann, op. cit., p. 37.

7   Op. cit., p. 53.

8   Op. cit., pp. 11–14.

CHAPTER 9: THE LIFE OF A COMMUNITY

1   Cited in Vorgrimler, H. (1968), *Commentary on the Documents of Vatican II: Volume II*, 2nd edition, Herder & Herder, p. 64.

2   Mt. 14.15-21; 15.32-38; Mk 6.35-44; 8.1-9; Lk. 9.10-17; Jn 6.

3   Mt. 8.11; Lk. 12.35ff.; 13.29; 14.15-24; 22.28f.

4   Mt. 22.1-14; 25.1-13; Rev. 19.7.

5   See, for example, Mt. 9.10-13; Mk 2.15ff.; Lk. 15.1-2; 19.1-10.

6   Lk. 24.28-35, 36-43; Jn 21.9-14.

7   See, for example, the international Catholic review called *Communio* (1972), founded by Hans Urs von Balthasar, Henri de Lubac and Joseph Ratzinger. See also Ratzinger, J. (1996), *Called to Communion: Understanding the Church Today*, San Francisco: Ignatius Press and the Congregation for the Doctrine of the Faith, *Letter on Some Aspects of the Church Understood as Communion* (1992).

8   Barth, K. (1936), *The Church and the Churches*, Grand Rapids, MI: Eerdmans, pp. 18–20.

CHAPTER 10: WITH THE SON: CHRIST, THE HEAD OF HUMANITY

1   See Chapter 1, note 1, on p. 259–60 above.

2   *Epistle* 72, 21 (Migne, *Patrologia Latina* 3:1123). This is generally regarded as the earliest statement of the principle.

3   *De Fide* 38–39 (Migne, *Patrologia Latina* 65:704). This text is quoted in a decree of the Council of Florence in 1442, thereby taking on a greater weight of authority.
4   *Mystici corporis Christi* (1943), n. 102.
5   Letter to Cardinal Cushing, 8 August 1949.
6   *Redemptoris missio* (1990), n. 10. For a full consideration of this point see Francis A. Sullivan SJ (1992), *Salvation Outside the Church? Tracing the History of the Catholic Response*, London: Chapman.
7   *Ecclesiam suam*, nn. 97–113.
8   *LG* 14. See also Vatican II's *Decree on the Eastern Catholic Churches*.
9   *LG* 15. See also Vatican II's *Decree on Ecumenism*, nn. 14–18.
10 A document published by the Pontifical Biblical Commission in 2002.
11 *Decree on Non-Christian Religions*, n. 3. See also *Document on Human Fraternity*, Abu Dhabi, 4 February 2019.

Chapter 11: In the Spirit: The Love of Christ Urges Us On

1   Apostolic Exhortation *Evangelii Nuntiandi*, n. 41.
2   Apostolic Exhortation *Evangelii Nuntiandi*, nn. 70–7.
3   Chrism consists of olive oil mixed with balsam, which gives it its aroma.

Chapter 12: To the Father: From Glory to Glory

1   Boff, L. (2009), *Saint Joseph: The Father of Jesus in a Fatherless Society*, Eugene OR: Cascade Books, p. 8.
2   Peguy, C. (1996), *The Portal of the Mystery of Hope*, Edinburgh: T&T Clark.
3   Brueggemann, op. cit., Chapter 7, 'Rethinking Church Models through Scripture'.
4   Mt. 7.21, 12.50; Jn 6.38, 40, 44; Acts 1.6-7; Heb. 10.7, 9.
5   *ST* I.II 91, 2. See also Chapter 11, pp. 238–39 above.
6   Brueggemann, op. cit., pp. 8–9, 15, 132–4. Note particularly his reference to the sacramental as a way to 'host the holy' in a context of profane absence (p. 8).

INDEX

Abraham   17, 28, 31, 33 164, 178, 217–8, 231
Ad Petri Cathedram (John XXIII)   182
Adam
  first Adam   41–6
  last Adam   28, 41, 46–9, 51
Adam, Karl   7–8, 13, 17
ambition and tyranny   14
analogies   12, 15, 91, 103, 137, 189
angels   96, 134–5, 166, 178, 205
Anglican Communion   181–2, 183, 217
Anointing of the sick, sacrament of   52, 135
anti-intellectualism   153–5, 158, 169
apostles   25–6, 33, 67, 96, 122, 130, 131, 133,
        138, 141, 144–6, 150, 155, 166, 172, 173,
        180, 183, 186, 192, 226, 235
  pseudo-apostles   95
  super-apostles   95
  see also Paul, Saint
Apostles' Creed   67
Aquinas, Thomas   9, 11, 16, 24, 44, 52, 61, 68,
        92, 116–17, 136, 151, 184, 190, 227,
        251
  on the Church as a body   78–9, 80, 81–4, 91,
        141, 198
  Corpus Christi antiphon   253
  on hierarchies in Church   130–7
  on Holy Spirit   139, 224, 238–9
  human beings as pilgrims   246
  moral responsibility   44–5
  and Paul   165
  on Paul's letters   198–206, 220
  and philosophy   159
  Summa theologiae   103, 117–18, 130–2, 200,
        203–6, 223
  on theology   160, 165
  thinking and faith   24
  and truth   158
Aristotle   91–2, 159–60
ark of the covenant   85, 188
Athenagoras I of Constantinople   216–17
Augustine of Hippo   68, 151, 164, 206, 214
authority   63, 76, 93, 129ff, 150, 161, 232–5
  and obedience   14
  Paul on   150, 166, 168

Bach, Johann Sebastian   163
Bakhita, Josephine   257–8
Balthasar, Hans Urs von   101–5, 149
baptism   11, 36, 51, 64–7, 69–70, 82, 88, 135,
        169, 184, 209, 211–3, 236, 260
Barth, Karl   184
beauty   131–2, 140, 164, 213, 219, 254–7
Bedouelle, Guy   74, 76
belief
  in Church   62–71
  levels of   68
Benedict XVI, Pope   206, 257–8
  Spe salvi   245, 258
biblical references
  Genesis   31, 41–2, 43, 44, 45, 47, 143, 164,
        166, 178, 231
  Exodus   32, 85, 115, 175, 177, 178
  Numbers   165, 175
  Deuteronomy   125–6, 165, 175, 237
  Joshua   175
  2 Samuel   85
  1 Kings   85, 131–2
  2 Kings   191
  Job   107
  Psalms   25, 26, 153–4, 163, 165, 175
  Proverbs   175
  Song of Songs   175, 185
  Wisdom   165, 168, 175, 185
  Sirach (Ecclesiasticus)   45–6, 175
  Isaiah   25, 26, 32, 164, 178, 186, 191, 201,
        249, 255–6
  Jeremiah   115, 116, 177, 186, 191, 238,
        249
  Lamentations   191
  Baruch   117
  Ezekiel   25, 86, 88, 176, 186
  Daniel   62, 116
  Hosea   32, 168, 186
  Zechariah   88
  Malachi   61, 249
  Matthew   26, 33, 36–7, 62, 86, 105, 142, 153,
        154, 177, 186, 187, 206, 238
  Mark   26, 36–7, 86, 105, 142, 150, 153, 177,
        186, 207, 214, 231

Luke 23, 25, 33, 36–7, 86, 87, 94, 98, 105, 142, 153, 177, 179–80, 186, 230

John 11, 14, 25, 36–7, 50, 53, 54, 58, 60, 61, 62, 65, 82, 86–7, 88, 109, 142, 145, 153, 164, 175–6, 178, 179–80, 182, 186–7, 188, 190–1, 198, 204, 207, 212, 219, 221, 224, 228, 230, 231, 235, 237, 243, 255

Acts 26, 34, 48–50, 87, 126, 133, 164, 172, 183, 207, 214, 251, 256, 257

Romans 25, 33, 48, 79, 80–1, 83, 97, 106, 108, 115, 131, 141, 154, 156, 164, 165, 168, 173, 199, 204, 217–18, 221, 224, 230, 239, 243, 245, 252

1 Corinthians 12, 25, 34, 47–8, 58, 60–1, 63, 79, 83, 93, 96, 97, 106, 108, 125, 126, 132, 137–9, 140, 141, 142, 149–50, 154, 156, 157, 174, 177, 178, 199, 201, 234, 239, 252, 255–6

2 Corinthians 13, 25, 36, 37, 41, 46, 48, 53, 63, 88, 93–6, 97, 98, 105, 106, 108, 125, 154, 166–8, 173, 174, 187, 199, 206, 221, 224, 235–6, 237, 238, 256

Galatians 26, 33, 34, 36, 47, 126, 141, 154, 165, 168, 173, 188, 199, 221, 231, 239, 243, 255

Ephesians 25–7, 34, 36, 60–1, 79, 81–3, 131, 132, 154, 157, 164, 168, 178, 187, 199, 200, 201, 205, 220, 221, 229

Philippians 27, 33, 36, 51, 94, 154, 156, 173, 174, 199, 255

Colossians 27, 36, 46, 48, 79, 164, 199, 200, 201, 202–3, 205, 220, 221

1 Thessalonians 108, 154, 199

2 Thessalonians 199

1 Timothy 154, 198, 199

2 Timothy 35, 131, 154, 199

Titus 154, 199

Philemon 154, 173, 199

Hebrews 26, 37, 46, 54, 87, 88, 154, 157, 199, 207, 220, 221, 245, 253

James 33, 46–7, 83, 158, 164

1 Peter 26, 32, 33, 115, 118, 141, 153–5, 154, 156, 157, 220

2 Peter 35, 228, 244

1 John 33, 34, 48, 49, 50, 87, 88, 92, 143, 154, 163, 172–3, 221, 229, 240, 252, 256, 257

2 John 35, 191–2

Revelation 25–7, 67, 178, 187–8, 192

bishops 129, 133, 135, 137, 180, 227, 206
and infallibility 147–8
power of 143–5

Blessed Virgin Mary, see Mary

Blondel, Maurice 119

Body of Christ: see Church; metaphors; Paul; Aquinas

Boff, Leonardo 243–4

Brémond, Henri 119

Brueggemann, Walter 16–17, 162, 163, 250, 252
on wandering/settlement/exile/ homecoming 247–9

Buddhism 17, 217, 218–19, 240

Cabrini, Frances 136

Calvary 9, 87, 150, 179, 255

Calvin, John 118

catechism 51

Catherine of Siena 136

Certeau, Michel de 197

charismatic gifts 124, 137,139, 204, 228: see also Paul: gifts, ministries, services; spiritual gifts

charismatic movement 75–8, 226

charity 136, 140, 180, 233, 239
Christ and 203–4
and Church unity 81, 132, 171, 182, 183, 202, 203, 205, 212

Chesterton, G. K. 9, 11, 76–7

childlikeness 153–5, 157

children 33, 44, 49, 92, 164, 193, 243, 252, 256
protection of 23

chrism, oil of 236

Christ
as bridegroom 178–9, 186–7, 192
Chartres cathedral sculpture 41
cleansing of temple 86–7
crucifixion 106, 190–1, 257
See also Calvary
and grace 62, 71, 130–1, 167, 183
as head of Church 198–203
as head of humanity 203–6
as image of God 46–9, 50, 54, 58, 256
as lumen gentium 33
as sacrament 49–55
threefold office of 14–5, 114–15, 116–18, 124, 126–7

Christian humanism 161, 164

Church
belief in 62–71
as body of Christ 13, 15, 28, 29, 57, 60–1, 67, 69, 70, 77, 78–84, 127, 132, 137, 138, 141, 174, 177, 200–3, 208, 220, 224, 234, 239, 244
and care 22, 136, 138, 141, 188, 192–3, 197, 216–19, 234
Christ as head of 28, 79, 82, 125, 141, 184, 198–206, 219, 220, 224, 241
circles of humanity 211–19, 225, 231, 232

and corruption   12, 91–109, 146
definitions of   16, 57, 61, 193, 207
diversity of   80, 82, 84, 130–3, 138, 140, 180
experiences of   21–5, 233, 251, 255
images for   15, 25–30, 33, 37, 57, 61, 73,
    77, 80, 82, 84–5, 91, 97, 103, 185, 187,
    217, 224, 237, 244–5 See also analogies;
    Church: models approach; images;
    metaphors
many faces of   27, 225, 232–5
membership of   34–7, 183
models approach   15, 25, 29–30, 37, 58, 77,
    101–2, 103, 113, 124
moon as symbol of   61–2, 98
as mystery   30, 57–8, 113
in pilgrimage   27, 101, 103, 187, 202, 244,
    247–50, 254, 257
and prayer   211–15
as sacrament   29, 33, 51, 54, 57–71, 78, 98,
    101–2, 182, 189, 205, 220, 244, 257
and State   101, 162
tension and conflict   93, 98, 101–5, 106, 116,
    124, 144, 158, 161–2
Clément, Olivier   8, 16
Clement XI, Pope   208
communio (koinonia)   13, 21–2, 171–3, 180–1,
    200
community   13, 21–2, 51, 59, 62, 80–1, 84, 108,
    113, 131, 135, 171–93, 220, 237, 245
of disciples   21, 30
confirmation, sacrament of   51, 227
Congar, Yves   103, 104, 182
    Divided Christendom   182
    on reform   99–101
contemplation   146, 152, 256, 257
contemporary issues, engagement with   8, 16,
    151, 161–2, 228, 250
contraception   24
corruption   12, 14, 91–109, 114, 142, 146
covenants   177–8
    with Israel   26, 31, 32, 85, 87, 116, 186, 212,
        231, 248
    new covenant   54, 115, 117, 174, 179, 188,
        217, 238
    post–Flood   45
Covid-19 pandemic   106, 186
creation   9, 28–9, 41–9, 64, 67, 165, 169, 191,
    200, 205, 235, 243, 256
    and gender equality   47
creeds   64–9, 92, 254
    Apostles' Creed   67
    Nicene Creed   67
culture   14, 24, 100, 153, 160–4, 167, 218, 250
crucifixion   106, 190–1
Cyprian of Carthage   16, 57, 61, 69, 207–8

Dalai Lama   239–40
Day, Dorothy   136
deacon   31, 143, 180
de Lubac, Henri   7, 8, 17, 101–4, 240
Declaration on Non-Christian Religions
    (Vatican II)   217, 218–19
Decree on Ecumenism (Vatican II)   183–4, 217
Decree on Religious Freedom (Vatican II)   217
Dei verbum: Dogmatic Constitution on Divine
    Revelation (Vatican II)   135, 146
devotion   8, 14, 114, 186, 189, 192, 197
    and spirituality   14
diakonia, see service (diakonia)
dialogue   158, 182, 216–19, 226, 234, 239
    theology of   228–32
disciples   14, 28, 32, 35, 36, 37, 49–50, 54, 74,
    76, 87, 93, 142, 143, 145, 153, 155, 179,
    180, 182, 188, 221, 224, 226, 229, 237,
    247, 257
    community of   21, 30, 190
    missionary discipleship   197, 227
    of Lady Wisdom   175, 178, 185
Divided Christendom (Congar)   182
Dominic, Saint   75–6
Dominicans   76, 226
Dominus Iesus (Congregation for the Doctrine of
    the Faith)   183, 184
Duchesne, Louis   119
Dulles, Avery   25
    five models of the Church   29–30
    mega-/meta-model (community of
        disciples)   30

Eastern Orthodox Christianity   16, 181, 216
    Great Schism (1054)   11, 181, 216–17
ecclesia/ekklesia   21, 26, 28, 29, 75, 183, 185,
    188, 189, 206
ecclesial conditions   247–50
Ecclesiam suam (Paul VI)   102, 216, 228
ecclesiology   24, 77, 78
    communio ecclesiology   171–2, 200
ecumenical
    council   144, 147
    movement   181–4, 216–17
education   122, 136, 152, 158, 234, 250
    universities   152, 159–60
embodiment   12–13, 74–89, 91, 113, 130
    Eucharist   9–10
    Mary   9, 10
    papacy   9, 10
    see also incarnation; incorporation;
        sacramentality
En una noche oscura (John of the Cross)   213
enthusiasm   75
    superstition and   14

epiclesis 244
Essay in Aid of a Grammar of Assent, An
    (Newman) 159
Essay on the Development of Christian Doctrine,
    An (Newman) 7
Eucharist 9–10, 51, 54, 59, 70, 77–8, 88, 135,
    161,171, 172, 174–80, 183, 187, 192,
    220, 244, 252, 253
Evangelii gaudium (Francis) 197, 227
Evangelii nuntiandi (Paul VI) 227, 229
evangelization 75, 197, 225–7
evolution 245, 246
exile/exiles 17, 27, 28, 162–3, 244, 248, 249,
    250, 252
    Babylonian Exile 86, 116, 162–4, 247–50, 251

Faber, Peter 197
faith 7, 13, 14, 24, 35, 48, 50, 54, 62–70, 78, 81,
    82, 83, 106, 120, 132, 136, 147, 153, 154,
    155, 203–5, 213
    rationality of 151–2, 159, 214, 254
    thinking and 24, 157, 162, 189
family life 21, 26–7, 185
fellowship 29, 49, 50, 172–4, 180, 181, 183: see
    also *koinonia* (*communio*)
Fides et ratio (John Paul II) 152
Foucauld, Charles de 119
Francis, Pope 24, 149, 197, 206, 218, 236
    Evangelii gaudium 197, 227
    Fratelli tutti 197
    Laudato sí 161, 197
    missionary discipleship 197, 227
Francis of Assisi, Saint 9, 11, 75
Franciscans 76, 226
freedom 68–9, 126, 142, 143, 158, 168, 227,
    233, 247
    of action 42–6, 163, 230–1, 245–6
    and grace 161, 238–9, 251
Fulgentius of Ruspe 208

Galileo Galilei 151
Gandhi, Mahatma 70
gender equality 47
Gentiles: reconciliation with Jews 25, 28, 217,
    219–21
God
    glory of 28, 41, 47, 48, 54, 85, 86, 87, 94, 98,
        130–1, 179, 184, 248, 255–8
    grace of 14, 24, 37, 50, 60, 83, 87, 97, 230
    images of 41–9, 50, 51, 54
'God's Grandeur' (Hopkins) 52
Good Friday liturgy 211–15
grace 33, 41, 51, 60, 70, 100, 131, 139, 141, 161,
    203–4, 205, 220, 227, 235, 253
    capital grace of Christ 200, 205

Christ and 62, 71, 130–1, 167, 183, 199–206
    grace of God 14, 24, 37, 50, 83, 87, 97, 230
    Holy Spirit and 81, 238
    Mary and 188–9, 192
    sacramental grace 51, 58–9, 60–1
    and salvation 208, 210
    sin and 106
Grand Imam of al-Azhar 218
Greek Catholics 181
Guardini, Romano 8

healers 138, 141
Healy, Nicholas 17, 101–2, 103–5, 113
hell 67, 206
Herbert, George 244
hierarchies 9, 10, 13, 30–1, 99, 129–31, 133–7,
    143–4, 149–50, 234
    Aquinas on 130–1, 133, 135
Hildegard of Bingen 136,153
Hillesum, Etty 17
Hinduism 17, 217, 218
history 8, 12, 13, 21, 25, 31, 32, 33, 41, 45–6,
    51, 57, 67, 69, 77, 82, 102, 103, 104–5,
    108, 206, 230, 231, 245–6, 247, 248,
    250, 257
    and providence 251–2
holiness 36, 61, 62, 92, 93, 102, 115, 132–3,
    135, 136, 137, 140, 142, 150, 157, 163,
    164, 165, 180, 186, 213, 227
    sin and 96, 105–9
Holy Office (later Congregation for the Doctrine
    of the Faith) 208–9
Holy Orders, sacrament of 52 *See also* priest
Holy Spirit 12, 34, 36, 57, 61, 64–70, 75, 77, 78,
    81, 82, 83, 87, 95, 132, 144, 145, 146,
    147, 157, 163, 168, 171, 173, 174, 184,
    197, 207, 210, 211, 221, 223–4, 234–7,
    243–4, 249–50, 253, 255
    Aquinas on 139–40, 238–9
    heart as symbol 204
    and oil of chrism 236
    and truth 158
homecoming 248–9
homosexuality 24
hope 13, 62–3, 64, 69, 81, 88, 156, 168, 171, 204,
    207, 244–6, 250, 252, 254, 255, 257–8
Hopkins, Gerard Manley 52
Hügel, Friedrich von, *see* von Hügel, Friedrich
humanism 161, 164
humankind 8, 33, 44, 45, 47, 117, 244
    Christ as head of 197–8, 203–6, 241
    as image of God 13, 41–5, 46–9
humility 94, 102, 155
Huvelin, Henri 119
hypocrites 23

'I see his blood upon the rose' (Plunkett)   52
Idea of a University (Newman)   159–60
images   15, 57–8, 103, 224
   for Church   25–30, 61, 77, 80, 97, 237, 244–5
   of God   13, 41–9, 50, 51, 54, 256
   human beings as image of God   41–6
   human relationships, marriage and family
      life   26–7, 185, 187
   pastoral and agricultural   25, 217
   see also metaphors
image of God
   human being as   41–6
   Jesus as   46–9, 50–5, 58, 256–7
incarnation   12, 47, 229, 240
incorporation   11
infallibility   13, 145–8
initiative/action   42–6, 75, 163, 229, 239
institutional charism   74–8
intellectual work and teaching   14, 16, 113, 118,
   123, 152, 153, 155, 162, 192, 234
Islam   17, 158, 217–8, 228
Israel: threefold organization of   115–16, 118

Jerusalem   26, 88, 118, 152–5, 172, 173, 187–8,
   191, 219, 249, 253
   Temple   84, 85–7, 164
Jesuits   226
Jesus, *see* Christ
*Jewish People and their Sacred Scriptures in the
   Christian Bible, The*   218
Jews: reconciliation with Gentiles   219–21
John XXIII, Pope: *Ad Petri Cathedram*   182
John of the Cross   213
John Paul II, Pope   24, 75
   on evangelization   226
   Fides et ratio   152
   Redemptoris missio   210
Jones, David   51
journeys   27, 95, 166, 247: *see also* exile/exiles
Judaism   17, 80, 217–18, 228, 251
   reference to, in liturgy   212
Julian of Norwich   105, 106
Justin Martyr   214

Kemp Smith, Norman   119
Kenny, Anthony   152
kerygma (proclamation)   48, 127, 180, 219, 226,
   229, 232
king   86, 130, 131, 132
   prophet, priest and king   14, 15, 114–18,
      124, 125, 126, 127, 130, 132, 133, 137,
      180, 227
kingdom   10, 28, 29, 32, 35, 57, 62, 67, 82, 100,
   115, 127, 130, 140, 155, 156, 178, 179,
   180, 187, 207, 244, 254, 257

Knox, Ronald   121
koinonia (*communio*)   13, 21–2, 171–3, 180–1,
   200 *See also* fellowship; participation;
   partnership; sharing

Laberthonière, Lucien   119
language   43–4, 53, 59–60, 152, 162, 163, 218
   theological   257
Lash, Nicholas   114, 123–4
Last Supper   174–6, 177, 178, 244
Laudato sí (Francis)   161, 197
Leo the Great, Pope   55
Leo XIII, Pope
   Rerum novarum   233
liberation theology   32, 175, 219, 250
liturgy (*leitourgia*)   33, 53, 93, 105, 127, 178,
   180, 181
   Good Friday liturgy   211–15
   reference to Judaism   212
Loisy, Alfred   119
London Society for the Study of Religion   119
love   62–3, 83, 223–4, 230
Lubac, Henri de, *see* de Lubac, Henri
Lumen gentium (Vatican II)   25–7, 30–3, 57, 61,
   101, 142, 143–5, 184, 216–17
   communion   172
   infallibility   146–8
   on salvation   209
   threefold office of Christ   114–15
Lutherans   183

McCabe, Herbert   51, 53, 59, 190
Macmillan, James   163, 254
magisteria   135–6, 147, 150, 234
Mariology   189
marriage   22, 26–7, 52, 178, 186, 187, 253
   remarriage after divorce   24
   sex outside marriage   24
Mary   67, 92, 183, 185–93
   as *ekklesia*   189
   embodiment   9–11
   and grace   188
   Mother of the Church   190–1, 192
   as sacrament   188
   theotokos   188–9
meditation   166, 218, 239–40, 256
mendicant movement   74–6, 78, 226
   institutional charism   74–8
   see also Dominicans; Franciscans
metaphors   15, 34, 37, 57, 58, 73, 74, 91, 103,
   235–7
   ambassadors   28, 168, 235
   aroma of Christ   15, 28, 236–7
   bride of Christ   26–7, 29, 67, 74, 178, 185,
      187, 191–2

buildings and cities   25–6, 27, 28, 73, 74,
    81–2, 84–9, 188, 244–5, 253
Christ as bridegroom   74, 178–9, 186–7, 192
Church as a body   29, 79–84, 137–8, 198,
    200–3
cultivation and husbandry   73, 74
heart (Holy Spirit)   204, 224
human relationships   26, 73, 74, 185, 245
letter of recommendation   237
primal metaphors   28–30
  (*see also* analogies; Church: models approach;
    images; symbols)
ministry   13, 36, 82, 141–2, 171, 235
  of Jesus   14, 50, 87, 118, 189
  of Paul   94–5, 107–8, 237
miracles   35, 175, 178
  Cana wedding feast   179, 190–1
miracle workers   117, 138, 141
mission   225–7, 234–5, 239, 240–1
Möhler, J. A.   7
Moore, Brian   151
moral responsibility   44–5
Moses   32, 88, 115
Mount Zion   84, 86
Murray, Les   254
Mystical Element of Religion, The
    (von Hügel)   119–20, 122
mystical theology   257
Mystici corporis Christi (Pius XII)   79

Newman, Jeremiah   129
Newman, John Henry   14–15, 137
  on corruption   98–9
  An Essay in Aid of a Grammar of Assent   159
  *An Essay on the Development of Christian
    Doctrine*   7
  Idea of a University   159–60
  rationality of faith   159
  three elements of religion   113–14
Nicene Creed   67

obedience: authority and   14
O'Connor, Flannery   10 , 59, 254
office holders   135–6, 141–8
  with sacred power   143–8
On Generation and Corruption (Aristotle)   91–2

papacy   144–5, 183, 206
  embodiment   9, 10
  and infallibility   148
parables   23
  wise and foolish virgins   187
participation   16, 173, 174, 203, 206, 221, 233,
    239, 246: see also *koinonia* (*communio*)
particularity   11, 103, 104

partnership   44, 173, 230: see also *koinonia*
    (*communio*)
Passionists   226
pastoral care   22
Paul, Saint   12–13, 16, 25, 27, 34, 35–6, 51, 58,
    64, 88, 105–6, 107, 108, 172, 173, 174,
    224, 236–7, 251, 252, 255
  anti-rhetorical rhetoric   153–8
  as apostle   49–50, 122, 127, 130, 164, 192
  on his authority   150, 235
  Christ as image/icon of God   46, 98, 256
  Church as body of Christ   79–84, 91, 92,
    132, 137–8, 187, 198, 199–205
  on the Eucharist   174–7
  first/last Adam   41
  on gender equality   47
  on gifts, ministries, services   137–42: see also
    charismatic gifts; spiritual gifts
  on Holy Spirit   139, 238–9, 243
  humankind as image of God   47–9
  on Judaism   47, 80, 81, 125–6, 156, 202, 217,
    218, 219–21, 226
  letters   198–203, 220: see also *under* biblical
    references
  own struggles/weaknesses   93–7
  as Saul   165–6, 168
  speech at Athens   48, 126, 214
  and tensions in religion   124–6
  zeal of   165–9
Paul VI, Pope   239
  Ecclesiam suam   102, 216, 228
  on evangelization   227
  theology of dialogue   228, 229, 230, 231
Péguy, Charles   246
Penance, sacrament of   52
Phinehas   165
philosophy   91, 121, 126, 151–60, 169, 218
  Catholicism and   14, 108, 114, 122, 159
Pieper, Josef   246
pilgrims   215, 245, 246, 252, 253, 254, 255
  and beauty   254–5
  Church in pilgrimage   27, 101, 103, 187, 202,
    206, 209, 244, 247–50, 254, 257
Pius XII, Pope   184, 208
  Mystici corporis Christi   79
Plunkett, Joseph Mary   52
pneumatika   139
poiesis   189
power   46, 54, 64, 65, 67, 70, 82, 83, 92, 93, 94,
    95, 96, 97, 100, 103, 105, 106, 108, 114,
    117, 121, 125, 126, 130, 134, 139, 142–9,
    154, 155, 162, 163, 165, 168, 188, 200,
    201, 204, 205, 206, 218, 227, 231, 233,
    234, 239, 250
  of bishops   143–5

Catholicism as political power   14
  sacred power   142–8
prayer   85–7, 116, 118, 132, 136, 166, 172, 180,
    183, 190, 218, 243–4, 257
  and circles of humanity   211–15
  epiclesis   244
  and hope   244–6
'Prayer' (Herbert)   244
Preston, Geoffrey   27–9, 30, 73
pride   92, 96, 98, 143, 156, 255
priest   28, 31, 32, 73, 86, 87, 127, 141, 143, 157,
    173, 187, 236, 248
  ministerial priesthood   133, 149
  prophet, priest and king   14, 15, 114–18,
    124, 125, 126, 127, 130, 132, 133, 137,
    180, 227
progress   146, 181–2, 184, 199, 215, 231
  contrasted with hope   245, 246
prophet   17, 25, 32, 54, 61, 62, 64–5, 67, 69, 73,
    86, 88, 103, 114–18, 131, 137, 138, 141,
    161, 162–4, 168, 177, 186, 191, 204, 206,
    218, 248–9
  prophet, priest and king   14, 15, 114–18,
    124, 125, 126, 127, 130, 132, 133, 137,
    180, 227
Protestant Christianity   16–17, 162, 182, 183,
    184, 198, 217, 228, 250, 252
Protestant Reformation   11, 181
providence   105, 140, 210
  history and   251–2
pseudo-apostles   95
Pseudo-Dionysius the Areopagite   133–5

qahal   21
Quesnel, Paschasius   208

Rahner, Karl   123–4, 188
rationalism   14, 121
rationality   152, 223
  of faith   156, 159, 214
Ratzinger, Joseph (Benedict XVI)   62
realized eschatology   252
reason   13, 14, 63, 68, 120, 151, 152, 153,
    156–60, 169, 254
reconciliation   53, 86, 168, 202, 235, 248
  Jews and Gentiles   28, 219–21
Redemptoris missio (John Paul II)   210
Redemptorists   226
relationships   26–7, 43, 45, 73, 74, 80, 93, 129,
    134, 140, 143, 144, 159, 166, 185, 188, 245
religion   7, 10, 17, 22, 60, 153, 183, 212, 215,
    217, 218, 219, 228
  elements of   14–15, 105, 113–14, 118–24,
    126, 130, 192
  tensions in   124–5

religion-theology-faith triad   151–2, 158–9
remarriage after divorce   24
remembrance   145, 174, 252–3
Rerum novarum (Leo XIII)   233
res catholica   13
responsibilities
  apostolic responsibilities   141, 142, 143, 168
  moral responsibility   13, 44–5, 199
rites of passage   22
ritual celebrations   23, 51, 77, 86

sacramentality   12–15, 52, 58, 113, 205, 253
  Church as sacrament   29, 51, 57–71
  definition of sacrament   51–2
  Jesus as sacrament   49–55
  Mary as sacrament   189–90
sacraments   12–14, 33, 50, 51–4, 58–60, 77–8,
    253
  see also anointing of the sick, baptism,
    confirmation, Eucharist, Holy Orders,
    marriage, Penance
salvation   35, 67, 102, 103, 108, 126, 145, 186,
    188, 211, 212, 213, 215
  outside the Church   206–10, 231
San Clemente, Rome   219
Santa Sabina, Rome   219
Schütz, Heinrich   163
science-philosophy-reason triad   151–2,
    158–9
Selene, goddess of the Moon   61, 188
service (*diakonia*)   32, 69, 100, 115, 127, 132,
    129–50, 156, 160, 165–6, 168, 180,
    224–7
  mission and   188, 197, 225–7, 232, 233,
    234–5, 239, 240–1
sexual morality   23–4, 93, 161, 168
sexuality: Catholic teaching on   23–4
sharing   16, 22, 53, 69, 74, 103, 104, 117, 130,
    172–3, 180, 181, 225, 229, 236 : see also
    koinonia (*communio*)
shekinah   85
signs   12, 51, 53–5, 58–60, 87, 190, 214, 226,
    254
sin   13, 41, 45, 47, 64, 65, 66, 67, 69, 70, 86, 87,
    88, 91, 93, 103, 114, 118, 143, 163, 167,
    173, 177, 179, 188, 207, 209–10, 221,
    229, 230, 239, 248
  and holiness   96, 105–9
  and suffering   107
smell, sense of   50, 52, 236–7, 255
social teaching   7, 23, 232, 233, 234
Spe salvi (Benedict XVI)   245, 258
spiritual gifts   139, 141, 201, 204: *see also*
    charismatic gifts; Paul: gifts, ministries,
    services

spirituality 9, 11, 102–3, 134, 162, 228, 240
  and devotion 14
State: Church and 101, 162
Stein, Edith (Teresa Benedicta of the
  Cross) 136
Summa theologiae (Aquinas) 103, 117–18,
  130–2, 200, 203–6, 223
super-apostles 95
superstition and enthusiasm 14, 121
symbols 10, 37, 52, 53, 54, 58–61, 69, 71, 85,
  185, 189, 190, 191, 192, 236, 253, 257
  heart as symbol of Holy Spirit 204
  moon as symbol of Church 61–2, 98
  See also images, metaphors

Talbot, George 137
teachers 23, 33, 34, 54, 75, 83, 117, 122,
  131,134, 135, 138, 141, 158, 185, 191,
  204, 225, 227, 234
  bishops as 144, 147
Teresa Benedicta of the Cross (Edith Stein)
  136
Teresa of Avila 12, 136
Teresa of Calcutta 136
Tertullian 152, 153, 155
theologians 7, 14, 29, 78, 134, 135, 136, 137,
  152, 157, 166, 181, 184, 208, 216, 243
theology 8, 60, 134, 151, 153, 158, 159, 160,
  161, 162, 165, 166, 181
  of the body 24
  of the Church 77, 78
  of dialogue 216, 228–32
  liberation theology 250
  of Mary 188, 192
  mystical theology 257
Thérèse of Lisieux 136, 213
Thils, Gustave 171–2
thinking and faith 24
Thomas Aquinas, *see* Aquinas, Thomas
threefold office, *see* Christ, Israel
transubstantiation 9–10, 11, 244
Trent, Council of 209
Trinity of Persons 16, 57, 64, 139, 184, 223,
  243–4, 157
Troelstch, Ernest 119

truth 119, 14, 17, 24, 34, 54, 58, 60, 83, 95, 99,
  103, 104, 106, 108, 117, 118, 125, 135,
  145–7, 152, 156, 157, 159, 160, 162, 173,
  198, 207, 209, 212, 213, 214, 219, 221,
  225, 226, 231, 256, 258
  Holy Spirit and 158
tyranny and ambition 14, 121
Tyrrell, George 119

ultimate reality 240
unity 7, 16, 25–6, 33, 57, 61, 69, 71, 75, 77,
  80–2, 84, 92, 101, 123, 132, 138, 140,
  144, 167, 171, 175, 177, 199, 200, 202,
  204, 207, 220, 235, 244
  restoration of 180–4, 212, 216
Unity in the Church (Möhler) 7, 13
universities 152, 159–60

Vatican I 143, 145, 148
Vatican II 30, 36, 79, 101, 114–5, 129, 143, 144,
  181, 182, 247
  Declaration on Non–Christian Religions 217,
    218–19
  Decree on Ecumenism 183–4, 217
  Decree on Religious Freedom 217
  *Dei verbum: Dogmatic Constitution on Divine
    Revelation* 135, 146
  *Lumen gentium: Dogmatic Constitution on
    the Church* 25–7, 30–3, 57, 61, 101,
    114–15, 142, 143–5, 146–8, 172, 209,
    216–17
Virgin Mary, *see* Mary
von Hügel, Friedrich 14–15, 17, 105, 113,
  118–24, 126
  The Mystical Element of Religion 119–20,
    122
  three elements of religion 114, 119–23
vulnerable adults, protection of 23

Ward, Wilfrid 119
Weil, Simone 17
wisdom literature 46, 165, 168, 175, 178, 179,
  185
women, ordination of 183
World Council of Churches 182–3